Female Entrepreneurship

Over recent years, the promotion of female entrepreneurship has become a key area of debate amongst academics, policy makers and support agencies. Today, woman entrepreneurs represent a third of all business start-ups, and the need to understand the why, what and how of women entrepreneurs has increased the need for a well-researched, comprehensive publication on this important topic.

At last, this book presents the subject of female entrepreneurship in a systematic way, capable of separate and detailed analysis. Featuring contributions by Sara Carter, Candida G. Brush, John Watson and Elisabet Ljunggren, as well as international scholars based in the UK, mainland Europe, the USA and Australia, *Female Entrepreneurship* provides a comprehensive analysis of the challenges and opportunities facing female entrepreneurs worldwide. The book advances the general understanding of female entrepreneurship, and sets a research agenda on how best to promote female-owned/led businesses both nationally and internationally.

Providing a much-needed, insightful analysis into the complex range of issues facing female entrepreneurs throughout the world, this book also provides recommendations as to how support agencies, educators and trainers can best respond to the challenge of encouraging more women to get involved in new business creation. It will also be of benefit to those working in the areas of Business Studies, Entrepreneurship, Gender Studies and Business Development.

Nancy M. Carter is Vice President of Catalyst Inc., and was Leverhulme Visiting Professor at the London Business School. **Colette Henry** is Head of the Department of Business Studies, and Director of the Centre for Entrepreneurship Research at Dundalk Institute of Technology in Ireland. **Barra Ó Cinnéide** is Professor Emeritus, University of Limerick. **Kate Johnston** is Senior Researcher, also at the Centre for Entrepreneurship Research, Dundalk Institute of Technology.

Routledge advances in management and business studies

Female Entrepreneurship

Implications for education, training and policy

**Edited by Nancy M. Carter,
Colette Henry, Barra Ó Cinnéide
and Kate Johnston**

LONDON AND NEW YORK

First published 2007
by Routledge
2 Park Square, Milton Park, Abingdon, Oxon OX14 4RN

Simultaneously published in the USA and Canada
by Routledge
270 Madison Ave, New York, NY 10016

Routledge is an imprint of the Taylor & Francis Group, an informa business

© 2007 Selection and editorial matter Nancy M. Carter, Colette Henry,
Barra Ó Cinnéide and Kate Johnston; individual chapters, the contributors

Typeset in Times by Wearset Ltd, Boldon, Tyne and Wear
Printed and bound in Great Britain by TJI Digital, Padstow, Cornwall

British Library Cataloguing in Publication Data
A catalogue record for this book is available from the British Library

Library of Congress Cataloging in Publication Data
A catalog record for this book has been requested

ISBN10: 0-415-36317-9 (hbk)
ISBN10: 0-203-01353-0 (ebk)

ISBN13: 978-0-415-36317-4 (hbk)
ISBN13: 978-0-203-01353-3 (ebk)

Contents

PART II
Promoting female entrepreneurship   135

Illustrations

x *List of illustrations*

Contributors

Gry Agnete Alsos, Senior Researcher, Nordland Research Institute, Bodo, Norway.

Clare Brindley, Head of Department of Strategy and Innovation, Lancashire Business School, University of Central Lancashire, Preston, England.

Candida G. Brush, President's Chair in Entrepreneurship, Chair-Entrepreneurship Division, Babson College, Wellesley, USA.

Nancy M. Carter, Vice President, Research and Information Centre, Catalyst Inc., New York, USA.

Sara Carter, Professor of Entrepreneurship, University of Stirling, Scotland.

Christine Diegelmann, Ministry of Economic Affairs Baden-Wuerttemberg, Stuttgart, Germany.

Elizabeth J. Gatewood, Director of the University Office of Entrepreneurship and Liberal Arts, Wake Forest University, Winston-Salem, North Carolina.

Patricia G. Greene, Provost, Babson College, Babson Park, USA.

Alison Hampton, PhD Researcher, University of Ulster, Newtownabbey, Northern Ireland.

Myra M. Hart, MBA Class of 1961, Professor of Management Practice, Harvard Business School, Boston, USA.

Shirley-Ann Hazlett, School of Management and Economics, Queen's University Belfast, Belfast, Northern Ireland.

Joan Henderson, School of Management and Economics, Queen's University Belfast, Belfast, Northern Ireland.

Colette Henry, Head of Department of Business Studies and Director of the Centre for Entrepreneurship Research, Dundalk Institute of Technology, Ireland.

Frances Hill, Director, Executive MBA Programme, School of Management and Economics, Queen's University Belfast, Belfast, Northern Ireland.

Briga Hynes, Department of Management and Marketing, University of Limerick, Limerick, Ireland.

Kate Johnston, Senior Researcher, Centre for Entrepreneurship Research, Dundalk Institute of Technology, Ireland.

Claire Leitch, Senior Lecturer, School of Management and Economics, Queen's University Belfast, Belfast, Northern Ireland.

Elisabet Ljunggren, Research Manager and Senior Researcher, Nordland Research Institute, Norway.

Pauric McGowan, Director of NICENT (Northern Ireland Centre For Entrepreneurship), University of Ulster, Jordonstown, Newtownabbey, Northern Ireland.

Susan Marlow, Professor of Small Business and Entrepreneurship, De Montfort University, Leicester, England.

Rick Newby, Lecturer in Accounting and Finance, School of Economics and Commerce, University of Western Australia, Crawley, Australia.

Barra Ó Cinnéide, Visiting Professor of Entrepreneurship, Dundalk Institute of Technology, Professor Emeritus, University of Limerick, Limerick, Ireland.

Petra Puechner, Managing Director, Steinbeis-Europa-Zentrum, Coordinator Innovation Relay Centre, Stuttgart-Erfurt-Zürich, Haus der Wirtschaft, Stuttgart, Germany.

Ita Richardson, Head of Department of Computer Science and Information Systems, University of Limerick, Limerick, Ireland.

John Watson, Associate Professor of Accounting and Finance, School of Economics and Commerce, University of Western Australia, Crawley, Australia.

Reviewers

Maria Aggestam, School of Economics and Management, Lund University, Lund, Sweden.

Sally Arkley, Director of Women's Business Development Agency (WBDA), United Kingdom and a director of PROWESS, the national trade association for organisations offering enterprise support for women.

Patricia Barker, Accounting Group Director, Dublin City University Business School, Ireland.

Josephine Browne, Head of School of Business and Humanities, Dun Laoghaire Institute of Art Design and Technology, Ireland.

Mark Cowling, Chief Economist, The Work Foundation, London, United Kingdom.

Patricia Fleming, Associate Dean, Postgraduate Programmes and Executive Education and PRO-TEM Director, MBA Programmes, Kemmy Business School, University of Limerick, Ireland.

Jennifer Jennings, Assistant Professor, Department of Strategic Management and Organization, School of Business, University of Alberta, Edmonton, Canada.

Deveraux Jennings, Professor of Strategic Management and Organization, School of Business, University of Alberta, Edmonton, Canada.

Patricia Lewis, Senior Lecturer, Brunel University, London, United Kingdom.

William Mayfield, Dean of the School of Business, East Central University, Oklahoma, USA.

Barra Ó Cinnéide, Professor Emeritus, University of Limerick, and Visiting Research Fellow, Centre for Entrepreneurship Research, Dundalk Institute of Technology, Ireland.

Friederike Welter, Chair 'SMEs and Entrepreneurship', University of Siegen, Germany.

Fiona Wilson, Professor of Organizational Behaviour in the School of Business and Management, University of Glasgow, Scotland.

Foreword

As a successful business person, who can also be categorised as both a female and an entrepreneur, I was delighted when I was approached to write the foreword to this book. I was somewhat daunted by the target market for the book which, I was told, is academics, researchers and postgraduate students. But, after much internal debate, my conclusion was that this book would also benefit the budding female entrepreneur, and that was *me* twenty years ago. I understand the obstacles women face in business. I was at the sharp end when my company was a start-up, operating from my lounge at home, my previous home having being sold in order to finance the business.

Almost twenty years on, I am Managing Director of that company which manufactures electronic security equipment (one of the first rules of entrepreneurship – never miss a marketing opportunity), and with a superb team behind me, I am able to put my experience and abilities to good use by becoming involved in support agencies to help others towards similar goals. I accept that many things have changed during those twenty years, but the change in ideas and policy must continue. By highlighting the key issues facing women entrepreneurs, this book aims to illustrate how educators, trainers and support agencies can best encourage female entrepreneurship.

Female entrepreneurship is a phenomenon whose time has come. It has reached a point of no return, having gained that all-important critical mass. It is well and truly on the radar and is a cause for celebration. It has defied many of its critics. It has a voice (which is demonstrated in this book) and it is global.

It has liberated the lives of many women who are financially independent, from women's micro businesses in the developing world to the multi-million dollar businesses of successful women entrepreneurs across the world. I hope that millions of women will be liberated by their own enterprise in the foreseeable future.

Women often do things differently and for different reasons from men. They are usually holistic, inclusive, long-term, customer-focused and work to high standards of ethics and integrity. Profit is not usually the main goal. Women set up more social enterprises; and they often start their own business to get a better work–life balance or because they have reached the 'glass ceiling' at work. Or they start a business to fill a gap in the products and services they use for their family. However, they are more risk averse and, as a result, they grow their businesses more slowly. Women tend to have businesses employing fewer than five staff.

Ironically, momentum is now also coming from government, which has realised that there is a considerable economic case for women's enterprise and that the UK is lagging behind other key nations in this respect. The government believes that women should be making a greater contribution to the nation's wealth and, frankly, if that mobilises the action and resources required to help women do this, then that's fine by me!

In 2003, the Department of Trade and Industry launched the Strategic Framework for Women's Enterprise, which outlines a plan to reach the government target of 20 per cent majority female-owned businesses by 2006. This is a tough target, but this is just the start. The government's regional development agencies (RDAs) are taking responsibility for making business services more available to women.

The agenda for women entrepreneurs is wide and includes, *inter alia*, making access to finance more accessible; stimulating the reduction of barriers for women; creating an innovative and entrepreneurial culture; and encouraging leadership and management skills training with an emphasis on life-long learning. All of this support is geared towards improving the performance of our entrepreneurial women and their companies.

Whatever comes next, we can rest assured that there is plenty of muscle now to move the women's enterprise agenda forward. The private and voluntary sectors are also doing their bit, with the proliferation of professional women's networks and women representatives in the Chamber of Commerce, Institute of Directors and CBI. Recently, a new venture capital firm has been launched to raise finance for women entrepreneurs. The balance of power in business has, for a long time, been a male domain. While great advances have been made in the quality of life and its technical sophistication, the flip side is daunting. Startling extremes exist of wealth and poverty, regulation burdens and an increasing culture of litigation, environmental abuse and more. Women, with their ability to listen, their consensus style of management and their sensitivity to the bigger picture, will do much to help us achieve a better balance in business, and thus, in life generally. Women entrepreneurs have a long way to go, but we have certainly made a start.

It has been a privilege to write the foreword for such an important book, which aims to highlight the key issues facing women entrepreneurs and illustrate how educators, trainers and support agencies can best understand and promote female entrepreneurship. I sincerely hope that readers can use the learning in this book to develop and promote the issues of women entrepreneurs.

Julie Kenny, CBE
Managing Director of Pyronix Limited
Chair of the Small Business Council (SBC),
United Kingdom

Acknowledgements

The authors and publishers would like to thank the following for granting permission to reproduce material in this work: Emerald Group Publishing Limited for permission to reprint material from Clare Brindley, 'Barriers to women achieving their entrepreneurial potential: women and risk', *International Journal of Entrepreneurial Behaviour and Research*, special issue on Female Entrepreneurship, Vol. 1, No. 2, 2005, pp. 144–161.

Every effort has been made to contact copyright holders for their permission to reprint material in this book. The publishers would be grateful to hear from any copyright holder who is not here acknowledged and will undertake to rectify any errors or omissions in future editions of this book.

The editors are extremely grateful to all those who have contributed to this monograph. We are especially delighted to have had the opportunity to work with such a reputable team of academic scholars who have drawn on their particular specialist research experiences within the field of Female Entrepreneurship. Without their expertise, dedication and patience, this international collection would not have been possible.

We would also like to thank those who formed part of our refereeing process. Their comments were most instructive. Our thanks are also due to Angela Hamouda and the team at the Centre for Entrepreneurship Research who provided the administrative and typesetting support, and to Naomi Birdthistle, Paula Reilly and Valerie O'Connor who assisted with the proofreading.

Finally, we are grateful to InterTradeIreland and Enterprise Ireland, whose sponsorship of our Research Forum on Female Entrepreneurship in 2002 provided the inspiration for this monograph.

Nancy Carter
Colette Henry
Barra Ó Cinnéide
Kate Johnston

1 Introduction

Colette Henry and Kate Johnston

Female entrepreneurship, as a subject of academic research, has attracted a considerable amount of attention in recent years, and is fast becoming a primary focus for scholars, practitioners and governments alike. This phenomenal increase in gender specific entrepreneurship would appear to be due as much to the increase in entrepreneurship research activity overall (Fiet, 2000; Henry *et al.*, 2003), as to the growing recognition that women now make a valuable contribution to national economies worldwide in terms of job creation, economic growth and wealth generation (Macaulay, 2003; Prowess Report, 2005; Centre for Women's Business Research, 2005). It is estimated that there are currently ten million self-employed women in Europe, with female-owned firms comprising between a quarter and a third of the business population worldwide (NFWBO, 1997; OECD, 2000; OECD, 2004). This, combined with the fact that twenty-first century women are now setting up the so-called "new economy companies", with success in high technology, life sciences and professional services (Carlassare, 2000; Langowitz, 2001; Ernst and Young, 2005), has led to women becoming important agents of economic and social change.

Female entrepreneurs often provide innovative and new solutions to organizational problems and, because they tend to be well educated and experienced (Maysami and Goby, 1999; Carter, 2005) are now, in response to the impenetrable glass ceiling, trading successful corporate careers for more exciting and less discriminatory entrepreneurial endeavours (Hansard, 1990; Mattis, 2000). It would appear that female entrepreneurship is well and truly in vogue!

But despite the impact that female entrepreneurs have in terms of economic activity and new job creation, the role of female entrepreneurs is often undervalued and underplayed. Women still have an alarmingly poor share in the new venture creation market and, compared to their male counterparts, tend to start and manage their businesses differently, opting for unconventional industries, mainly in the services sector (Women's Unit, 2001; Carter *et al.*, 2001; Orhan and Scott, 2001; Forson and Özbilgin, 2003). Furthermore, according to the literature, women entrepreneurs are both risk and debt averse and, whether due to market failure or direct impediments, typically fail to attract the level of capital investment considered vital for major business growth. This despite the fact that women now make up half the European population (Women's Unit, 2001, as cited in Henry and Kennedy, 2003:205).

While commentators have, for the most part, sought to emphasize the particular difficulties associated with female entrepreneurship, the specific differences associated with women entrepreneurs and how they contrast with their male counterparts have received less attention from the academic community. Women behave differently from men, and their entrepreneurial endeavours reflect this. However, the valuable contribution that gender can make in terms of stimulating economic progress, providing innovative solutions to existing problems and exploiting new opportunities needs to be recognized. Rigorous research which offers insights into the practice of female entrepreneurship and provides practical examples of successful initiatives, can serve as a powerful tool for effecting change.

This book aims to advance understanding and effect real change in the field of female entrepreneurship in a number of strategic ways. First, it aims to promote the study of female entrepreneurship as an issue capable of separate and detailed analysis, thereby facilitating its development as an academic discipline in its own right. Second, by examining a number of pertinent themes which embed the female entrepreneurship literature, the book uncovers the nature of women entrepreneurs; their characteristics, their behaviour patterns and the challenges they face as they manoeuvre through the new venture creation process. Third, by examining female entrepreneurship in different country contexts, and by identifying some successful initiatives which have been specifically designed to encourage more women to participate in new venture creation, the book aims to inform educators, trainers and policy makers about what can be done to effectively promote female entrepreneurship at local and national level.

Accepting that differences exist in the nature of female entrepreneurship in different countries, as well as in different economic and social contexts, the editors have adopted a strong international perspective in their choice of material. This research monograph presents a collection of edited, research-based contributions from leading international scholars and researchers within the field of female entrepreneurship. The chapters that make up this volume combine the theoretical with the empirical to offer valuable insights into the very essence of female entrepreneurship.

Following this introductory chapter, the monograph is divided into two parts: Part I deals with our understanding of female entrepreneurship and contains five, mainly empirically-based, chapters, each exploring a pertinent aspect of the current research agenda in this field. Part II considers the promotion of female entrepreneurship and contains four chapters, with a mixture of empirically and experientially-based contributions which aim to identify and share good practice in promoting female entrepreneurs. A Conclusions chapter (Chapter 11) reviews the contributions in the context of what can and should be done to encourage and promote female entrepreneurship.

In Chapter 2, Sara Carter and Susan Marlow lay the foundation for the monograph by reviewing the existing literature on female entrepreneurship and highlighting the key themes to emerge from the early 1980s and into the new millennium and beyond. The characteristics and motivations of female entrepreneurs, their start-up patterns and resources, their management style and the various constraints they face are all considered by the authors. The complex, and sometimes controversial issues concerning access to finance, growth and performance are also examined. The authors illustrate how research on female entrepreneurship has not only expanded but matured in recent years, with much of the contemporary literature on entrepreneurship and new venture creation now more sensitive to the nuances of gender.

In Chapter 3, John Watson and Rick Newby further develop some of the particular nuances of gender discussed in the previous chapter by focusing on the differences in the goals of owner-operated small to medium-sized enterprises (SMEs). The authors argue that traditionally masculine values and concepts have tended to dominate the management and organization literature and, as a consequence, such concepts have influenced our thinking on business success and performance. This in turn has impacted upon studies which consider the differences between male- and female-led SMEs. While the literature has suggested that male entrepreneurs outperform their female counterparts, there is evidence to suggest that there are considerable sex-based differences in both the desire for and achievement of business growth. Thus, Watson and Newby question the validity of using traditional "hard" economic measures alone to assess and contrast the performance of female- and male-led firms. Their study, which involved 474 male and 137 female SME owner–operators in Western Australia, argues that future SME studies which seek to examine the impact of gender might be better served by the use of masculinity and femininity scores, rather than biological sex.

The issue of attitudes towards entrepreneurship is examined in Chapter 4 by Shirley-Ann Hazlett, Joan Henderson, Frances Hill and Claire Leitch. The authors explore the differences in attitudes towards entrepreneurship among female and male students, based on a sample of 596 undergraduates, across a variety of business related subjects. The chapter reports on the first part of a three-year longitudinal study to assess students' understanding and perceptions of, as well as their attitudes towards, self-employment and new venture creation. The authors report that the females in the study appeared to place considerable value on networking, were more likely than men to perceive risk as a barrier to starting a business and that considerably fewer men than women perceived not having the necessary business skills as a potential barrier. The study also found that, overall, female students are less confident about their entrepreneurial abilities than their male counterparts. The authors conclude that, in the absence of further data, there is a need to tailor educational curricula to raise the total entrepreneurial activity particularly for female students at third level.

In Chapter 5, the theme of the general perception of female entrepreneurship is explored in greater depth by Elisabet Ljunggren and Gry Agnete Alsos. In their study, the authors focus on the discourse in newspapers and the different treatment afforded to male and female entrepreneurs in the Norwegian media to explore how media coverage can significantly influence society's perception of women entrepreneurs overall. Using discourse analysis based on 117 newspaper articles in leading business papers, the authors demonstrate that current media discourse on entrepreneurs is highly masculine in nature. When portrayed in the media, male entrepreneurs are strongly associated with risk-taking behaviour, stock market involvement, ambitious goals, and are representative of strong, high growth firms. In contrast, female entrepreneurs are described in terms of their personal characteristics, being motivated by lifestyle, often having other "soft" goals such as a caring attitude and as individuals who have a life outside that of an entrepreneur. Echoing Watson and Newby's chapter, the authors conclude that the male portrayal of an entrepreneur is very much the "*norm*", with the female entrepreneur considered as the "other" or something different, which is, unfortunately, sometimes perceived as something "subordinate", contributing something less than their male equivalents.

Chapter 6 explores the networking behaviour of female entrepreneurs at the start-up and growth stages of the new venture creation process. The role and importance of networking, as well as the different types of networking approaches adopted at the various stages of the business life cycle, are discussed. Consideration is also given to how the effectiveness of women entrepreneurs' networking behaviour can be improved. Based on research from a pilot study, the chapter authors – Pauric McGowan and Alison Hampton – develop a tentative model of the networking practices of female-owned SMEs. Their study illustrates how the length of time a female entrepreneur is in business impacts on her level of knowledge and confidence, thus affecting her networking style and abilities.

Having focused on understanding the very nature of female entrepreneurship by reviewing extant trends in the literature worldwide, exploring the differences between the goals of male- and female-led SMEs in Western Australia, assessing the attitudes towards entrepreneurship among male and female undergraduates in Northern Ireland, reviewing the portrayal of female entrepreneurs in the Norwegian business media and evaluating the evolving networking behaviour of female entrepreneurs, Part II of the monograph shifts the focus to what can actually be done to encourage more women into new venture creation.

Chapter 7, by Clare Brindley, lays the foundation for Part II by considering the various barriers women entrepreneurs face in the new venture creation process. In this regard, risk is platformed as a key barrier which, according to the author, significantly impacts on the ability of women entrepreneurs to gain access to social supports, build networks and access finance. While Brindley reiterates the point that women are not a homogeneous group, her discussion of the relevant themes from the literature serves to remind us that women behave differently from men. Quite simply, the fact that success for self-employed women is not solely related to finance but can also mean the effective maintenance of home/work balance, suggests that women will remain disadvantaged as this view of success does not fit with conventional thinking. The author argues that there is a need to remove or reduce the barriers hindering women in their efforts to become self-employed. She calls for specific initiatives to be introduced to address the "complex system of interacting motivations" that prevent women from entering the world of entrepreneurship in greater numbers.

Picking up on the concept of finance as a key barrier to female entrepreneurship, Chapter 8, by Candida G. Brush, Nancy M. Carter, Elizabeth J. Gatewood, Patricia G. Greene and Myra M. Hart, considers women's financial strategies for growth. The authors suggest that women are typically disadvantaged when starting a business because they have been unable to accumulate savings similar to their male counterparts, due to having lower incomes. As such, men and women employ different financing strategies and this can affect women entrepreneurs' ability to grow their business. From their study of ninety-two women entrepreneurs who had applied to Springboard 2000 Venture Forums in Silicon Valley and the Mid-Atlantic, Brush *et al.* highlighted a range of financing strategies. The study showed that those with equity funding were significantly more likely to use bootstrapping to fund product development. The authors conclude that bootstrapping as a financing strategy can be highly effective in helping to position the business for external equity investment.

Chapter 9, by Ita Richardson and Briga Hynes, discusses the lack of women in both technical employment and entrepreneurship. While their research supports the literature in suggesting that a lack of women studying technical disciplines has a direct impact on the number of technology-based female entrepreneurs, their study traces the root of the problem back to the secondary education system. Based on the experiences of the University of Limerick in Ireland, three practical initiatives are examined which were designed to encourage more women to study engineering, science and technology based subjects and to consider self-employment as a viable career option. The simple structures of the initiatives render them valuable tools for positively impacting on women's technical entrepreneurship, and make them capable of being transferred into virtually any social or economic climate.

In Chapter 10, Petra Puechner and Christine Diegelmann report on an international study conducted by the ProWomEn network, an EU initiative established in 2001 to promote women entrepreneurs. The authors describe the work of the ProWomEn project, outline the international project team membership and explain the project objectives. The research undertaken by the ProWomEn team considered the state of female entrepreneurship across a range of European countries in an effort to gather data on the varying levels of female entrepreneurial activity and, more specifically, to identify good practice examples in the promotion of female entrepreneurship. Several examples of good practice are mentioned by the authors, and four specific examples are detailed across the thematic areas of problem awareness, instruments of support, regional networks, and education and training.

Finally, in Chapter 11, Nancy M. Carter and Barra Ó Cinnéide draw conclusions from the contributions and consider the way forward. The authors recognize that the sudden increase in research into female entrepreneurship in the last two decades is presenting significant challenges to educators, trainers and policy makers. The authors seek to identify the key implications of this research for the education, training and policy agenda, and thus the text concludes with some practical recommendations designed to facilitate the task of promoting female entrepreneurship at regional and national level. It is hoped that the insights into the practice of female entrepreneurship and the examples of successful initiatives presented in this book can serve as a tool for effecting change.

References

Carlassare, E. (2000). *DotCom Divas*, New York, McGraw Hill.

Carter, S. (2005). *The Role and Contribution of Women's Entrepreneurship*, Presentation to the RSA/DTI, 27 June 2005, London.

Carter, S., Anderson, S. and Shaw, E. (2001). *Women Business Ownership: A Review of the Academic, Popular and Internet Literature.* London. Small Business Service. Census 2001, available: www.statistics.gov.uk/census2001/default.asp.

Centre for Women's Business Research (2005). *Key Facts about Women Owned Businesses*, available: www.womensbusinessresearch.org/researchstudies.html (3 October 2005).

Ernst and Young, (2005). 2005 South Region Award recipients, available: www.ey.com/GLOBAL/content.nsf/UK/EOY_-_2005_Awards_-_South (3 October 2005).

Fiet, J.O. (2000). "The Pedagogical Side of Entrepreneurship Theory". *Journal of Business Venturing*, 16, 2, 101–117.

Forson, C. and Özbilgin, M. (2003). "Dot-com women entrepreneurs in the UK". *International Journal of Entrepreneurship and Innovation*, 4, 1, February, 13–24.

Hansard Society (1990). *Women at the Top*, London, A.L. Publishing Services.

Henry, C. and Kennedy, S. (2003). "In Search of a New Celtic Tiger – Promoting Female Entrepreneurship in Ireland". In Butler, J. (ed.), *New Perspectives on Women Entrepreneurs*, Vol. 3 in Research in Entrepreneurship and Management. Hong Kong: Information Age Publishing Inc.

Henry, C., Hill, F. and Leitch, C. (2003). *Entrepreneurship Education and Training*, Aldershot, Ashgate.

Langowitz, N. (2001). "The Top Women-Led Business in Massachusetts". Babson Park, MA, Centre for Women's Leadership, Babson College.

Macaulay, C. (2003). "Changes to Self-Employment in the UK: 2002 to 2003". *Labour Market Trends*. London: Office for National Statistics.

Mattis, M.C. (2000). "Women Entrepreneurs in the United States". In Davidson, M.J. and Burke, R. (eds), *Journal of Women in Management: Current Research Issues Volume II*. London: Sage.

Maysami, R.C. and Goby, V.P. (1999). "Female Business Owners in Singapore and Elsewhere: A Review of Studies". *Journal of Small Business Management*, 2, 96.

NFWBO (National Foundation for Women Business Owners) (1997). "Women Entrepreneurs are a Growing International Trend", Washington, DC.

OECD (Organisation for Economic Co-operation and Development) (2000). "OECD Small and Medium Enterprises Outlook", Paris, OECD.

OECD (Organisation for Economic Co-operation and Development) (2004). "OECD Promoting Entrepreneurship and Innovative SMEs in a Global Economy: Women's Entrepreneurship: Issues and Policies", Paris, OECD.

Orhan, M. and Scott, D. (2001). "Why Women Enter into Entrepreneurship: an Explanatory Model". *Women in Management Review*, 16, 5, 232–243.

Prowess (2005). "The Regional State of Women's Enterprise in England", available: www.prowess.org.uk/documents/TheStateofWomensEnglandintheEnglishRegionsthisis theonetodistribute.pdf (29 September 2005).

Women's Unit (2001). *Women as Entrepreneurs in Sweden and the UK*, London, The Women's Unit, Cabinet Office.

Part I

Understanding female entrepreneurship

2 Female entrepreneurship

Theoretical perspectives and empirical evidence

Sara Carter and Susan Marlow

Introduction

The past thirty years have seen the development of a burgeoning academic literature investigating the small firms sector from a range of different disciplinary perspectives. In a diverse and increasingly specialised research area, it is notable that relatively few studies consider the position of women as business owners. A notable assessment of the literature argued that female entrepreneurship had been 'neglected' both by the mass media and the academic community (Baker *et al.*, 1997). Scholars have contested that the research literature assumes entrepreneurship to be a male activity (Brush, 1992; Berg, 1997), describing theories of entrepreneurship as being 'created by men, for men and applied to men' (Holmquist and Sundin, 1989:1). As this chapter will attempt to demonstrate, women's entrepreneurship may be regarded as a minority interest, but the issue is far from neglected. The most recent review of the gender and enterprise research literature sponsored by the UK Small Business Service revealed over 400 peer-reviewed academic papers and numerous popular articles (Carter *et al.*, 2001). The gender and enterprise research field is perhaps more accurately portrayed as under-developed. Despite a growing enthusiasm among researchers and policy makers to focus on issues relating to gender and enterprise, and a marked increase in the number of studies investigating the area, there has been a failure to build adequate explanatory theories, particularly around the concept of gender and how the experiences of female entrepreneurs reflect those within the wider socio-economic context.

Following this introduction, the chapter provides an assessment of current estimates of the number of women entrepreneurs, prior to exploring the key themes within the research literature. The chapter highlights several studies of gender and enterprise that have been undertaken throughout the world. While there has been a strong focus on the collection of empirical data, researchers have paid less attention to the theoretical dimensions that underpin the analysis of gender and entrepreneurship. This chapter discusses the potential contribution of gender-based analyses to the study of entrepreneurship and makes suggestions for a new strand of research enquiry based on gendered perspectives.

Female entrepreneurship: numbers and trends

While there are no official statistics that disaggregate enterprise ownership by gender in the UK, it is generally considered that about 15 per cent of enterprises are female-owned, 50 per cent are male-owned and 35 per cent are co-owned by males and females (Small Business Service, 2003; Carter *et al.*, 2004). Since 1992, there has been a 6.5 per cent growth in the number of self-employed women in the UK, from 899,000 in 1992 (Q1), to 962,000 in 2004 (Q1). However, in the same period, both the female share of self-employment (26 per cent) and the proportion of economically active women in self-employment (7 per cent) have remained largely static. Research suggests that not only are women in the UK less likely to become self-employed, their experience of business ownership differs substantially from that of men; most female self-employment is confined to traditionally female occupational sectors, such as education, health, finance and business services; more than half of self-employed women work part-time (less than thirty hours per week); and over a third of women, compared with 12 per cent of men, use their home as a business base (Small Business Service, 2003).

The proportion of female business owners in the UK is comparable with other Northern European countries (Holmquist, 1997; Nilsson, 1997), but considerably lower than in the USA, where there are an estimated 10.1 million businesses in which a woman owns at least 50 per cent of the company, and women-owned firms account for 28 per cent of all businesses (National Women's Business Council, 2004). Estimates suggest that the majority of women-owned firms employ 9.2 million workers and generate $1.2 trillion in sales revenue (National Women's Business Council, 2004). While the majority (53 per cent) still operate within the services sectors, there is evidence that women-owned businesses in the USA are moving out of traditionally 'female' sectors, such as retailing and low-order services, and into construction, production and technology-based sectors (Carter and Allen, 1997; Brush and Hisrich, 1999). This, too, contrasts with the UK, where female enterprise is still predominantly located within the service economy (Marlow, 1997; Marlow and Carter, 2004), and 'new economy' businesses, initially believed to present the potential for gender-neutral entrepreneurial action, have emerged as a masculine province. The number of 'new economy' firms owned by men substantially outnumber those owned by women, and traditional patterns of gender representation and stereotyping appear to persist (Wilkinson, 2001).

The extraordinary success of the USA in fostering female self-employment is often cited by government and policy officers from other countries, in particular European nations, as a role model for replication (Small Business Service, 2003). However, it should be recognised that there are a number of distinctive features of the US economy that, while encouraging to female entrepreneurship, may be less desirable and replicable elsewhere. Welfare provision in the USA, while differing between the states, is limited in scope and is time-constrained, so does not facilitate non-waged work options, such as full-time caring, for any period of time. Consequently, self-employment for groups such as lone mothers is one option that becomes more attractive in the face of no income or inflexible, minimum wage work (Stoesz, 2002). By comparison, Europe's more comprehensive, though much criticised, welfare provision system ensures that women with no other source of income are less often forced into either employment or self-employment (Marlow *et al.*, 2003). Moreover, inward migration stimulates enterprise as new and existing ethnic minorities turn to self-employment to counter labour market discrimination or unemployment (Frazier, 1997). Even the most cursory examination of migration policies in the USA indicates a far more dynamic approach over time towards inward migration than in Europe, with associated impacts upon enterprise. These are just two notable socioeconomic factors that help to explain the differences between nations with regard to entrepreneurship rates. An important research challenge is to identify initiatives that may lead European economies to become more conducive to new and growing enterprises for both men and women, while learning from best practice examples in the USA.

The characteristics and motivations of female business owners

Table 2.1 highlights some of the main themes of the research literature pertaining to female entrepreneurship. The first of the six main themes concentrates on the characteristics and motivations of women business owners. This theme was particularly apparent within the early exploratory studies, influenced by the existing small business literature. Many of these early studies emerged from North America and concentrated on describing the characteristics of women owners and their motivations for self-employment. Overall, these studies presented a prima facie picture of businesswomen with more similarities than differences to their male counterparts. Like men, the most frequently cited reason for starting in business was the search for independence and control over one's destiny. The greatest barriers to business formation and success were access to capital and mobilising start up resources. Few of the early studies developed sophisticated taxonomies, preferring to identify female proprietors as a homogeneous group, and there was an implicit acceptance by researchers that, beyond the start-up phase, few significant differences existed between male- and female-owned and managed companies.

In an early attempt to convey the heterogeneity of women entrepreneurs, Goffee and Scase (1985) analysed the experiences of 54 female proprietors in the UK. Central to this study was the development of a typology of female entrepreneurs based on two factors. First, their relative attachment to conventional entrepreneurial ideals in the form of individualism and self-reliance and, second, their willingness to accept conventional gender roles, often subordinate to men. Four types of self-employed women emerged in this taxonomy: 'conventional' owners who were highly committed to both entrepreneurial ideals and conventional gender roles; 'innovative' owners who held a strong belief in entrepreneurial ideals but had a relatively low attachment to conventional gender

Table 2.1 Overview of the academic research literature on female entrepreneurship

Main themes	Sub-themes
Characteristics and motivations of women entrepreneurs	Differences in psychological characteristics between women and men Social background and business differences between women and men The effect of the labour market/glass ceiling on women's decision to start in business
Start-up: patterns, resources and constraints	Motivations, processes and structures used at start-up Resource acquisition and mobilisation: including finance, social and human capital Resource lack: including credibility and track record The effect of start-up barriers on incubation, start-up and long-term business performance Programmes and policies to foster women entrepreneurs
Management of female-owned firms	Women's management style and approach to leadership The business–family nexus Copreneurship The effect of gender on business performance
Finance and related issues	Access to start-up finance Guarantees on loans and external finance Access to growth and ongoing finance Relationship with external lenders and women's credibility
Business networks	Gender differences in types of networks created Gender differences in network content, i.e. the uses made of networks
Business performance and growth	Gender differences in criteria used to assess business performance Gender differences in actual business performance

roles; 'domestic' owners who organised their business life around the family situation and believed very strongly in conventional female roles, holding low attachment to entrepreneurial ideals; and 'radicals' who held low attachment to both, often organising their businesses on a political, collectivist basis.

While early studies provided valuable descriptions of a group of female business owners who had, hitherto, been overlooked by the mainstream small business research effort, critics of the research drew attention to the exploratory nature of this research. Criticism was levelled, in particular, at the small size of the samples used and their lack of representativeness and reliability (Curran, 1986; Carter, 1993), the general lack of rigour of the studies (Allen and Truman, 1993; Solomon and Fernald, 1988; Rosa and Hamilton, 1994) and the limited extent of the cumulative knowledge (Stevenson, 1983; Curran, 1986; Hamilton *et al.*, 1987). Indeed, by the late 1980s it was becoming clear that some of the research debates surrounding the issue of gender and business ownership were continuing largely because of the difficulties for researchers in providing clear and unequivocal evidence, either through empirical investigation or through more theoretical approaches. While several studies had suggested that it was considerably harder for women both to start and run their own enterprises, others had cited the gender literature to argue that start up problems tended to be equally great for men, and that many women 'far from being discriminated against, thought that being a woman gave them a positive advantage over men' (Birley, 1989).

Within this broad theme of characteristics and motivations of women entre-preneurs a number of sub-themes emerge. The first of these relates to the psy-chological characteristics of female business owners, usually considered in direct comparison to men or in relation to norms established using male samples. Research has compared the psychological profile of self-employed women according to their risk-taking propensity and achievement motivation (Masters and Meier, 1988; Sexton and Bowman-Upton, 1990; Langan-Fox and Roth, 1995), personal value systems (Olson and Currie, 1992; Fagenson, 1993) and in terms of sex-role stereotyping and career selection (Brenner *et al.*, 1989; Scherer *et al.*, 1990; Fagenson and Marcus, 1991). While research profiling the psychological dimensions of firm owners continues, recent articles have implic-itly challenged its relevance, arguing that the process of 'creating and growing wealth' is universal, and that small firm owners and non-owners cannot be dichotomised (Birley and Wright, 2001:129).

A further sub-theme within this literature compares the broader social back-ground and business differences between male and female business owners, in an effort to identify and portray the typical characteristics of self-employed women. This has been undertaken in very general terms, considering a range of comparative issues (Cromie, 1987; Carland and Carland, 1991; Catley and Hamilton, 1998), and in relation to specific criteria such as education (Dolinsky *et al.*, 1993), youthfulness (Kourlisky and Walstad, 1998), ethnicity (Dolinsky *et al.*, 1994; Shim and Eastlick, 1998), family background (Matthews and Moser, 1996; Caputo and Dolinsky, 1998) and type of industry (Anna *et al.*, 2000).

This sub-theme of the literature has been supplemented by country-specific research that has profiled the characteristics and motivations of self-employed women in a range of different national and regional settings. Research has examined the characteristics of women business owners in different western economies such as Canada, Norway, Sweden and Australia (Holmquist and Sundin, 1988; Belcourt, 1990; Collerette and Aubry, 1990; Lee-Gosselin and Grise, 1990; Loscocco and Robinson, 1991; Bennett and Dann, 2000; Spilling and Berg, 2000). Studies have also focused on the characteristics of self-employed women in transitional economies such as Russia (Izyumov and Razumnova, 2000), Poland (Mroczkowski, 1997) and Slovenia (Glas and Petrin, 1998), and in developing economies such as Brazil (Jones, 2000), the Philippines (Gordon, 1997) and Turkey (Hisrich and Ozturk, 1999). There has also been a range of studies profiling the characteristics of enterprising women in various Asian countries, from the less-developed economies of India, Pakistan and Nepal (Padaki, 1994; Premchander, 1994) to the more developed states of Singapore and Hong Kong (Lee, 1996; Weeks, 1998; Maysami and Goby, 1999). A common trend has been the reliance, in even very recent studies, on descriptive profiles of demographic and personal characteristics, which are then often compared with results derived from similar studies in different country settings. Maysami and Goby's (1999) article, for example, describes Singaporean women entrepreneurs as 'an average age of 41, are mostly married, and have an average of two children [p. 97] . . . Australian females are not so different [p. 99] . . . Studies of female owner/managers in Singapore and elsewhere show remarkably similar results [p. 102]'.

A further sub-theme that is particularly apparent within, but not exclusive to, the European research literature has been the attempt to establish linkages between motivations for self-employment and the overall position of women in the labour market (Goffee and Scase, 1985; van der Wees and Romijn, 1987; Cromie and Hayes, 1988; Carter and Cannon, 1992; Marlow, 2002). In particular, researchers have analysed patterns of female business ownership and questioned whether this presents a rejection of traditional corporate careers or simply reproduces existing labour market patterns under a guise of independence (Goffee and Scase, 1987; Lee-Gosselin and Grise, 1990; Green and Cohen, 1995; Marlow and Carter, 2004).

A surprising absence in this literature is the use of very large scale data sets to inform descriptions of entrepreneurial characteristics and demographics. Curran and Burrows' (1988) analysis of the UK General Household Survey represents one of the few studies that can be seen to provide an accurate, though now dated, demographic profile of female participation in self-employment. While the use of national data sets, such as the Labour Force Survey, would appear to be an appropriate way forward in investigating issues of gender and enterprise, their utility is restricted by the limited depth of the data which is collected. For example, national data sets can provide no assistance in investigating some of the most interesting and the most controversial of the research themes, such as the existence and extent of female disadvantage in starting and running a business. Neither can they assist in developing an understanding of the processes and practices of gender relations, a prerequisite to the development of theories of gender and enterprise.

Start-up: patterns, resources and constraints

Linked strongly to the research literature that considers the characteristics and motivations of women business owners, is the analysis of start-up patterns and goals. Indeed, a preoccupation with start-ups permeates the literature, but is particularly noticeable within the more descriptive analyses where there is a widespread and generally unquestioned acceptance that start-up is more difficult for women. A key debate, however, is whether the barriers encountered by women at start-up have a long-term effect on business performance or whether these constraints dissipate after start-up has been successfully negotiated. Among those studies that focus predominantly on the start-up situation, four broad sub-themes emerge. First, a focus upon the various factors, such as motivations, goals, processes and structures, that are an integral part of the start-up experience (Shane *et al.*, 1991; Shabbir and Di Gregorio, 1996; Alsos and Ljunggren, 1998). The experiences of women starting in business have generally been drawn from comparative analyses: either contrasting female start-ups with those of men (Shane *et al.*, 1991; Ljunggren and Kolvereid, 1996; Alsos and Ljunggren, 1998); analysing the different experiences of female start-ups in a variety of different cultural settings (Shane *et al.*, 1991; Kolvereid *et al.*, 1993; Carter and Kolvereid, 1997); or contrasting the start-up experience of different groups of women, as in Dolinsky *et al.*'s (1994) analysis of gender and ethnicity.

The second sub-theme relates to the acquisition and mobilisation of start-up resources. This issue initially gained prominence in the very early, exploratory studies of self-employed women (cf. Schreier, 1973 and Schwartz, 1976) and has been a persistent element of the discourse surrounding gender and enterprise. Early studies tended to focus solely on the acquisition of start-up finance and the social systems that endowed women with a lack of business credibility. As Hisrich and Brush (1986:17) described:

> For a woman entrepreneur who lacks experience in executive management, has had limited financial responsibilities, and proposes a non-proprietary product, the task of persuading a loan officer to lend start-up capital is not an easy one. As a result, a woman must often have her husband co-sign a note, seek a co-owner, or use personal assets or savings. Many women entrepreneurs feel strongly that they have been discriminated against in this financial area.

Highlighting an issue of female credibility that would recur in several later studies, Hisrich and Brush (1986) also reported that half of their respondents reported difficulties in overcoming some of the social beliefs that women are not as serious as men about business.

While research focusing on gender and finance has developed into a highly specialised area, more recent studies of resource acquisition at start-up have focused on gender differences in access to human and social capital. Building on the work of Goffee and Scase (1985), it has been argued that women's enterprise can be seen both as a reaction to and a means of escaping from the persistent inequalities and the occupational confines of the labour market (Marlow, 1997). There is now a growing body of evidence that suggests that a woman's pre-venture labour market experience has a profound effect on her ability to mobilise appropriate start-up resources. In comparison with men, when women enter self-employment they do so with fewer financial assets, with less experience in management and under-resourced in terms of their human and social capital. Women generally lack both hard resources, such as finance and capital assets, and soft resources, such as management experience, networks and family support. A key issue in the debate is the extent to which this initial resource shortage affects long-term business performance (Brush, 1997; Collins-Dodd *et al.*, 2004).

The third sub-theme is concerned with the role and effect of start-up on business survival and performance. Most of this literature focuses on the limited choices facing most women, for example in determining an appropriate business sector (Carter *et al.*, 1997), and the constraints they face in mobilising initial resources, for example financial backing (Marlow and Patton, 2005).

The final sub-theme focuses on programmes and policies to increase the number of women in self-employment. This literature tends to emanate either from evaluations of specific programmes and initiatives, for example the UK's Women's Enterprise Roadshow (Hartshorn, 1996), or from broad appeals to refocus policy initiatives to support women-owned start-ups (Carter, 2000).

The management of female-owned firms

As the field of study developed, the research effort moved beyond broad descriptions of the personal and business characteristics of women to focus on the nature of management differences in female-owned firms. Early studies examining the management of female-owned firms drew on contemporaneous debates within the mainstream small firms literature to focus on issues such as employment relations, generic small business management issues and broad descriptions of management processes (Hisrich and Brush, 1983; Goffee and Scase, 1985; Carter and Cannon, 1992; Allen and Truman, 1993). More recent studies have continued to examine issues of management within female-owned enterprises, but the field has become more specialised and concentrated around a number of distinctive themes.

A recurrent issue within the research has been the assessment of women's management style and approaches to leadership. Echoing the gender and leadership debates within the field of management science in the 1980s, researchers have attempted to investigate whether women manage their firms in a qualitatively different way from men (Chaganti, 1986; Holmquist and Sundin, 1988; Brush, 1992; Stanford *et al.*, 1995; Brush, 1997; Gardiner and Tiggemann, 1999). The assumption that women are 'better at relationship-oriented skills, while men excel at task-oriented skills' has been refuted by some researchers (Leahy and Eggers, 1998), although the stereotypical view persists. Buttner (2001) reported that the management styles of self-employed women were best described using relational dimensions such as mutual empowering, collaboration, sharing of information, empathy and nurturing. Importantly, these dimensions, which have also been associated with women in different professional occupations, were deemed to be associated with firm performance, particularly with regard to employee retention and *esprit de corps*.

A perhaps more interesting element of the management literature has been an examination of the connections between women, business ownership and the family. Informed by sociological perspectives, researchers such as Baines and Wheelock (1998), and Ram and Holliday (1992), have explored these connections by 'pushing the family to the forefront of the analysis' (Baines and Wheelock, 1998:32). While the business–home nexus had been explored in earlier analyses, specifically from the perspective of role conflict (Stoner *et al.*, 1990), contribution of spouses (Nelson, 1989) and career development (Cromie and O'Sullivan, 1999), this new strand of research draws on qualitative and contextual case study data to tease out the more nuanced dimensions and processes of the interaction. A rather different strand of the family-women's business literature has focused on 'copreneurial' marital partners who own and manage a small business together (Marshak, 1994; Smith, 2000). While focusing on similar issues such as work–home boundaries and the persistence of traditional gender roles, this strand highlights the inherent difficulties in precisely defining women's involvement in enterprise. The predominance of family ownership within the small and medium enterprise sector makes it impossible to precisely delineate the extent of women's involvement in enterprise and differentiate gender-based management styles and processes.

Over the past ten years, research investigating gender and enterprise has developed to encompass more sophisticated methodologies and more robust sampling procedures. An increasing theoretical sophistication, particularly noticeable in the engagement with sociological and feminist approaches which have opened up the field to include insights into race, class and family issues, is starting to produce a more complete and nuanced picture of women's participation in the small firms sector. At the same time, the research effort has improved as a result of growing research specialisation. Within the area of gender and enterprise management, the focus of investigation has evolved to concentrate on smaller, but more precisely defined aspects. An important development in the contemporary field is the focus on the effect of gender on both the experience of self-employment and the relative performance of small businesses (Rosa and Hamilton, 1994; Rosa *et al.*, 1996; Berg, 1997; Carter and Allen, 1997; Marlow, 1997; Collins-Dodd *et al.*, 2004). Two recurrent themes have emerged from this work. Following work by Buttner and Rosen (1989), Riding and Swift (1990) in North America, and Fay and Williams (1993) in New Zealand, a major research theme has been the effect of gender differences in business financing (Read, 1994; Carter and Rosa, 1998; Marlow and Patton, 2005). Developments have also been seen in the analysis of female entrepreneurs' use of business networks (Olm *et al.*, 1988; Katz and Williams, 1997).

Finance and related issues

Studies of women's enterprise have consistently reported that women find it particularly difficult to access capital to start and sustain their ventures. While the research in this area is quite extensive, there is still conflicting evidence about whether finance poses problems for women starting and running businesses. Several studies have suggested that it is both more difficult for women to raise start-up and recurrent finance for business ownership and that women encounter credibility problems when dealing with bankers (Schwartz, 1976; Hisrich and Brush, 1984; Goffee and Scase, 1985; van der Wees and Romijn, 1987; Carr, 1990; Brush, 1992; Carter and Cannon, 1992; Orser and Foster, 1994; Carter and Rosa, 1998). Other studies have not confirmed this (Buttner and Rosen, 1988; 1989; Chrisman et al., 1990; Riding and Swift, 1990; Haines et al., 1999; Haynes and Haynes, 1999). The debate has continued largely because of the difficulties for researchers in providing clear and unequivocal evidence (Mahoot, 1997). Nevertheless, within the most recent research there are signs that a consensus is beginning to emerge, at least within some of the issues.

Four areas of the financing process have been consistently noted as posing particular problems for women. First, women may be disadvantaged in their ability to raise start-up finance (Schwartz, 1976; Carter and Cannon, 1992; Johnson and Storey, 1993; Koper, 1993; Van Auken et al., 1993; Carter and Rosa, 1998). Second, guarantees required for external financing may be beyond the scope of most women's personal assets and credit track record (Hisrich and Brush, 1986; Riding and Swift, 1990; Marlow and Patton, 2005). Third, finance for the ongoing business may be less available for female-owned firms than it is for male enterprises, largely due to women's inability to penetrate informal financial networks (Olm et al., 1988; Aldrich, 1989; Greene et al., 1999). Finally, female entrepreneurs' relationships with bankers may suffer because of sexual stereotyping and discrimination (Hisrich and Brush, 1986; Buttner and Rosen, 1988, 1989). Placing these arguments in a broader analytical framework, Marlow and Patton (2005) link the financing of women-owned firms to wider issues regarding experiences of gender-based discrimination and subordination. Using feminist analyses as a conceptual framework, it is argued that the ascription of gendered stereotypes devalues women in the socio-economic context. As such, the combination of stereotypical ascriptions plus a poorer accumulation of social and human capital leads to gender-based barriers which women have to overcome.

The gender and finance debate has also been analysed from the supply side, with explorations of the role of banks in providing finance to female business owners. Taking an 'asymmetric information' approach, a number of studies have explored whether banks have (unstated) differential lending policies to male and female business owners and, if so, whether these policies are a result of unwitting socialisation or outright discrimination (Koper, 1993; Coleman, 1998, 2000). In an example drawn from New Zealand, Fay and Williams (1993:365) found some evidence that women encounter credit discrimination in seeking start-up funding, but concluded that this was not necessarily the fault of the banks:

Commercial banks are risk averse institutions. Confronted by applications for finance from individuals with limited education and experience in the area they wish to operate and low proposed personal equity, as is commonly the case for would be female proprietors, loan officers not surprisingly refuse requests for finance. Bank staff are not guilty of discrimination in such situations. Rather, applicants' socialisation and work related experiences have disadvantaged them compared to male proprietors.

Gender and business networks

The important role of networks in the survival and success of individual firms has been a recurrent theme in the small firms literature (Aldrich *et al.*, 1989; Rosa and Hamilton, 1994; Aldrich *et al.*, 1997). Gender differences in the way networks are created and used have been cited as having an influence on certain aspects of the management process, for example, enabling improved access to finance and the development of strong relationships with financial backers (Millman, 1997; Carter and Rosa, 1998). This view has been influenced by studies that have demonstrated that the quantity and quality of external linkages between a firm and its environment are crucial to its success. Some have suggested that distinct gender differences might exist both in the establishment and management of social networks (i.e. the process of networking) and in the contents of social networks (i.e. what networks are used for) (Olm *et al.*, 1988; Aldrich, 1989). This view has been contested however. Starr and Yudkin (1996:40) concluded that: 'The few studies that compare the networking activities of women and men business owners show differences in the sex composition of the networks of women, but not in how men and women use their networks.'

The influence of gender on the networking activities of business owners has been subject to very little dedicated investigation, and remains contentious, largely because of conflicting guidance in the literature that has separately considered gender effects on business ownership and the influence of gender on networking activities. Researchers such as Rosa and Hamilton (1994) have argued that networking is both more critical and should be greater amongst women firm owners than amongst their male counterparts. This approach is, however, countered by earlier research conducted by Aldrich (1989) which suggested that self-employed women's networking levels are lower than those of self-employed men.

While it is clear that this remains a seriously under-researched area, the range of studies that have investigated gender differences in networking activities has enabled the emergence of a consensus on some elements of the networking debate. Studies undertaken in a diverse variety of contexts and countries, including the USA, Italy and Northern Ireland, have all concluded that there is a great deal of similarity in the networking behaviour of men and women, although the sex composition of networks does vary by gender. Women are more likely to have networks composed entirely of other women, and men are more likely to have networks composed entirely of other men (Aldrich *et al.*, 1989; Smeltzer and Fann, 1989; Cromie and Birley, 1992; Aldrich *et al.*, 1997). Hence, it might be more productive to consider the power and influence of gendered networks in terms of supporting either career progression or business support, rather than their reach and depth.

Performance and growth

The performance of small businesses, usually determined in terms of their economic contribution to job and wealth creation through business start-up and growth, has become an important area of recent policy and academic debate. Comparatively little rigorous and in-depth research, however, has been undertaken on the issue of gender and business performance. Although many studies have made some mention of it, most shy away from direct examination of quantitative performance measures, preferring instead to engage in discursive debate concerning gender differences in qualitative assessments of success. These studies suggest that women perform less well on quantitative measures such as job creation, sales turnover and profitability (Cliff, 1998; Fasci and Valdez, 1998). This, it is often argued, is usually because women do not enter business for financial gain but to pursue intrinsic goals (for example, independence and the flexibility to run business and domestic lives). Implicitly, women are deemed to assess success in relation to their achievement in attaining personal goals (i.e. self-fulfilment, goal attainment, etc.), while men are assumed to measure success using quantitative criteria (i.e. profits, growth, etc.) (Buttner and Moore, 1997; Lerner *et al.*, 1997; Marlow, 1997; Still and Timms, 2000; Collins-Dodd *et al.*, 2004). Elsewhere, it has been argued that the structural disadvantages facing women and their consequent lack of human, social and financial capital constrains their business performance from the outset (Marlow and Strange, 1994; Chell and Baines, 1998; Boden and Nucci, 2000).

The few studies that have used more sophisticated methodologies in pursuing issues of gender and performance have presented less clear-cut results (Chaganti and Parasuraman, 1996; Hisrich *et al.*, 1997). In a longitudinal study of 298 UK businesses, of which sixty-seven were female-owned, Johnson and Storey (1993) found that women proprietors in their study had created more stable enterprises than had their male sample, although, on average, the sales turnover for women was lower than for males. Fischer *et al.*'s (1993) study found that women's businesses tended to perform less well on measures such as sales, employment and growth, but concluded that determinants of gender differences in business performance were far more complex than had been recognised in earlier studies. Carter *et al.*'s (1997) analysis based on the US retail sector found that women were more likely to exit business and related this to the low level of initial start-up resources and the founding strategies of the owner. One of the few large-scale studies (Rosa *et al.*, 1996), specifically designed to investigate the impact of gender on small business management outlined four different measures of comparative performance of businesses by gender: primary performance measures (number of employees, growth in employees, sales turnover, value of capital assets); proxy performance measures (geographical range of markets, VAT registration); subjective measures (including the ability of the business to meet business and domestic needs); and finally, entrepreneurial performance measures (the desire for growth, the ownership of multiple businesses).

Rosa *et al.*'s (1996) analysis of primary performance measures suggested that women's businesses employed fewer core staff, were less likely to have grown substantially in employment (more than twenty employees) after twelve months in business, had a lower sales turnover and were valued at a lower level than male-owned businesses. The analysis of proxy performance measures also indicated that women-owned businesses were more likely to serve only local markets, although gender differences in export sales were non-significant. Male-owned businesses were also more likely to be registered for VAT. The subjective measures of performance, however, were less clearly divided by gender. In considering how well their businesses had performed in the previous two years, men and women gave comparable responses. Women did, however, appear to be less optimistic than men in their expectation of future business success. Women were also less likely to believe that their business created sufficient income to meet domestic needs, perhaps reflecting the fact that women's businesses tended to be substantially smaller than male-owned businesses in the sample. Male respondents whose businesses had a similar sized turnover were equally dissatisfied with their ability to meet domestic financial needs. The final measure, entrepreneurial performance, also demonstrated marked gender differences. Men were significantly more likely to own other businesses (19.6 per cent compared with 8.6 per cent) and also to have strong growth ambitions in so far as they wanted to expand their businesses 'as far as they could (43 per cent versus 34 per cent)' (Rosa *et al.*, 1996:469).

Although these results appear to demonstrate marked gender differences in business performance, they should be treated with caution. Not only are conclusions potentially premature given the scarcity of previous research, there are a number of complicating factors (such as industrial sector, prior experience, founding strategy, business age and presence of co-owners) which, depending on how they are treated methodologically, appear to produce widely differing results in business performance (Rosa *et al.*, 1996). Confirming Marlow and Strange's (1994) view, Rosa *et al.* (1996) argue that, while the performance of women-owned businesses appears at first sight to be substantially lower than for their male counterparts, women have only recently emerged as an entrepreneurial group and their businesses are much younger and, therefore, less established. This need for caution is reinforced by a recent study drawing upon an extensive Australian data set (Watson, 2002) which compared returns upon investment in firms owned by men and women. It was found that returns were broadly consistent but that women had poorer levels of investment in their firms in the first instance. So, while female-owned businesses underperformed compared to their male counterparts, this arose from a lack of initial investment and not from managerial or strategic failures associated with gender.

Collectively, the results of the various studies comparing male and female performance differences offer mixed results. Overall, there is little evidence to suggest that men are more profit orientated than women. However, it would appear that female-owned businesses are more likely to experience 'under-capitalisation' (Carter *et al.*, 2001), as well as a lack of initial human, social and economic resources, which in turn leads to underperformance over the longer term.

Explaining the evidence

From the evidence explored above, it is apparent that there is now a distinct body of literature and empirical evidence exploring the specific link between gender and entrepreneurship. However, when this material is carefully considered, there appears to be an overemphasis upon the end result of the impact of gender upon entrepreneurship, rather than any studied conceptual analysis of the process that creates disadvantage. For example, it has been argued that women's businesses generally underperform compared to those owned by men, and that underlying factors such as the lack of human, social and financial capital have been identified. Yet the reasons why women lack these attributes, which in turn, impact upon their enterprises, has rarely been considered. When reading the literature pertaining to gender and self-employment, there is a sense that gender is not understood as femininity or masculinity (see Chell, 2001 as an exception), and that the world of the entrepreneur is somehow immune to many of the broader social and economic influences that shape life chances in general. By locating the debate concerning gender and entrepreneurship largely within the boundaries of the small firms sector, that is with the economic unit of the firm as the key determinant, there is a serious failure to place self-employed women within the complex debate concerning female subordination in broader terms. As Mirchandani (1999:224) argues succinctly:

> Much of the literature on women and entrepreneurship does not address the consequences of adapting theories of entrepreneurship, developed through analyses of men's lives, to the experiences of women. Approaches to women and entrepreneurship would benefit greatly from theoretical insight on the gendered processes in work settings developed within feminist theory.

It is evident that a critical framework for analysing female entrepreneurship is through the concept of gender but only rarely is this notion engaged with on any analytical basis and used to support arguments or findings. The articulation of gender occurs through a binary division where stereotypical behaviours are associated with masculine and feminine traits where the former is more valued. As Cranny-Francis *et al.* (2003:2) describe: 'The male side of the equation is generally coded as the positive one and so becomes the standard by which all others are judged, in effect it becomes the norm. This privileging of the masculine is generally the case in Western societies.'

Given the social context in which gendered behaviours are cited, there is broad conformity with gendered expectations. As West and Zimmerman (1987) describe it, we all 'do gender'. Moreover, even those who adopt a gendered persona reflecting characteristics of the other sex are still, in effect, doing gender. Given the manner in which, as individuals, we engage with gendered behaviour, this also influences how we perceive and experience society. It leads to what Berger (1972) refers to as 'ways of seeing', or Bem (1993) describes as the 'lens of gender', in that our gender shapes our perception of the world and particularly our assumptions of how we, and others, should act. In turn, gender then acts in conjunction with other influences and characterisations such as race, age and class ensuring that men and women do not experience their masculinity and femininity in a homogeneous manner. Hence, unravelling the influence of gender is challenging and complex and requires care in application, but it undoubtedly moulds socio-economic interaction, albeit in different guises and to differing extents.

The outcome of a subordinating sex–gender system, which prioritises the heterosexual male, generates what Shakeshaft and Nowell (1984:187–188) describe as an androcentric society which appears neutral, but in fact is premised upon the

> elevation of the masculine to the level of the universal and the ideal, it is the honouring of men and the male principle above women and the female. This perception creates a belief in male superiority and a value system in which female values, experiences and behaviours are viewed as inferior.

Supporting this assertion, Cockburn (1991) argues that most societies are underpinned by a masculinist hegemony where a domination of male culture and ideas results in a specific form of common sense which is cited within the heterosexual male. Thus, the things that such men do, the ways that they act and think are ascribed as the norm, with other forms of behaviour deemed in terms of the 'other'.

Such an analysis of gender within the socio-economic environment is supported by empirical evidence from a comprehensive range of disciplines. For example, any consideration of the contemporary labour market exposes a persistent pay gap between men and women. In the UK, the pay gap is about 20 per cent and has hardly changed since the widespread enactment of the Sex Discrimination Act in 1975 (EOC, 2004). Much of this difference arises from the continued influence of horizontal and vertical occupational segregation (Hakim, 1979). Horizontal segregation refers to the clustering of men and women into different occupations where those dominated by women are defined by lower pay, skill and status than those dominated by men. Vertical segregation refers to the clustering of women in the lowest tiers of occupations where integration between the sexes occurs. Drawing upon a range of studies and surveys, Bradley

(1999) finds substantial evidence that such segregation persists in contemporary society, even given recent labour market changes such as the expansion of women into managerial posts and the increased entry of women into full-time work.

The issue of waged work disadvantage is particularly apposite for any consideration of entrepreneurship. It is well established that most entrants to entrepreneurship do so on the basis of work-based experiences, bringing their human, social and financial capital into the new venture (Wynarczk et al., 1993; Storey, 1994). If, due to the larger influence of gendered subordination, women have fewer resources to deploy, it is axiomatic that their business will reflect this. As Diamantopoulou (1997) notes, there is a fantasy that 'business has no gender', which suggests that all who enter the field are equally well equipped to act. However, the evidence regarding the impact of gender upon men and women would indicate that this is not so. Further to the example of subordination in waged labour, there is a considerable body of literature that explores the unequal responsibilities men and women experience as carers and as domestic labourers, which again shape their life chances in terms of engaging with the contemporary market economy in a positive fashion.

It is evident that women struggle to conform to the standards that advantage men but subordinate women (Bradley, 1999; Cranny-Francis et al., 2003). So, women must attain levels of performance drawn from male norms of work and achievement while beginning from a point of fundamental disadvantage. Entrepreneurship is not removed from other areas of work such that firm owners, by some magical act, separate themselves from existing norms and values in society. So it is simplistic to suggest that entrepreneurship can be somehow removed from prevailing systems of gendered subordination or disadvantage. Thus, analyses of entrepreneurship must take account of wider theoretical concepts associated with the specific circumstances of the self-employed individual and how this impinges upon the market position and perception of the firm. A key research task must now be to consider how, rather than if, the impact of gender is articulated within entrepreneurship with appropriate sensitivity to heterogeneity amongst women. The point here is not to argue deterministically that all women will experience gender-related subordination in a uniform fashion. This would be absurd. Rather, the complex and sophisticated analyses that have been developed regarding gender-related disadvantage for women should not be ignored. It is the manner in which women use individual agency to negotiate through and around disadvantage that now requires consideration.

Conclusions

As this chapter has demonstrated, research investigating gender and enterprise has expanded and matured considerably over the past fifteen years. There has been a refocusing of attention from early studies of women's business ownership which considered female experiences entirely in relation to male norms, towards an increasing awareness of gender differences within entrepreneurship which are socially constructed and negotiated. On this basis, therefore, the field has developed and matured. Although many of the early studies which examined the demographic characteristics and motivations of female entrepreneurs were subsequently criticised for their small scale and their lack of rigour, their importance cannot be underestimated in identifying and clearly delineating a hitherto 'invisible' group (Baker *et al.*, 1997:221). Although exploratory, these studies challenged for the first time the view that entrepreneurship is a gender-neutral activity. More recent research has moved towards large-scale studies, often utilising quantitative methods. However, developments have not only occurred in the growing trend towards empiricism. Engagement with sociological approaches, in particular, has enabled a more insightful, qualitative analysis of the entrepreneurial principles and processes used by both men and women.

It was stated in the introduction that, in comparison with the volume of academic research that has been undertaken on the small firms' sector, the female business owner has been 'neglected' by both the mass media and the academic community (Baker *et al.*, 1997:221). For some researchers, the lack of attention given to women's enterprise is indicative of a wider problem of gender effects being omitted from mainstream research studies into social phenomena. Carter (1993:151), for example, notes that: 'Historically women have been left off the small business research agenda or made invisible by research practices or in other ways written out of the analysis of self-employment.'

Others have argued that the neglect of a focus on women is part of a much wider problem which has resulted in the social sciences being structured in a manner which favours the male experience. Concepts of entrepreneurship are traditionally assumed to be gender-neutral, but as Berg (1997:261) points out: 'rely in fact on notions of humanity and rationality that are masculinist'. Dualities such as the rational–irrational distinction, seen most clearly within studies examining gender and business performance, may appear to have no apparent gender bias, but in reality are 'thoroughly imbued with gender connotations, one side being socially characterized as masculine, the other as feminine, and the former being socially valorised' (Massey, 1996:113).

There can be little doubt that self-employed women, as a relatively new group operating significantly younger businesses, may not yet have attained the same level of achievement as those owned by men, but over time they are catching up. Contemporary literature regarding the links between gender and self employment (Carter *et al.*, 2001; Watson, 2002; Collins-Dodd *et al.*, 2004; Marlow and Patton, 2005) is now far more sensitive to the nuances of gender and how it interacts with other socio-economic influences. This represents considerable progress. Using gender in a generalised, almost blunt instrument fashion is no longer useful in attempting to fully explore how women and men engage with enterprise. However, there is still considerable scope for further progress in refining and developing our understanding of how gender works, particularly with respect to wider feminist debates regarding subordination and discrimination. Otherwise, from prevailing debate, it might be assumed that the key characteristic women require to succeed in self-employment is the ability to be an 'honorary' man, and the more they pursue the male model, the more likely they are to succeed. We must be wary of lauding this as progress.

References

Aldrich, H. (1989). 'Networking Among Women Entrepreneurs'. In Hagen, O., Rivchum, C. and Sexton, D. (eds), *Women Owned Businesses*. New York: Praeger, 103–132.

Aldrich, H., Reese, P. and Dubini, P. (1989). 'Women on the Verge of a Breakthrough? Networking Among Entrepreneurs in the United States and Italy'. *Entrepreneurship and Regional Development*, 1, 339–356.

Aldrich, H.E., Elam, A.B. and Reece, P.R. (1997). 'Strong Ties, Weak Ties and Strangers: Do Women Owners Differ from Men in their Use of Networking to Obtain Assistance?' In Birley, S. and MacMillan, I.C. (eds), *Entrepreneurship in a Global Context*. London: Routledge.

Allen, S. and Truman, C. (1993). 'Women and Men Entrepreneurs: Life Strategies, Business Strategies'. In Allen, S. and Truman, C. (eds), W*omen in Business: Perspectives on Women Entrepreneurs*. London: Routledge, 1–13.

Alsos, G. and Ljunggren, E. (1998). 'Does the Business Start-Up Process Differ by Gender? A Longitudinal Study of Nascent Entrepreneurs'. *Frontiers of Entrepreneurship Research.* Wellesley, MA: Babson College. Available: www.babson.edu/entrep/fer.

Anna, A., Chandler, G., Jansen, E. and Mero, N. (2000). 'Women Business Owners in Traditional and Non-Traditional Industries'. *Journal of Business Venturing*, 15, 3, 279–303.

Baines, S. and Wheelock, J. (1998). 'Working for Each Other: Gender, the Household and Micro-business Survival and Growth'. *International Small Business Journal*, 17, 1, 16–35.

Baker, T., Aldrich, H.E. and Liou, N. (1997). 'Invisible Entrepreneurs: the Neglect of Women Business Owners by Mass Media and Scholarly Journals in the United States'. *Entrepreneurship and Regional Development*, 9, 3, 221–238.

Belcourt, M. (1990). 'A Family Portrait of Canada's Most Successful Female Entrepreneurs'. *Journal of Business Ethics*, 9, 4/5, 435–438.

Bem, S. (1993). *The Lens of Gender*, New Haven, CT, Yale University Press.

Bennett, R. and Dann, S. (2000). 'The Changing Experience of Australian Female Entrepreneurs'. *Gender, Work and Organisation (UK)*, 7, 2, 75–83.

Berg, N.G. (1997). 'Gender, Place and Entrepreneurship'. *Entrepreneurship and Regional Development*, 9, 3, 259–268.

Berger, J. (1972). *Ways of Seeing*, London, BBC and Penguin.

Birley, S. (1989). 'Female Entrepreneurs: Are They Really any Different?' *Journal of Small Business Management*, 2, 1, 7–31.

Birley, S. and Wright, M. (2001). 'Entrepreneurship and Wealth Creation: Sue Birley Reflects on Creating and Growing Wealth'. *European Management Journal*, 19, 2, 128–139.

Boden, R.J. and Nucci, A.R. (2000). 'On the Survival Prospects of Men's and Women's New Business Ventures'. *Journal of Business Venturing*, 15, 4, 347–362.

Bradley, H. (1999). *Gender and Power in the Workplace*, Basingstoke, Macmillan.

Brenner, O.C., Tomkiewicz, J. and Schein, V. (1989). 'The Relationship Between Sex Role Stereotypes and Requisite Management Characteristics Revisited'. *Academy of Management Journal*, 32, 3, 662–669.

Brush, C. (1992). 'Research on Women Business Owners: Past Trends, a New Perspective and Future Directions'. *Entrepreneurship Theory and Practice*, 16, 4, 5–30.

Brush, C. (1997). 'Women-Owned Businesses: Obstacles and Opportunities'. *Journal of Developmental Entrepreneurship*, 2, 1, 1–25.

Brush, C.G. and Hisrich, R.D. (1999). 'Women-Owned Businesses: Why Do They Matter?' In Acs, Z.J. (ed.), *Are Small Firms Important? Their Role and Impact*. Norwell MA: Kluwer Academic Publishers, 111–127.

Buttner, E.H. (2001). 'Examining Female Entrepreneurs' Management Style: An Application of a Relational Frame'. *Journal of Business Ethics*, Dordrecht, February, 263–269.

Buttner, E. and Rosen, B. (1988). 'Bank Loan Officers' Perceptions of the Characteristics of Men, Women, and Successful Entrepreneurs'. *Journal of Business Venturing*, 3, 3, 249–258.

Buttner, E. and Rosen, B. (1989). 'Funding New Business Ventures: Are Decision Makers Biased Against Women Entrepreneurs?' *Journal of Business Venturing*, 4, 4, 249–261.

Buttner, E. and Moore, D. (1997). 'Women's Organisational Exodus to Entrepreneurship: Self Reported Motivations and Correlates with Success'. *Journal of Small Business Management*, 35, 1, 34–46.

Caputo, R.K. and Dolinsky, A. (1998). 'Women's Choice to Pursue Self-Employment: The Role of Financial and Human Capital of Household Members'. *Journal of Small Business Management*, 36, 3, 8–17.

Carland, J.A. and Carland, J.W. (1991). 'An Empirical Investigation into the Distinction Between Male and Female Entrepreneurs and Managers'. *International Small Business Journal*, 9, 3, 62–72.

Carr, M. (1990). 'Women in Small-Scale Industries – Some Lessons from Africa'. *Small Enterprise Development*, 1, 1, 47–51.

Carter, N. and Allan, K.R. (1997). 'Size Determinants of Women-Owned Businesses: Choice or Barriers to Resources?' *Entrepreneurship and Regional Development*, 9, 3, 211–220.

Carter, N.M. and Kolvereid, L. (1997). 'Women Starting New Businesses: The Experiences in Norway and the US'. *Proceedings from the OECD Conference on Women Entrepreneurs in Small and Medium Enterprises: A Major Force in Innovation and Job Creation*, Paris, April, 185–202.

Carter, N.M., Williams, M. and Reynolds, P.D. (1997). 'Discontinuance Among New Firms in Retail: The Influence of Initial Resources, Strategy, and Gender'. *Journal of Business Venturing*, 12, 2, 125–145.

Carter, S. (1993). 'Female Business Ownership: Current Research and Possibilities for the Future'. In Allen, S. and Truman, C. (eds), *Women in Business: Perspectives on Women Entrepreneurs*. London: Routledge, 148–160.

Carter, S. (2000). 'Improving the Numbers and Performance of Women-Owned Businesses: Some Implications for Training and Advisory Services'. *Education and Training*, 42, 4/5, 326–333.

Carter, S. and Cannon, T. (1992). *Women as Entrepreneurs*, London, Academic Press.

Carter, S. and Rosa, P. (1998). 'The Financing of Male and Female-Owned Businesses'. *Entrepreneurship and Regional Development*, 10, 3, 225–241.

Carter, S., Anderson, S. and Shaw, E. (2001). 'Women's Business Ownership: A Review of the Academic, Popular and Internet Literature'. Report to the Small Business Service, RR002/01.

Carter, S., Mason, C. and Tagg, S. (2004). *Lifting the Barriers to Business Survival and Growth: The FSB Biennial Survey 2004*, London, Federation of Small Businesses.

Catley, S. and Hamilton, R.T. (1998). 'Small Business Development and Gender of Owner'. *Journal of Management Development*, 17, 1, 75–82.

Chaganti, R. (1986). 'Management in Women-Owned Enterprises'. *Journal of Small Business Management*, 24, 4, 18–29.

Chaganti, R. and Parasuraman, S. (1996). 'A Study of the Impact of Gender on Business Performance and Management Patterns in Small Business'. *Entrepreneurship Theory and Practice*, 21, 2, 73–76.

Chell, E. (2001). *Entrepreneurship, Globalization, Innovation and Development*, London, Thompson Learning.

Chell, E. and Baines, S. (1998). 'Does Gender Affect Business Performance? A Study of Microbusiness in Business Services in the UK'. *Entrepreneurship and Regional Development*, 10, 2, 117–135.

Chrisman, J.J., Carsrud, A.L., DeCastro, J. and Herron, L. (1990). 'A Comparison of the Assistance Needs of Male and Female Pre-Venture Entrepreneurs'. *Journal of Business Venturing*, 5, 235–248.

Cliff, J.E. (1998). 'Does One Size Fit All? – Exploring the Relationship Between Attitudes Towards Growth, Gender and Business Size'. *Journal of Business Venturing*, 13, 6, 523–542.

Cockburn, C. (1991). *In the Way of Women*, London, Methuen.

Coleman, S. (1998). 'Access to Capital: A Comparison of Men and Women-Owned Small Businesses'. *Frontiers of Entrepreneurship Research*. Wellesley, MA: Babson College. Available: www.babson.edu/entrep/fer.

Coleman, S. (2000). 'Access to Capital: A Comparison of Men and Women-Owned Small Businesses'. *Journal of Small Business Management*, 38, 3, 37–52.

Collerette, P. and Aubry, P. (1990). 'Socio-Economic Evolution of Women Business Owners in Quebec'. *Journal of Business Ethics* (Netherlands), 9, 4/5, 417–422.

Collins-Dodd, C., Gordon, I. and Smart, C. (2004). 'Further Evidence on the Role of Gender in Financial Performance'. *Journal of Small Business Management*, 42, 4, 395–417.

Cranny-Francis, A., Waring, W., Stavropoulos, P. and Kirky, J. (2003). *Gender Studies: Terms and Debates*, Basingstoke: Palgrave.

Cromie, S. (1987). 'Similarities and Differences Between Women and Men Who Choose Business Proprietorship'. *International Small Business Journal*, 5, 3, 43–60.

Cromie, S. and Birley, S. (1992). 'Networking by Female Business Owners in Northern Ireland'. *Journal of Business Venturing*, 7, 3, 237–251.

Cromie, S. and Hayes, J. (1988). 'Towards a Typology of Female Entrepreneurs'. *Sociological Review*, 36, 1, 87–113.

Cromie, S. and O'Sullivan, S. (1999). 'Women as Managers in Family Firms'. *Women in Management Review*, 14, 3, 76–88.

Curran, J. (1986). 'Bolton Fifteen Years on: a Review and Analysis of Small Business Research in Britain 1971–1986', London: Small Business Research Trust.

Curran, J. and Burrows, R. (1988). 'Enterprise in Britain: a National Profile of Small Business Owners and the Self-Employed', London: Small Business Research Trust.

Diamantopoulou, A. (1997). Address to the Women in Small and Medium Sized Enterprises Conference, OECD, Paris.

Dolinsky, A., Caputo, R.K. and Pasumarty, K. (1994). 'Long-Term Entrepreneurship

Patterns: A National Study of Black and White Female Entry and Stayer Status Differences'. *Journal of Small Business Management*, 32, 1, 18–25.

Dolinsky, A., Caputo, R.K., Parsumarty, K. and Quazi, H. (1993). 'The Effects of Education on Business Ownership: A Longitudinal Study of Women'. *Entrepreneurship Theory and Practice*, 18, 1, 43–54.

Equal Opportunities Commission (2004). *Women and Men at Work*, available: www.eoc.org.uk.

Fagenson, E. (1993). 'Personal Value Systems of Men and Women Entrepreneurs Versus Managers'. *Journal of Business Venturing*, 8, 5, 409–430.

Fagenson, E. and Marcus, E. (1991). 'Perceptions of the Sex-Role Stereotypic Characteristics of Entrepreneurs: Women's Evaluations'. *Entrepreneurship Theory and Practice*, 15, 4, 33–47.

Fasci, M.A. and Valdex, J. (1998). 'A Performance Contrast of Male and Female-Owned Small Accounting Practices'. *Journal of Small Business Management*, 36, 3, 1–7.

Fay, M. and Williams, L. (1993). 'Gender Bias and the Availability of Business Loans'. *Journal of Business Venturing*, 8, 4, 363–376.

Fischer, E., Reuber, A.R. and Dyke, L. (1993). 'A Theoretical Overview and Extension of Research on Sex, Gender and Entrepreneurship'. *Journal of Business Venturing*, 8, 2, 151–168.

Frazier, E.F. (1997). *Black Bourgeoisie: The Rise of a New Middle Class*, New York, The Free Press.

Gardiner, M. and Tiggemann, M. (1999). 'Gender Differences in Leadership Style, Job Stress and Mental Health in Male and Female Dominated Industries'. *Journal of Occupational and Organisational Psychology*, 72, 301–315.

Glas, M. and Petrin, T. (1998). 'Entrepreneurship: New Challenge for Slovene Women'. Abstract Summary presented at the 21st ISBA National Small Firms Policy and Research Conference, November 1998.

Goffee, R. and Scase, R. (1985). *Women in Charge: The Experiences of Female Entrepreneurs*, London, George Allen & Unwin.

Goffee, R. and Scase, R. (1987). 'Patterns of Business Proprietorship Among Women in Britain'. In Goffee, R. and Scase, R. (eds), *Entrepreneurship in Europe: The Social Processes*. London: Crook Helmm, Chapter 5.

Gordon, Z.G. (1997). 'SMEs in the Philippines'. *Proceedings of the OECD Conference on Women Entrepreneurs in Small and Medium Enterprises: A Major Force in Innovation and Job Creation*, Paris, April, 237–250.

Green, E. and Cohen, L. (1995). 'Women's Business – are Women Entrepreneurs Breaking New Ground or Simply Balancing the Demands of Women's Work in a New Way?' *Journal of Gender Studies*, 4, 3, 297–314.

Greene, P., Brush, C., Hart, M. and Saparito, P. (1999). 'Exploration of the Venture Capital Industry: is Gender an issue?' *Frontiers of Entrepreneurship Research*. Wellesley, MA: Babson College. Available: www.babson.edu/entrep/fer.

Greer, G. (1999). *The Whole Woman*, London, Doubleday.

Haines, G., Orser, A. and Riding, L. (1999). 'Myths and Realities: an Empirical Study of Banks and the Gender of Small Business Clients'. *Canadian Journal of Administrative Sciences*, 16, 4, 291–307.

Hakim, C. (1979). 'Occupational Segregation by Sex'. Research paper no. 9, Department of Employment, UK.

Hamilton, D., Rosa, P. and Carter, S. (1987). 'The Impact of Gender on the Management of Small Business: Some Fundamental Problems'. In Welford, R. (ed.), *Small Business and Small Business Development – a Practical Approach*. Bradford: European Research Press, 33–40.

Hartshorn, C. (1996). 'Raising Entrepreneurial Awareness: Some Issues Relating to Rural Women'. In Briley, S. (ed.), *Women in the Workplace: Human Resource Development Strategies into the Next Century*. Edinburgh: HMSO, Chapter 4.

Haynes, G.W. and Haynes, D.C. (1999). 'The Debt Structure of Small Businesses Owned by Women in 1987 and 1993'. *Journal of Small Business Management*, 37, 2, 1–19.

Hisrich, R. and Brush, C. (1983). 'The Woman Entrepreneur: Implications of Family, Educational, and Occupational Experience'. In Hornaday, J., Timmons, J. and Vesper, K. (eds), *Frontiers of Entrepreneurship Research*. Wellesley, MA: Babson College, 255–270.

Hisrich, R. and Brush, C. (1984). 'The Woman Entrepreneur: Implications of Family, Educational, and Occupational Experience'. *Journal of Small Business Management*, 33 (January).

Hisrich, R. and Brush, C. (1986). *The Woman Entrepreneur: Starting, Financing and Managing a Successful New Business*, Lexington, MA, Lexington Books.

Hisrich, R.D. and Ozturk, S. (1999). 'Women Entrepreneurs in a Developing Economy'. *Journal of Management Development*, 18, 2, 114–124.

Hisrich, R.D., Brush, C.G., Good, D. and DeSouza, G. (1997). 'Performance in Entrepreneurial Ventures: Does Gender Matter?' *Frontiers of Entrepreneurship Research*. Wellesley, MA: Babson College. Available: www.babson.edu/entrep/fer.

Holmquist, C. (1997). 'The Other Side of the Coin or Another Coin? – Women's Entrepreneurship as a Complement or an Alternative?' *Entrepreneurship and Regional Development*, 9, 3, 179–182.

Holmquist, C. and Sundin, E. (1988). 'Women as Entrepreneurs in Sweden – Conclusions from a Survey'. In Kirchoff, B., Long, W., McMullan, W., Vesper, K. and Wetzel, W. Jr (eds), *Frontiers of Entrepreneurship Research*. Wellesley, MA: Babson College, 643–653.

Holmquist, C. and Sundin, E. (1989). 'The Growth of Women's Entrepreneurship – Push or Pull Factors?' Paper presented to the EIASM Conference on Small Business, University of Durham Business School.

Izyumov, A. and Razumnova, I. (2000). 'Women Entrepreneurs in Russia: Learning to Survive the Market'. *Journal of Developmental Entrepreneurship*, 5, 1, 1–19.

Johnson, S. and Storey, D. (1993). 'Male and Female Entrepreneurs and their Businesses: A Comparative Study'. In Allen, S. and Truman, C. (eds), *Women in Business: Perspectives on Women Entrepreneurs*. London: Routledge, 70–85.

Jones, K. (2000). 'Psychodynamics, Gender and Reactionary Entrepreneurship in Metropolitan Sao Paulo, Brazil'. *Women in Management Review*, 15, 4, 207–220.

Katz, J.A. and Williams, P.M. (1997). 'Gender, Self-Employment and Weak-Tie Networking through Formal Organisations'. *Entrepreneurship and Regional Development*, 9, 3, 183–197.

Kolvereid, L., Shane, S. and Westhead, P. (1993). 'Is it Equally Difficult for Female Entrepreneurs to Start Businesses in all Countries?' *Journal of Small Business Management*, 31, 4, 42–51.

Koper, G. (1993). 'Women Entrepreneurs and the Granting of Business Credit'. In Allen, S. and Truman, C. (eds), *Women in Business: Perspectives on Women Entrepreneurs*. London: Routledge, 57–69.

Kourilsky, M.L. and Walstad, W.B. (1998). 'Entrepreneurship and Female Youth: Knowledge, Attitudes, Gender Differences and Educational Practices'. *Journal of Business Venturing*, 13, 1, 77–88.

Langan-Fox, J. and Roth, S. (1995). 'Achievement, Motivation and Female Entrepreneurs'. *Journal of Occupational and Organisational Psychology*, 3, 68, 209–218.

Leahy, K.T. and Eggers, J.H. (1998). 'Is Gender Still a Factor in Entrepreneurial Leader Behaviour?' Poster Summary presented at the 21st ISBA National Small Firms Policy and Research Conference, November.

Lee, J. (1996). 'The Motivation of Women Entrepreneurs in Singapore'. *Women in Management Review*, 11, 2, 18–29.

Lee-Gosselin, H. and Grise, J. (1990). 'Are Women Owner–Managers Challenging our Definitions of Entrepreneurship? An In-depth study'. *Journal of Business Ethics*, 9, 4/5, 423–433.

Lerner, M., Brush, C. and Hisrich, R. (1997). 'Israeli Women Entrepreneurs: An Examination of Factors Affecting Performance'. *Journal of Business Venturing*, 12, 4, 315–339.

Ljunggren, E. and Kolvereid, L. (1996). 'New Business Formation: Does Gender Make a Difference?' *Women in Management Review*, 11, 4, 3–12.

Loscocco, K.A. and Robinson, J. (1991). 'Barriers to Women's Small Business Success in the United States'. *Gender and Society*, 5, 4, 511–532.

Mahoot, P. (1997). 'Funding for Women Entrepreneurs: A Real, Though Disputed, Problem'. *Proceedings of the OECD Conference on Women Entrepreneurs in Small and Medium Enterprises: A Major Force in Innovation and Job Creation*, Paris, April, 217–226.

Marlow, S. (1997). 'Self-Employed Women – Do they Mean Business?' *Entrepreneurship and Regional Development*, 9, 3, 199–210.

Marlow, S. (2002). 'Women in Self Employment; A Part of, or Apart from, Theoretical Construct?' *Entrepreneurship and Innovation*, 3, 2, 83–91.

Marlow, S. and Carter, S. (2004) 'Accounting for Change: Professional Status, Gender Disadvantage and Self-Employment'. *Women in Management Review*, 19, 1, 5–16.

Marlow, S. and Patton, D. (2005). 'All Credit to Men? Entrepreneurship, Finance and Gender'. *Entrepreneurship Theory and Practice*, 29, 6, 717–736.

Marlow, S. and Strange, A. (1994). 'Female Entrepreneurs – Success by Whose Standards?' In Tanton, M. (ed.), *Women in Management: A Developing Presence*. London: Routledge, 172–184.

Marlow, S., Westall, A. and Watson, E. (2003). *Who Benefits?* London, New Economics Foundation.

Marshack, K.J. (1994). 'Copreneurs and Dual-Career Couples: Are They Different?' *Entrepreneurship Theory and Practice*, 19, 1, 46–69.

Massey, D. (1996). 'Masculinity, Dualisms and High Technology'. In Duncan, N. (ed.), *Bodyspace – Destabilizing Geographies of Gender and Sexuality*. London: Routledge, 109–126.

Masters, R. and Meier, R. (1988). 'Sex Differences and Risk-Taking Propensity of Entrepreneurs'. *Journal of Small Business Management*, 26, 1, 31–35.

Matthews, C. and Moser, S. (1996). 'A Longitudinal Investigation of the Impact of Family Background and Gender on Interest in Small Firm Ownership'. *Journal of Small Business Management*, 34, 2, 29–43.

Maysami, C. and Goby, V.P. (1999). 'Female Business Owners in Singapore and Elsewhere: A Review of Studies'. *Journal of Small Business Management*, 37, 2, 96–105.

Millman, A. (1997). 'The Role of Networks'. *Proceedings of the OECD Conference on Women Entrepreneurs in Small and Medium Enterprises: A Major Force in Innovation and Job Creation*, Paris, April, 121–128.

Mirchandani, K. (1999). 'Feminist Insight on Gendered Work: New Directions in Research on Women and Entrepreneurship'. *Gender, Work and Organisation*, 6, 4, 224–235.

Mroczkowski, T. (1997). 'Women as Employees and Entrepreneurs in the Polish Transformation'. *Industrial Relations Journal*, 28, 2, 83–91.

National Women's Business Council (2004). *Key Facts About Women Business Owners and Their Enterprises*. Washington DC, National Women's Business Council.

Nelson, G. (1989). 'Factors of Friendship: Relevance of Significant Others to Female Business Owners'. *Entrepreneurship Theory and Practice*, 13, 4, 7–18.

Nilsson, P. (1997). 'Business Counselling Services Directed Towards Female Entrepreneurs – Some Legitimacy Dilemmas'. *Entrepreneurship and Regional Development*, 9, 3, 239–257.

Olm, K., Carsrud, A. and Alvey, L. (1988). 'The Role of Networks in New Venture Funding for the Female Entrepreneur: A Continuing Analysis'. In Kirchoff, B.A., Long, W.A., McMullan, W.E., Vesper, K.H. and Wetzel, W.E. Jr (eds), *Frontiers of Entrepreneurship Research.* Wellesley, MA: Babson College.

Olson, S. and Currie, H. (1992). 'Female Entrepreneurs: Personal Value Systems and Business Strategies in a Male-Dominated Industry'. *Journal of Small Business Management*, 30, 1, 49–57.

Orser, B.J. and Foster, M.K. (1994). 'Lending Practices and Canadian Women in Micro-Based Businesses'. *Women in Management Review*, 9, 5, 11–19.

Padaki, R. (1994). *Women and her Enterprise: a Study of Karnataka State*, Bangalore, The P & P Group.

Premchander, S. (1994). 'Income Generating Programmes for Rural Women – Examining the Role of NGOs'. *Small Enterprise Development*, 5, 1.

Ram, M. and Holliday, R. (1992). 'Keeping it in the Family, Small Firms and Familial Culture'. Paper presented at the 13th National Small Firms Policy and Research Conference, Southampton.

Read, L. (1994). 'The Financing of Women-Owned Businesses: A Review and Research Agenda'. Working Paper No. 8. Urban Policy Research Unit, University of Southampton, May.

Riding, A. and Swift, C. (1990). 'Women Business Owners and Terms of Credit: Some Empirical Findings of the Canadian Experience'. *Journal of Business Venturing*, 5, 327–340.

Rosa, P. and Hamilton, D. (1994). 'Gender and Ownership in UK Small Firms'. *Entrepreneurship Theory and Practice*, 18, 311–28.

Rosa, P., Carter, S. and Hamilton, D. (1996). 'Gender as a Determinant of Small Business Performance: Insights from a British study'. *Small Business Economics*, 8, 463–478.

Scherer, R.F., Brodzinski, J.D. and Wiebe, F.A. (1990). 'Entrepreneurship Career Selection and Gender: A Socialization approach'. *Journal of Small Business Management*, 28, 2, 37–44.

Schreier, J. (1973). *The Female Entrepreneur: A Pilot Study*, Milwaukee, WI, Centre for Venture Management.

Schwartz, E.B. (1976). 'Entrepreneurship: a New Female Frontier'. *Journal of Contemporary Business*, Winter, 47–76.

Sexton, D. and Bowman-Upton, N. (1990). 'Female and Male Entrepreneurs: Psychological Characteristics and their Role in Gender-Related Discrimination'. *Journal of Business Venturing*, 5, 1, 29–36.

Shabbir, A. and Di Gregorio, S. (1996). 'An Examination of the Relationship Between Women's Personal Goals and Structural Factors Influencing their Decision to Start a Business: the Case of Pakistan'. *Journal of Business Venturing*, 11, 6, 507–529.

Shakeshaft, C. and Nowell, I. (1984) 'Research on Themes, Concepts and Models of Organisational Behaviour: the Influence of Gender'. *Issues in Education*, 2, 3, 186–203.

Shane, S., Kolvereid, L. and Westhead, A. (1991). 'An Exploratory Examination of the Reasons Leading to New Firm Formation Across Country and Gender'. *Journal of Business Venturing*, 6, 6, 431–46.

Shim, S. and Eastlick, M.A. (1998). 'Characteristics of Hispanic Female Business Owners: An Exploratory Study'. *Journal of Small Business Management*, 36, 3, 18–34.

Small Business Service, (2003). *A Strategic Framework for Women's Enterprise*, London, DTI/5000k/04/03.

Smeltzer, L.R. and Fann, G.L. (1989). 'Gender Differences in External Networks of Small Business Owners/Managers'. *Journal of Small Business Management*, 27, 2, 25–32.

Smith, C.R. (2000). 'Managing Work and Family in Small "Copreneurial" Business: an Australian study'. *Women in Management Review*, 15, 5/6, 283–289.

Solomon, G.T. and Fernald, L.W. (1988). 'Value Profiles of Male and Female Entrepreneurs'. *International Small Business Journal*, 6, 120–131.

Spilling, O.R. and Berg, N. (2000). 'Gender and Small Business Management: The Case of Norway in the 1990s'. *International Small Business Journal*, 18, 2, 38–59.

Stanford, J., Oates, B. and Flores, D. (1995). 'Women's Leadership Styles: a Heuristic Analysis'. *Women in Management Review*, 10, 2, 9–16.

Starr, J. and Yudkin, M. (1996). *Women Entrepreneurs: A Review of Current Research*, Wellesley, MA, Centre for Research on Women.

Stevenson, L. (1983). 'An Investigation into the Entrepreneurial Experience of Women: Implications for Small Business Policy in Canada'. Paper presented to the ASAC Conference, Vancouver: University of British Columbia.

Still, L.V. and Timms, W. (2000). 'Women's Business: the Flexible Alternative Workstyle for Women'. *Women in Management Review*, 15, 5/6, 272–282.

Stoesz, D. (2002). 'The American Welfare State at Twilight'. *Journal of Social Policy*, 31, 3, 487–503.

Stoner, C.R., Hartman, R.I. and Arora, R. (1990). 'Work–Home Role Conflict in Female Owners of Small Businesses: An Exploratory Study'. *Journal of Small Business Management*, 28, 1, 30–38.

Storey, D. (1994). *Understanding the Small Business Sector*, London, Routledge.

Van Auken, H., Gaskill, L. and Kao, S. (1993). 'Acquisition of Capital by Women Entrepreneurs: Patterns of Initial and Refinancing Capitalization'. *Journal of Small Business and Entrepreneurship*, 10, 4, 44–55.

van der Wees, C. and Romijn, H. (1987). *Entrepreneurship and Small Enterprise Development for Women in Developing Countries*, Geneva, ILO Management Development Branch.

Watson, J. (2002). 'Comparing the Performance of Male and Female Controlled Businesses: Relating Outputs to Inputs'. *Entrepreneurship Theory and Practice*, 26, 3, 91–100.

Weeks, J.R. (1998). *A Study on Women Entrepreneurs in SMEs in the APEC Region:*

Report from the US. Asia-Pacific Economic Cooperation Project No SME 02/98. Silver Spring, MD: NFWBO.

West, C. and Zimmerman, D. (1987). 'Doing Gender'. *Gender and Society*, 1, 125–152.

Wilkinson, H. (2001). *Dot Bombshell: Women, E-quality and the New Economy*, London, The Industrial Society.

Wynarczk, P., Watson, D., Storey, D. and Keasey, K. (1993). *Managerial Labour Markets*, London, Routledge.

3 Gender differences in the goals of owner-operated SMEs

John Watson and Rick Newby

Introduction

Modern management and organisation theory is often criticised for being based on masculine values and concepts. "Men seem to be the norm and women are 'the other' " (Lamsa *et al.*, 2000:203) and the business media "reverberates with the great male sagas of conquest of new markets and ... campaigns to launch new products" (Gherardi, 1994:591). Such viewpoints reflect Hofstede's (1980, 1983, 1991, 1993, 1998) various works which classify Western cultures as individualistic and highly masculine, causing traditional social values to become "the importance of showing off, of performing, of achieving something visible, of making money, of 'big is beautiful' " (Hofstede, 1983:85). These culturally prevailing masculine principles have, therefore, heavily influenced our perspective of business success, where financial measures of performance (such as business size, rate of growth and profitability) have become dominant. While there can be no dispute with the routine use of financial measures to assess the performance of large businesses, it has been argued that economic measures alone might not be appropriate in assessing the performance, or success, of owner-operated small and medium enterprises (SMEs) (Keats and Bracker, 1988; Wärneryd, 1988).

This questioning of conventional performance measurement for owner-operated firms comes from the lack of separation between ownership and management in SMEs. In being their own boss, the goals of the owner–operator become the goals of the firm. Therefore, each firm might have a unique set of goals related to the individual circumstances of its owner (Naffziger *et al.*, 1994). Given that many of the stated motivations for entering and remaining in small business are non-financial in nature (for example, see discussions in Stanworth and Curran, 1976; Smith and Miner, 1983; Bird and Jelinek, 1988; Bird, 1988; Hankinson *et al.*, 1997; Miner, 1997; Zhuplev *et al.*, 1998; Culkin and Smith, 2000), the use of *hard* (objective) financial measures to assess SME performance might not be valid in gauging these *softer* (subjective) intrinsic constructs (Poiesz and von Grumbkow, 1988; Parasuraman *et al.*, 1996). Recent studies of SME owner–operator goals appear to support this contention. For example, Kuratko *et al.* (1997), McGregor and Tweed (2001), Newby *et al.*

(2003) and Robichaud *et al.* (2001) all found that the desire for economic (extrinsic) rewards comprised only one part of an owner–operator's set of motivations, goals and aspirations. Indeed, Kuratko *et al.* (1997:31) explicitly stated that the relative importance of subjective (intrinsic) goals underlined the view that "entrepreneurial success should not be solely measured in financial terms". This indicates that any assessment of the (financial) performance of owner-operated SMEs should control for the effects of these additional (non-financial) goals.

This chapter considers the extent to which male and female SME owner–operators differ in terms of the importance they attach to various financial and non-financial goals, and suggests that biological sex might not be an appropriate proxy to use when testing for the influence of gender on an entrepreneur's goals and expectations. Following this introductory section, the chapter gives further consideration to the research context that led us to our research questions. We then describe our sample and how our variables are measured. Finally, we present our results and draw some conclusions that we hope will guide future research in the area.

Research context

The pervasive masculine perspective of business has impacted studies on the differences between male- and female-controlled SMEs. This research has typically, but not always, found that male-owned businesses outperform female-owned businesses in economic terms, even after controlling for variables such as: industry; business age; business size; owner–operator experience; desire for business growth; and ownership structure (for example, see Cooper *et al.*, 1994; Rosa *et al.*, 1996; du Rietz and Henrekson, 2000; Bird *et al.*, 2001). Watson (2002) argued that this apparent underperformance was a function of male-owned enterprises having greater economic inputs and, therefore, greater economic outputs. Watson and Robinson (2003) further suggested that the apparent underperformance might also be a function of female-owned enterprises (on average) having less risk and, therefore, lower returns. We offer a third alternative, namely, that male and female business owners attach different levels of importance to *hard* (objective/financial) and *soft* (subjective/intrinsic) goals.

The argument that female business owners consider *subjective* goals relatively more important than their male counterparts is both long held and well established (Geoffee and Scase, 1983; Scott, 1986; Brush, 1992; Olson and Currie, 1992; Buttner and Moore, 1997; Mukhtar, 1998). Although the differences in goals for men and women has primarily been examined in relation to business entry (Stevenson, 1986; Shane *et al.*, 1991; Brodie and Stanworth, 1998; Mallon and Cohen, 2001), Cliff (1998) and Orser and Hogarth-Scott (2002) revealed significant sex-based differences in the desire for (and achievement of) business growth, while Mukhtar (1998:50) found that "male and female owners/managers choose to run their businesses very differently in the post-formation stage". Given these differences between men and women, using *hard* economic measures alone to assess and contrast the performances of female- and male-controlled SMEs would seem to be fundamentally flawed, especially given Buttner and Moore's (1997:34) finding that female entrepreneurs measured success in terms of "self-fulfilment and goal achievement. Profits and business growth, while important, were less substantial measures of their success".

Is gender the same as biological sex?

Central to any comparison between males and females is the expectation that biological sex either directly impacts the concept under study, or that sex appropriately proxies for other, non-biological, factors expected to influence that concept. Given the limited number of areas where sex is critical to performance, the regular use of biological sex in SME performance studies must, therefore, be to proxy for the social and cultural construct of gender (Borna and White, 2003).[1]

Until the middle of the last century gender was considered a unidimensional construct, with males and females being complete opposites. Men were expected to be the providers and women the care-givers, with Schein's (1973, 1975) argument of "think manager – think male" seen to be a self-evident truth. The feminist movement of the 1960s helped change this perception, such that a lifetime working career and self-achievement became more acceptable for women (Helson *et al.*, 1995). This led a number of researchers to challenge the belief that psychological gender and biological sex were equivalent, with arguments suggesting that *maleness* (measured by psychological masculinity or task focus, i.e. "getting the job done", (O'Neill and Blake-Beard, 2002:55)) and *femaleness* (measured by psychological femininity or relationship focus, i.e. "concern for the welfare of others" (O'Neill and Blake-Beard, 2002:55)) were two separate dimensions (Constantinople, 1973). Development of the Bem Sex-Role Inventory (BSRI; Bem, 1977) was based on this belief that gender was a multi- rather than a unidimensional construct, with Bem (1974) finding empirical support for her claim that psychological masculinity and femininity did not necessarily correlate with biological sex (men and women self-rated themselves as high or low on both scales). Bem (1974) subsequently classified her respondents into four groups: *androgynous* (high masculinity, high femininity); *masculine* (high masculinity, low femininity); *feminine* (low masculinity, high femininity); and *undifferentiated* (low masculinity, low femininity). Psychologically *androgynous* types were argued to be more effective managers given their high task-motivation and high relationship-orientation (for example, see Powell and Butterfield, 1979; Baril *et al.*, 1989), leading to subsequent calls for managers within modern organisations to become more collaborative (feminine) in their leadership styles (Peters, 1987; Kanter, 1989; Mintzberg, 1989).

In conjunction with these appeals for the "feminization of management" (Willemsen, 2002:385), the role of men and women within the labour force has also changed noticeably since the early 1970s. Coupled with a dramatic rise in labour market participation rates and higher educational standards (Blau, 1998; Henkens *et al.*, 2002; Konrad and Harris, 2002; Jaumotte, 2003), women have increasingly become involved in previously male-dominated, task-oriented occupations (Auster and Ohm, 2000). At the same time, male participation in previously female-dominated, relationships-based, occupations has become more accepted (Goldberg, 1994; Cejka and Eagly, 1999), with men also becoming more concerned with daily domestic tasks (Bianchi *et al.*, 2000) including taking more direct care of their children (Milkie *et al.*, 2002).

Not surprisingly, this shift in workforce roles played by men and women has been paralleled by a liberalisation of gender roles, defined as "the attitudes, behaviors, rights and responsibilities that a society associates with each sex" (Konrad and Harris, 2002:260). Using a highly homogeneous (US undergraduate-based) sample of self-rating BSRI studies from 1973 to 1995, Twenge (1997) found that the masculinity scores for women showed a clear linear increase over time, significantly greater than a similarly clear linear increase in the masculinity scores for males. The femininity scores for men also increased over this period (consistent with the "liberalised" perspective that males can nurture) but the femininity scores for females remained virtually the same. The logical consequence of these movements was, therefore, an increasing similarity between the average BSRI scores for men and women (particularly on the masculinity score) over the period of Twenge's (1997) meta-analysis. Indeed, the narrowing of the difference between males and females for masculinity was so marked that, in her last two samples, Twenge (1997:316) reported that "men and women did not have significantly different mean scores on this measure".[2] This is consistent with more general evidence indicating that female managers follow the Schein (1973) stereotype in treating the display of masculine traits as important for their career progression (Kolb, 1999; Tharenou, 2001; Kirchmeyer, 2002) and more specific evidence that this might be the same for the female self-employed (Fagenson and Marcus, 1991).

Gender and psychological characteristics

The conceptualisation of managers as male (Schein, 1973) has also impacted SME research into the psychological antecedents of SME ownership and success. A review of the literature shows that many studies designed to identify psychological differences between entrepreneurial and non-entrepreneurial business owners have concentrated on personality aspects that reflect a masculine perspective (for example, see Begley and Boyd, 1987a, 1987b; Cromie, 1987; Cromie *et al.*, 1992; Cromie and O'Donaghue, 1992; Begley, 1995; Cromie, 2000; Stewart and Roth, 2001; Shane *et al.*, 2003; Vecchio, 2003; Collins *et al.*, 2004). If gender is indeed a two- (or multi-) dimensional construct (and not a unidimensional construct), and given the increasing similarity in the masculinity scores for men and women, then focusing on attributes such as task achievement, goal-accomplishment and assertiveness (masculine traits) is likely to ignore the potential impact of feminine traits on SME performance, resulting in the finding of no difference by biological sex.

Reference to the current psychology literature suggests that Norman's (1963) five-factor taxonomy of personality attributes could prove useful in moderating this possible masculinity bias. Commonly referred to as the Big Five (see, for example, Barrick and Mount, 1991; Lippa, 1991; Schmit and Ryan, 1993; de Fruyt and Merveide, 1999; Hurtz and Donovan, 2000; LePine and van Dyne, 2001; Judge *et al.*, 2002; Thoresen *et al.*, 2004), the constructs of: emotional stability (also known as negative emotion or neuroticism); extraversion (sociability, social adaptability, surgency); culture (intelligence, openness, openness to experience); agreeableness (conformity, empathy, friendliness, liability); and conscientiousness (achievement, orderliness, prudence, self-control) have all been found useful even though they subsume "more specific personal attributes, dispositions, habits and behaviors" (Bateman and Crant, 1993:106; see also Cannella and Monroe, 1997; Boudreau *et al.*, 2001; Olver and Mooradian, 2003).

The Big Five model has proved to be the most investigated psychological paradigm over the past two decades: "If a consensual structure of traits is ever to emerge, the five-factor model is probably it" (Judge and Ilies, 2002:798). Indeed, Roberts and Robins (2000:1284) noted that the Big Five "generalize across many different cultures, and predict a wide range of outcomes, including job performance, occupational status [and] academic achievement". While it has its sceptics (see, for example, McAdams, 1992; Block, 1995, 2001), it now appears to hold pre-eminence in personality research ("there is widespread agreement about the five personality dimensions and their content", Barrick *et al.*, 2003:46).

Besides its popularity, we had three further reasons for considering the use of Norman's (1963) Big Five. First, it has been shown to be free of any gender- (sex-) role bias in the wider population (for example, see Lippa, 1991; Marusic and Bratko, 1998). Second, it has been shown to be free of any self-reporting or instrument bias (McCrae and Costa, 1987, 1992). Finally, the concepts measured in the Big Five are not arcane or academically obscure but are interpretable in a general sense (Sneed *et al.*, 1998) and, therefore, are likely to be easily understood by those with an interest in the SME sector.

Research questions

Unfortunately, the apparent shift in the relationship between an individual's biological sex and his/her sex-role has rarely been recognised in SME research. Using the abstracting service ProQuest 5000 International (ProQuest Information and Learning Company, 2000) as our source, we found few SME-based articles where the part played by an owner–operator's sex-role was explicitly considered. Even where sex-roles were discussed, most studies still used biological sex to examine gender differences. This has the potential to cause studies examining the impact of owner–operator gender on SME management and performance to be self-defeating.

Therefore, our research sought to answer the following questions with respect to a sample of SME owner–operators:

1   What is the relationship between the biological sex of owner–operators and their sex-roles (that is, their psychological masculinity and femininity)?
2   Do the *traditional* psychological scales often used in SME research (locus of control, manifest needs, risk-taking propensity and preference for innovation) have a masculinity bias?
3   If so, would the masculinity and femininity scores of SME owners provide more insights with respect to these *traditional* psychological scales than simply using biological sex?
4   Do the higher-level concepts contained in Norman's (1963) Big Five avoid any masculinity bias?
5   How do the goals and expectations of male and female SME owner–operators differ?
6   Do measures of sex-roles provide greater insights into the goals and expectations of SME owner–operators than biological sex?
7   Do measures of sex-roles provide greater insights into the goals and expectations of SME owner–operators than biological sex when used in combination with:

  •   the *traditional* psychological scales?
  •   Norman's (1963) Big Five?
  •   both the *traditional* psychological scales and Norman's Big Five?

Answering these questions should provide a platform for future research into how the sex-roles of SME owner–operators, together with their personality attributes, affect their goals and expectations, their management styles and, ultimately, their firm's performance.

Methodology

Sample selection

Data for this study came from an *omnibus* survey of the attitudes and expectations of a random sample of SME owner–operators throughout Western Australia (based on a sampling frame drawn from *White Page* telephone directories). A total of 702 SME owner–operators responded to a mail questionnaire, 611 of which proved to be sufficiently complete for this analysis (474 males, 137 females). The overall response rate of 19.6 per cent was considered reasonable given the length of the questionnaire (sixteen pages containing 247 items) and the nature of the population. Tests for non-response bias were conducted using the usual proxy of comparing early and late respondents, with no significant differences detected.

Measurement of variables – gender

Sex

Respondents were asked to indicate their sex, with males coded one and females coded zero.

Sex-roles

We assessed an individual's sex-role using the short-form of Bem's (1977) Sex-Roles Inventory. This reduced version of the scale contained ten items each for the dimensions of masculinity and femininity. As each item was measured using a seven-point Likert-type scale ranging from one (never or almost never true) to seven (always or almost always true), the possible values for both masculinity and femininity ranged from ten to seventy. Scale reliabilities, as measured by Cronbach's (1951) alpha, were 0.85 for masculinity and 0.89 for femininity.

Measurement of variables – "traditional" psychological attributes

The *traditional* psychological scales used in this study were selected based on their prior use in the SME literature. In selecting the scales we concentrated on two types of prior studies, namely: those that explicitly sought to find differences between male and female SME owners (and their firms), and those that controlled for such differences by using owner–operator sex as a moderating variable. This review revealed seven common traits of interest: need for achievement (as used by Carland and Carland, 1991, in their analysis of differences between male and female entrepreneurs and managers); need for power (as applied by Lefkowitz, 1994, in his research of the general working population); risk-taking propensity (see the evaluation of SME owner–operators and managers by Masters and Meier, 1988); internal *locus of control* (as employed by Kalleberg and Leicht, 1991, in their investigation into the impact of owner–operator sex on business survival and success; see also Loscocco *et al.*, 1991); powerful others locus of control and chance locus of control (see the study of entrepreneurs by Kaufmann *et al.*, 1995); and preference for innovation (as used by Stewart *et al.*, 1999, in their differentiation between the entrepreneur and the small business owner). Following is a brief description of how these various attributes were measured in this study.

Manifest needs

The theoretical justification for including need for achievement and need for power comes from McClelland (1961, 1975). McClelland argued that, while high need for achievement was a primary stimulus for an individual to become entrepreneurial, the effectiveness of their organisation also depended upon the individual's level of power motivation. Both need for achievement and need for power were assessed with the relevant items from the frequently used Steers and Braunstein's (1976) Manifest Needs Questionnaire. Consisting of five items for each manifest need, measurement was by a seven-point Likert-type scale with responses ranging from one (strongly disagree) to seven (strongly agree). Therefore, the possible values for these two variables ranged from five to thirty-five. Cronbach's (1951) alpha was 0.44 and 0.65 for need for achievement and need for power, respectively.

Risk-taking propensity

"Conceptualised as one's orientation toward taking chances in a decision-making situation" (Sexton and Bowman, 1985:13), risk-taking propensity has been defined in the SME literature as a willingness to take moderate risks (Begley, 1995). Following the lead of Busenitz and Barney (1997) and Stewart *et al.* (1999), risk-taking propensity was assessed using statements from the risk sub-scale of the Jackson Personality Inventory (Jackson, 1976). Our data collection consisted of six items, each measured by a seven-point Likert-type scale ranging from one (strongly disagree) to seven (strongly agree), giving a possible value for this variable ranging from six to forty-two. Cronbach's (1951) alpha was 0.51.

Locus of control

This refers to the degree to which people believe they are in charge of their destiny. Locus of control has been applied in the SME domain on the assumption that entrepreneurs will presuppose they have a capacity to influence business outcomes through their own abilities, efforts or skills. Originally conceived by Rotter (1966) as a unidimensional scale with *internal* (I'm in charge) and *external* (I'm not in charge) end points, subsequent empirical work by Levenson (1974, 1981) suggested that locus of control comprises three dimensions, namely, the internal perspective of Rotter (1966) and two separate *external* factors (powerful others and chance). Internal, powerful others and chance locus of control were assessed with items from Lumpkin's (1988) abbreviated version of Levenson's (1981) Locus of Control Scale. This shortened version of the original scale contained three items from each of the internal, powerful others and chance sub-scales. Measurement was based on a seven-point Likert-type scale ranging from one (strongly disagree) to seven (strongly agree). Therefore, the possible value for each of the locus of control dimensions ranged from three to twenty-one. Cronbach's (1951) alpha was 0.52, 0.48 and 0.34 for internal, powerful others and chance locus of control, respectively.

Preference for innovation

Our conceptual justification for including this last variable in our list of *traditional* psychological attributes is based on the belief that desire for innovation is central to the Schumpeterian view of the entrepreneur (Schumpeter, 1934) and of entrepreneurial endeavour (Carland *et al.*, 1984). Consistent with previous SME studies (for example, see Stewart *et al.*, 1999; Mueller and Thomas, 2001), preference for innovation was assessed using statements from the innovativeness sub-scale of the Jackson Personality Inventory (Jackson, 1976). Our data collection consisted of seven items, each measured by a seven-point Likert-type scale ranging from one (strongly disagree) to seven (strongly agree), giving a possible value for this variable ranging from seven to forty-nine. Cronbach's (1951) alpha was 0.74.

Measurement of variables – Norman's Big Five personality traits

Norman's (1963) Big Five personality traits were measured by the short-form of Costa and McCrae's (1992) NEO-PIR scale. Previously applied in the SME setting by Morrison (1996, 1997) and Willock *et al.* (1999), this short-form version measures traits named: neuroticism (comprising the facets of anxiety, hostility, depression, self-consciousness, impulsiveness and vulnerability – higher values indicate higher levels of negativity); extraversion (warmth, gregariousness, assertiveness, activity, excitement seeking and positive emotions – higher values indicate more demonstrativeness); openness to experience (fantasy, aesthetics, feelings, actions, ideas and values – higher values suggest a greater willingness to receive ideas); agreeableness (trust, straightforwardness, altruism, compliance, modesty and tender-mindedness – higher values indicate increased affability); and conscientiousness (competence, order, dutifulness, achievement striving and self-discipline – higher values imply greater assiduousness). With twelve items for each trait and each item measured on a five-point Likert-type scale ranging from one (strongly disagree) to five (strongly agree), possible values for each trait ranged from twelve to sixty. Cronbach's (1951) alpha was 0.82, 0.72, 0.71, 0.67 and 0.80 for neuroticism, extraversion, openness to experience, agreeableness and conscientiousness, respectively.

Measurement of variables – owner–operator goals

Current business goals (objectives) for each owner–operator were measured using standardised scores derived from items previously used in SME studies. After using focus groups to confirm the robustness, credibility, conceptual validity and exhaustiveness of SME owner–operator objectives identified by Kuratko *et al.* (1997) and Woodliff *et al.* (1999),[3] thirteen goal statement items were incorporated into our questionnaire.[4] Our primary consideration in selecting and adapting the items was their face validity, that is, whether the items "look like they measure what they are supposed to measure" (Friedenberg, 1995:251). Each of the thirteen items was measured by a seven-point Likert-type scale with end points of *not important* (one) to *very important* (seven).

As previously reported in Newby *et al.* (2004), Nunnally's (1967) coefficient of comparability test (suggested by Everett, 1983) was initially used to determine the appropriate number of SME owner–operator objective factors for our sample. Applying Everett's (1983) procedure to our data produced four stable factor solutions; a two-factor model, a three-factor model, a five-factor model, and a seven-factor model. We rejected the two-factor model because it had lower average stability than the other models, without the potential additional benefit of the extra factors.

Conducting principal components analysis with Varimax rotation for each of the three remaining models, we found that the three-factor model, while stable and logical, had an unacceptably low level of explanation of total variance (at 57 per cent),[5] causing us to also reject this model. The five-factor model had an explained variance of 74 per cent and also complied with Kaiser's (1960) minimum eigenvalue criterion.[6] However, reliability tests (based on Cronbach's (1951) alpha) showed that the fourth factor in this model could be improved by the deletion of one of its three items, and the solution's fifth factor was unreliable.[7] This caused us to also reject the five-factor model.

In this research, therefore, our analysis of SME owner–operator objectives is based on the seven-factor model. While this model breached Kaiser's (1960) minimum eigenvalue criterion, it did comply with Cattell's (1966) scree-plot criterion as the unrotated eigenvalues straightened from the eighth factor onwards.[8] The resulting SME Objectives Scale (SOS) comprised four multi-item and three single item factors.[9] Factors identified by the scale are: extrinsic rewards (four items, Cronbach's (1951) alpha of 0.88); time flexibility (two items, Cronbach's alpha of 0.83); family (two items, Cronbach's alpha of 0.72); staff relations (two items, Cronbach's alpha of 0.68); quality/customer relations (a single item); independence (a single item) and intrinsic rewards (a single item). A copy of the SOS is provided in the Appendix to this chapter.[10]

Analysis and results

Descriptive details for the sample, grouped by biological sex, are provided in Table 3.1. The table shows no significant differences between the males and females in our sample based on whether they founded their business and whether their business was in a metropolitan or regional location. However, there were significant differences between the two groups in terms of the age of the owner (the males were older on average), the length of time they had operated their firms (a greater proportion of women had operated their firms for less than five years, with a greater proportion of men having operated their firms for more than ten years) and industrial classification (there was a greater proportion of men in construction, with proportionately more women in education, cultural and recreational services and in all other services). The male-owned businesses were also significantly larger than the female-owned businesses in terms of total revenue (but not in terms of the number of equivalent full-time employees).

In answer to our first research question (what is the relationship between biological sex and sex-roles?), Table 3.2 reports the outcomes of independent sample t-tests of the sex-role differences (masculinity and femininity) between

Table 3.1 Male/female demographic comparisons

Demographic variables	Males		Females		All firms	
Age of owner–operator						
Mean (years)	48.3		42.6		47.1	
	t-statistic = 5.900; two-tailed p-value = **0.000**					
Years current owner has operated the firm						
Less than 5 years	135	29%	61	45%	196	32%
5 years to 10 years	120	25%	24	17%	144	24%
10 years and over	219	46%	52	38%	271	44%
Total	474		137		611	
	χ^2 = 12.901; two-tailed p-value = **0.002**					
Establishment status						
Founders	292	62%	75	55%	367	60%
Non-founders	182	38%	62	45%	244	40%
Total	474		137		611	
	χ^2 = 2.084; two-tailed p-value = 0.149					
Location						
Metropolitan	340	72%	93	60%	433	71%
Rural	134	28%	44	40%	178	29%
Total	474		137		611	
	χ^2 = 0.762; two-tailed p-value = 0.383					
Industry						
Agriculture, forestry, fishing and hunting	25	5%	8	6%	33	5%
Manufacturing	38	8%	7	5%	45	7%
Construction	71	15%	7	5%	78	13%
Wholesale trade	27	6%	4	3%	31	5%
Retail trade	94	20%	32	23%	126	21%
Communication services, finance and insurance, property and business services	114	24%	29	21%	143	23%
Health and community services	25	5%	11	8%	36	6%
Education, cultural and recreational services	14	3%	13	10%	27	5%
All other services	38	8%	19	14%	57	9%
All other industries	28	6%	7	5%	35	6%
Total	474		137		611	
	χ^2 = 27.686; two-tailed p-value = **0.001**					
Size (revenue)						
Mean (000s)	$1,395		$604		$1,238	
	(416 firms)		(103 firms)		(519 firms)	
	t-statistic = 3.295; two-tailed p-value = **0.001**					
Size (equivalent full-time employees)						
Mean (full-time equivalents)	6.9		4.8		6.4	
	(474 firms)		(137 firms)		(611 firms)	
	t-statistic = 1.656; two-tailed p-value = 0.098					

Table 3.2 T-tests for sex-roles

| | Mean scores for | | | 2-tailed p-value |
	Males	Females	t-statistic	
Masculinity	50.13	49.12	1.268	0.205
Femininity	52.13	57.23	−6.613	**0.000**

the men and women in our sample. We found that the female SME owner–operators had significantly higher femininity scores than their male counterparts, but that there was no significant difference with respect to the masculinity scores (an outcome consistent with Twenge's (1997) meta-analysis). These results suggest that we could extend Schein's (1973, 1975) argument of *think manager – think male* to *think SME owner – think masculine*. Such a conclusion is certainly consistent with the evidence of Kolb (1999) and Kirchmeyer (2002)

Table 3.3 T-tests and Pearson correlations for "traditional" psychological scales by biological sex and sex-roles

| | Mean scores for | | | 2-tailed p-value |
	Males	Females	t-statistic	
Panel A: t-tests				
Internal locus of control	17.23	17.33	−0.434	0.664
Powerful others locus of control	9.09	8.76	1.044	0.297
Chance locus of control	11.82	11.60	0.918	0.359
Need for achievement	25.51	24.99	1.565	0.118
Need for power	25.02	24.54	1.179	0.239
Risk-taking propensity	28.02	26.74	2.383	**0.017**
Preference for innovation	32.24	32.10	0.232	0.816

| | Correlations for BSRI masculinity | | Correlations for BSRI femininity | |
	Pearson's r	2-tailed p-value	Pearson's r	2-tailed p-value
Panel B: Pearson correlations				
Internal locus of control	0.411	**0.000**	0.183	**0.000**
Powerful others locus of control	−0.212	**0.000**	−0.060	0.137
Chance locus of control	0.118	**0.003**	−0.014	0.728
Need for achievement	0.565	**0.000**	0.065	0.109
Need for power	0.592	**0.000**	0.045	0.266
Risk-taking propensity	0.355	**0.000**	−0.018	0.659
Preference for innovation	0.366	**0.000**	0.205	**0.000**

that the display of masculine traits is considered necessary for career advancement.

The results provided in Table 3.3 are designed to answer our second and third research questions (do the *traditional* psychological scales have a masculinity bias and, if so, would using masculinity and femininity scores, rather than biological sex, provide more insights?). Panel A of Table 3.3 presents the results of our tests of the relationship between the seven *traditional* psychological scales and biological sex. The table shows that the male and female SME owners in our sample were significantly different on only one scale, namely, the males scored higher on risk-taking propensity. Somewhat unexpectedly (given the stereotypical view of men), the males in our sample did not have a significantly higher need for achievement, need for power or internal locus of control (compared to the females). If, therefore, we assume that these *traditional* scales measure appropriate psychological traits affecting SME ownership and success, then either gender has limited impact on these traits, or biological sex poorly discriminates across these scales and, therefore, the use of sex-roles might be more appropriate for this purpose.

The results presented in Panel B of Table 3.3 support the latter interpretation. The Pearson correlations indicate that all seven *traditional* scales were significantly related to masculinity, with only two of the scales significantly correlated with femininity (internal locus of control and preference for innovation). Furthermore, for the two scales that were significantly correlated with femininity, their correlation with masculinity was significantly higher.[11] The high correlations between the *traditional* psychological scales and masculinity, together with our earlier finding of no significant difference in the masculinity scores for the males and females in our sample, means that it is not surprising there were few differences in these *traditional* psychological attributes by biological sex (in the results presented in Panel A). This finding suggests that any future SME research, incorporating gender differences and these *traditional* psychological scales, should consider defining gender using sex-roles rather than biological sex.

Given these findings, we conducted further tests to see if (consistent with previous findings in the general population) the higher-level attributes captured by Norman's (1963) Big Five personality traits avoided this masculinity bias (our fourth research question). Table 3.4 suggests they do, as all correlations between Norman's Big Five personality traits and both masculinity and femininity were significant. For three of the Big Five traits the correlations with masculinity and femininity did not differ significantly.[12] For neuroticism, the correlation with masculinity was significantly more negative than the correlation with femininity,[13] while for agreeableness, the correlation with masculinity was negative and the correlation with femininity was positive.

Panel A of Table 3.5 provides the results of our findings with respect to how SME owner goals differ by biological sex (our fifth research question). The independent sample t-tests show that the level of importance attached to five of the seven goals was significantly different for males compared to females and,

Table 3.4 Pearson correlations for Norman's (1963) Big Five by sex-roles

	Correlations for BSRI masculinity		Correlations for BSRI femininity	
	Pearson's r	2-tailed p-value	Pearson's r	2-tailed p-value
Neuroticism	−0.194	0.000	−0.101	0.012
Extraversion	0.354	0.000	0.319	0.000
Openness to experience	0.127	0.002	0.209	0.000
Agreeableness	−0.378	0.000	0.403	0.000
Conscientiousness	0.274	0.000	0.266	0.000

for all but one of these goals, the outcome was consistent with our a priori expectations. As expected, female owner–operators placed greater importance on time flexibility, customer relations and intrinsic rewards, while their male counterparts attached more weight to independence. The males, somewhat surprisingly, also attached greater importance to the family goal. However, it should be noted that the family goal (see Appendix) relates to the provision of development and employment opportunities for family members and, therefore, perhaps this result is not that surprising after all. The two goals that were found not to differ by biological sex were extrinsic rewards and staff relations. The result with respect to extrinsic rewards was also unexpected, given the prior literature suggesting that males are more likely (than females) to attach greater importance to *hard* (financial) goals.

Given that the males and females in our sample appeared to place equal importance on extrinsic rewards, the results suggest that any difference in the financial performances of male- and female-controlled SMEs is unlikely to stem from differences in the importance they attach to this (financial) goal. It is more likely, therefore, that any difference in the financial performances of male- and female-controlled SMEs is related to other variables, such as the desire for time flexibility and risk-taking propensity.

In answer to our sixth research question, the results in Panel B of Table 3.5 suggest that the use of sex-roles does provide greater insights into the goals and expectations of SME owner–operators than simply using biological sex. The results indicate that either masculinity or femininity is statistically significantly correlated with all seven goals (compared with only five of these goals being significantly different by biological sex – see Panel A). Given the unexpected result for the family goal by biological sex reported in Panel A, the findings for this factor with respect to sex-roles is of particular interest. Our results in Panel B suggest that the significantly higher value attached to the family goal by the male SME owner–operators (as reported in Panel A) comes from their relationship focus (femininity) and not their task focus (masculinity); a finding consistent with our expectations.

Of the remaining six goals, five were associated with either masculinity or

Table 3.5 T-tests and Pearson correlations for owner–operator goals by biological sex and sex-roles

	Mean standardised factor scores for			2-tailed p-value
	Males	Females	t-statistic	
Panel A: *t-tests*				
Extrinsic rewards	0.002	−0.034	0.372	0.710
Time flexibility	−0.042	0.272	−3.342	**0.001**
Family	0.031	−0.175	2.099	**0.036**
Staff relations	−0.010	0.066	−0.795	0.427
Customer relations	−0.062	0.179	−2.699	**0.007**
Independence	0.053	−0.209	2.677	**0.008**
Intrinsic rewards	−0.040	0.180	−2.623	**0.009**

	Correlations for BSRI masculinity		Correlations for BSRI femininity	
	Pearson's r	2-tailed p-value	Pearson's r	2-tailed p-value
Panel B: *Pearson correlations*				
Extrinsic rewards	0.181	**0.000**	0.033	0.410
Time flexibility	0.027	0.509	0.184	**0.000**
Family	0.056	0.166	0.148	**0.000**
Staff relations	0.043	0.289	0.173	**0.000**
Customer relations	0.070	0.082	0.180	**0.000**
Independence	0.245	**0.000**	−0.072	0.076
Intrinsic rewards	0.155	**0.000**	0.127	**0.002**

femininity in a manner consistent with our expectations based on the prior literature. Masculinity was significantly correlated with extrinsic rewards and independence, while femininity was significantly correlated with time flexibility, staff relations and customer relations. From the literature it was not clear whether intrinsic rewards should be more strongly associated with masculinity or femininity; and our results suggest that this goal was almost equally (significantly) associated with both dimensions.

To further investigate whether using sex-roles provides greater insights into the goals and expectations of SME owner–operators than biological sex, we separately regressed each of the owner–operator goals first against biological sex and then against sex-roles, testing for model improvement. The results presented in Table 3.6 confirm those provided in Table 3.5, indicating that sex-roles provide greater insights into the goals and expectations of SME owner–operators than biological sex. From the results in Table 3.6, it can be seen that while five of the seven owner–operator goals were significantly associated with biological sex (time flexibility, family, customer relations, independence and intrinsic rewards), all seven were significantly associated with masculinity and/or

Table 3.6 Linear regressions for owner–operator goals – biological sex v. sex-roles

r^2	Sex (p-value)	Masculinity (p-value)	Femininity (p-value)	F-statistic (p-value)
Extrinsic rewards				
0.000	0.036 (0.710)			
0.033		0.022 **(0.000)**	0.002 (0.723)	20.675 **(0.000)**
Time flexibility				
0.018	−0.314 **(0.001)**			
0.034		0.001 (0.859)	0.022 **(0.000)**	10.111 **(0.000)**
Family				
0.007	0.207 **(0.036)**			
0.024		0.005 (0.312)	0.018 **(0.000)**	10.239 **(0.000)**
Staff relations				
0.001	−0.076 (0.427)			
0.031		0.003 (0.537)	0.020 **(0.000)**	18.519 **(0.000)**
Customer relations				
0.010	−0.241 **(0.014)**			
0.035		0.006 (0.197)	0.021 **(0.000)**	15.817 **(0.000)**
Independence				
0.012	0.262 **(0.008)**			
0.070		0.032 **(0.000)**	−0.012 **(0.012)**	37.934 **(0.000)**
Intrinsic rewards				
0.008	−0.221 **(0.024)**			
0.036		0.018 **(0.000)**	0.014 **(0.005)**	17.617 **(0.000)**

femininity. Further, in all cases, there was a significant improvement in the model when biological sex was replaced with sex-roles; as can be seen from the F-statistic in the right-hand column.

The results presented in Tables 3.7, 3.8 and 3.9 help answer our final research question which sought to determine whether sex-roles continued to provide more explanatory power (than biological sex) with respect to owner–operator goals when the *traditional* psychological scales and Norman's Big Five are included in the analysis.

From Table 3.7 we can see that when the *traditional* psychological scales are included in the models, in every case the model with sex-roles is better than the model with biological sex. For example, with respect to extrinsic rewards (although neither biological sex nor the two sex-role dimensions were significant) the model with masculinity, femininity and the *traditional* psychological scales was significantly better than the model with biological sex and the *traditional* psychological scales. Also note that in both models, only two of the seven *traditional* psychological scales were significant in explaining the importance

Table 3.7 Linear regressions for owner–operator goals and "traditional" psychological scales – biological sex v. sex-roles

r²	Sex (p-value)	Masculinity (p-value)	Femininity (p-value)	Other significant variables (direction)	F-statistic (p-value)
Extrinsic rewards					
0.068	−0.011 (0.908)			Powerful others (+)	
0.072		0.010 (0.134)	0.003 (0.553)	Need for achievement (+)	2.674 (**0.000**)
Time flexibility					
0.046	−0.307 (**0.001**)			Powerful others (−)	
0.059		−0.010 (0.127)	0.020 (**0.000**)	Powerful others (−)	8.190 (**0.000**)
Family					
0.013	0.201 (**0.044**)				
0.033		0.007 (0.278)	0.020 (**0.000**)		12.291 (**0.000**)
Staff relations					
0.025	−0.075 (0.434)			Risk-taking propensity (−)	
0.056		−0.003 (0.633)	0.022 (**0.000**)	Risk-taking propensity (−)	19.426 (**0.000**)
Customer relations					
0.072	−0.222 (**0.022**)			Internal locus of control (+) Preference for innovation (+)	
0.081		−0.003 (0.693)	0.017 (**0.001**)	Internal locus of control (+)	5.739 (**0.000**)
Independence					
0.072	0.246 (**0.011**)			Internal locus of control (+) Powerful others (−)	
0.090		0.023 (**0.001**)	−0.014 (**0.007**)	Need for power (+)	12.031 (**0.000**)
Intrinsic rewards					
0.052	−0.213 (**0.028**)			Internal locus of control (+) Risk-taking propensity (−)	
0.058		0.016 (0.053)	0.015 (**0.029**)	Risk-taking propensity (−)	4.059 (**0.000**)

Table 3.8 Linear regressions for owner–operator goals and Norman's (1963) Big Five – biological sex v. sex-roles

r^2	Sex (p-value)	Masculinity (p-value)	Femininity (p-value)	Other significant variables (direction)	F-statistic (p-value)
Extrinsic rewards					
0.074	0.044 (0.655)			Neuroticism (+) Extraversion (+) Openness to experience (−) Agreeableness (−) Conscientiousness (+)	6.971 **(0.000)**
0.084		0.014 **(0.019)**	0.005 (0.362)	Neuroticism (+) Extraversion (+) Openness to experience (−) Agreeableness (−)	
Time flexibility					
0.068	−0.204 **(0.035)**			Openness to experience (+) Agreeableness (+)	0.750 (1.000)
0.069		0.005 (0.416)	0.011 **(0.048)**	Openness to experience (+) Agreeableness (+)	
Family					
0.024	0.200 (0.052)			Openness to experience (+)	16.717 **(0.000)**
0.050		0.005 (0.417)	0.025 **(0.000)**	Openness to experience (+)	

	Step 1	Step 2	Step 3		F (p)
Staff relations					
0.035	0.000 (0.996)			Neuroticism (+) Extraversion (+) Agreeableness (+)	} 10.891 **(0.000)**
0.052		0.008 (0.215)	0.016 **(0.005)**	Neuroticism (+) Extraversion (+)	
Customer relations					
0.043	−0.153 (0.133)			Conscientiousness (+)	} 7.350 **(0.000)**
0.055		0.000 (0.977)	0.018 **(0.002)**	Conscientiousness (+)	
Independence					
0.044	0.199 **(0.050)**			Neuroticism (−)	} 28.723 **(0.000)**
0.087		0.034 **(0.000)**	−0.013 **(0.030)**	Neuroticism (−)	
Intrinsic rewards					
0.046	−0.213 **(0.035)**			Extraversion (+) Openness to experience (−)	} 10.962 **(0.000)**
0.063		0.016 **(0.012)**	0.015 **(0.010)**	Conscientiousness (+) Openness to experience (−)	

Table 3.9 Linear regressions for owner–operator goals and both the "traditional" psychological scales and Norman's (1963) Big Five – biological sex v. sex-roles

r^2	Sex (p-value)	Masculinity (p-value)	Femininity (p-value)	Other significant variables (direction)	F-statistic (p-value)
Extrinsic rewards					
0.106	−0.006 (0.952)				
0.109		0.002 (0.733)	0.007 (0.260)	Need for achievement (+) Neuroticism (+) Extraversion (+) Openness to experience (−) Need for achievement (+) Neuroticism (+) Extraversion (+) Openness to experience (−)	1.583 (**0.000**)
Time flexibility					
0.081	−0.215 (**0.027**)				
0.081		−0.002 (0.799)	0.013 (**0.028**)	Openness to experience (+) Agreeableness (+) Powerful others (−) Openness to experience (+) Agreeableness (+)	0.028 (1.000)
Family					
0.027	0.189 (0.071)				
0.053		0.004 (0.597)	0.026 (**0.000**)	Openness to experience (+) Openness to experience (+)	16.188 (**0.000**)

Staff relations				
0.058	0.001 (0.993)		Risk-taking propensity (−)	
0.073	0.002 (0.831)	0.018 (**0.002**)	Extraversion (+)	10.040 (**0.000**)
			Agreeableness (+)	
			Risk-taking propensity (−)	
Customer relations				
0.083	−0.174 (0.086)		Internal locus of control (+)	
			Powerful others (+)	
			Conscientiousness (+)	3.988 (**0.000**)
0.089	−0.006 (0.424)	0.016 (**0.009**)	Internal locus of control (+)	
			Conscientiousness (+)	
Independence				
0.087	0.159 (0.115)		Internal locus of control (+)	
			Need for power (+)	13.212 (**0.000**)
0.107	0.027 (**0.000**)	−0.012 (**0.035**)	Neuroticism (−)	
			Neuroticism (−)	
Intrinsic rewards				
0.077	−0.244 (**0.016**)		Internal locus of control (+)	
			Preference for innovation (+)	
			Openness to experience (−)	2.548 (**0.000**)
0.081	0.009 (0.213)	0.014 (**0.020**)	Risk-taking propensity (−)	
			Openness to experience (−)	

placed by owner–operators on extrinsic rewards (powerful others locus of control and need for achievement). Indeed, in only one model (independence by biological sex) were more than two of the *traditional* psychological scales significant. Further, for the family goal, none of the *traditional* psychological scales was significant.

Similarly, in all but one case, when we introduced Norman's Big Five (instead of the *traditional* psychological scales) into the regression (see Table 3.8), the model combining sex roles and Norman's Big Five was significantly better than the comparable model using biological sex (time flexibility). Also note that at least one of Norman's Big Five dimensions was significant in explaining the importance attached to each of the seven owner–operator goals.

Finally, when we included both the *traditional* psychological scales and Norman's Big Five into the regression (see Table 3.9), we again find that the model with sex-roles outperforms the model with biological sex in all but one case (time flexibility). In no case did any model with biological sex outperform a model with sex-roles. Further, it is worth noting that the various dimensions from Norman's Big Five were more frequently significant than the various *traditional* psychological scales (particularly when looking at extrinsic rewards, time flexibility and family goals).

Conclusions

It would seem that over the last three decades the differences between men and women have narrowed such that, in today's society, male and female SME owners score similarly in terms of their *masculine* traits. This is consistent with evidence indicating that female managers follow the Schein (1973) stereotype in treating the display of *masculine* traits as important for their career progression (Kolvereid, 1995; Tharenou, 2001; Kirchmeyer, 2002) and also with the suggestion that the same might be true for the female self-employed (Fagenson and Marcus, 1991). This was certainly the case in our sample of male and female SME owner–operators, where we found no significant difference in their masculinity scores. Therefore, we suggest that the measurement of gender in future SME studies might be better served by the use of masculinity and femininity scores rather than biological sex.

A second conclusion from our results is that the *traditional* psychological attributes (locus of control, manifest needs, risk-taking propensity and preference for innovation) used in the SME literature appear to be biased towards masculinity. Given this finding, and the similarity in the masculinity scores for the males and females in our sample, it is not surprising that previous studies examining gender differences in terms of these psychological attributes within the SME setting have resulted in few significant findings. Further, use of these *traditional* constructs by SME researchers has ensured that any impact of femininity on the way SMEs operate has largely been ignored. This seems inconsistent with the argument that good managers should be androgynous, that is, high in terms of both masculinity and femininity (Powell and Butterfield, 1979), and suggests that the *traditional* psychological attributes often used in SME research should be replaced by attributes that are more gender neutral.

Based on our findings, we would argue that Norman's (1963) Big Five might be appropriate for this purpose, especially given the degree to which personality research has been impacted by this five-factor model over the past twenty years. For example, we found widespread use of Norman's Big Five in the leadership literature (see, for example, Cannella and Monroe, 1997; Judge and Bono, 2000; Kickul and Neuman, 2000) and we would expect that the attributes that make for a good leader might also be important for success as an SME owner. However, there has been limited use of Norman's Big Five in the SME literature. In our sample of SME owner–operators (and consistent with prior findings for the wider community) we found that Norman's Big Five did not appear to have a masculinity (or femininity) bias. As such, we suggest that using the Big Five, instead of the *traditional* psychological scales (internal, powerful others and chance locus of control; need for achievement; need for power; risk-taking propensity; and preference for innovation) might prove beneficial in future research into issues concerned with SME owner characteristics.

Finally, while the results presented in this study support the view that male and female SME owner–operators differ in terms of the importance they attach to various non-financial goals, the results do not support the proposition that females attach less importance (than males) to financial goals. The results also confirm our belief that biological sex might not be an appropriate proxy to use when testing for the influence of gender on SME owner–operator goals and expectations. In almost all cases the explanatory power of our regression models (with respect to owner–operator goals) was significantly improved when we replaced biological sex with masculinity and femininity scores.

Appendix: The SME Objectives Scale (SOS)[14]

Listed below are a series of potential objectives. Use the scale provided to indicate how important these objectives are to you.

1	2	3	4	5	6	7
Not important	Of little importance	Slightly important	Neutral	Somewhat important	Quite important	Very important

Extrinsic rewards
  Increasing your personal income[K]
  Building your personal wealth[K]
  Achieving financial security[W]
  Increasing your income opportunities[K]

Time flexibility
  Having free time for non-business activities[W]
  Having flexibility of time for non-business activities[W]

Family
  Providing development opportunities for your family[W]
  Giving employment opportunities to your family[W]

Appendix: continued

Listed below are a series of potential objectives. Use the scale provided to indicate how important these objectives are to you.

1	2	3	4	5	6	7
Not important	Of little importance	Slightly important	Neutral	Somewhat important	Quite important	Very important

Staff relations
Providing security of employment for your staff[W]
Having loyal staff[W]

Quality/customer relations
Providing high quality products and/or services[W]

Independence
Being your own boss[K]

Intrinsic rewards
Proving you can do it (i.e. you can achieve)[K]

Some suggested additional items:

Quality/customer relations
Having a sound reputation for quality[M]

Independence
Making your own decisions[R]

Intrinsic rewards
Meeting the challenge[K]

K   Selected from items in Kuratko *et al.* (1997).
M   Selected from items in McDowell (1995).
R   Selected from items in Robichaud *et al.* (2001).
W   Selected from items in Woodliff *et al.* (1999).

Notes

1 Defined by Gentile (1993:120) as "Traits or conditions that are causally linked with maleness or femaleness but are culturally based rather than biologically based".
2 The mean scores for femininity, however, remained significantly different for men and women.
3 Newby *et al.* (2003) provides details of this focus group study.
4 Eight of the items were adapted from Woodliff *et al.* (1999), in particular those relating to the following factors: financial security; family; time flexibility; and staff and customer relations. Five of the items were adapted from Kuratko *et al.* (1997), in particular those relating to the following factors: extrinsic rewards; independence/ autonomy; and intrinsic rewards.
5 Korth (1975) states that there are limited reasons for using principal components factor analysis unless it accounts for more than 70 per cent of the variance within the original correlation matrix, while Hair *et al.* (1998) suggest a minimum explanation of 60 per cent for the social sciences.
6 That is, the unrotated solution showed five factors with eigenvalues greater than one.
7 In that it failed Nunnally's (1978) minimum Cronbach's (1951) alpha criterion of 0.600 (the actual value was 0.468).
8 Cattell (1966:207) claims that the number of items analysed impacts on eigenvalues

in such a way that when there are fewer than twenty variables (in our case there are thirteen) the Kaiser (1960) rule "systematically underestimate[s] the number of factors". Humphreys (1964) also argues that, for large samples, the Kaiser (1960) criterion is too conservative in its estimation of interpretable factors.

9 Single item factors, while uncommon, have previously been found by SME researchers. For example, see Chaganti and Greene (2002), Fischer *et al.* (1993) and Verheul and Thurik (2001).

10 For those who are concerned by single item factors, we also list some suggested additional statements for quality/customer relations, independence and intrinsic rewards at the bottom of the Appendix.

11 For internal locus of control the z-score for the comparison of the Pearson's correlations was 4.389 ($p = 0.001$), while for preference for innovation the z-score was 3.066 ($p = 0.001$).

12 For extraversion the z-score for the comparison of the Pearson's correlations was 0.688 ($p = 0.246$); for openness to experience it was 1.472 ($p = 0.070$); and for conscientiousness it was 0.150 ($p = 0.440$).

13 The z-score for the comparison was 1.659 ($p = 0.050$).

14 Please note that the order of the SOS items should be randomised before inclusion in any survey questionnaire, and the headings should be removed.

References

Auster, C.J. and Ohm, S.C. (2000). "Masculinity and Femininity in Contemporary American Society: A Re-Evaluation Using the Bem Sex-Role Inventory". *Sex Roles*, 43, 7/8, 499–528.

Baril, G.L., Elbert, N., Mahar-Potter, S. and Reavy, G.C. (1989). "Are Androgynous Managers Really More Effective?" *Group and Organisation Studies*, 14, 2, 234–249.

Barrick, M.R. and Mount, M.K. (1991). "The Big Five Personality Dimensions and Job Performance: A Meta-Analysis". *Personnel Psychology*, 44, 1, 1–26.

Barrick, M.R., Mount, M.K. and Gupta, R. (2003). "Meta-Analysis of the Relationship Between the Five-Factor Model of Personality and Holland's Occupational Types". *Personnel Psychology*, 56, 1, 45–74.

Bateman, T.S. and Crant, J.M. (1993). "The Proactive Component of Organisational Behavior: A Measure and Correlates'. *Journal of Organisational Behavior*, 14, 2, 103–118.

Begley, T.M. (1995). "Using Founder Status, Age of Firm, and Company Growth-Rate as the Basis for Distinguishing Entrepreneurs from Managers of Smaller Businesses". *Journal of Business Venturing*, 10, 3, 249–263.

Begley, T.M. and Boyd, D.P. (1987a). "A Comparison of Entrepreneurs and Managers of Small Business Firms". *Journal of Management*, 13, 1, 99–108.

Begley, T.M. and Boyd, D.P. (1987b). "Psychological Characteristics Associated With Performance in Entrepreneurial Firms and Smaller Businesses". *Journal of Business Venturing*, 2, 1, 79–93.

Bem, S.L. (1974). "The Measurement of Psychological Androgyny". *Journal of Consulting and Clinical Psychology*, 42, 2, 155–162.

Bem, S.L. (1977). "Bem Sex-Role Inventory (BSRI)". In Pfeiffer, J.W. and Jones, J.E. *The 1977 Annual Handbook for Group Facilitors*. San Diego, CA: University Associates, 83–85.

Bianchi, S.M., Milkie, M.A., Sayer, L.C. and Robinson, J.P. (2000). "Is Anyone Doing the Housework? Trends in the Gender Division of Household Labour". *Social Forces*, 79, 1, 191–228.

Bird, B.J. (1988). "Implementing Entrepreneurial Ideas: The Case for Intention". *Academy of Management Review*, 13, 3, 442–453.

Bird, B. and Jelinek, M. (1988). "The Operation of Entrepreneurial Intentions". *Entrepreneurship Theory and Practice*, 13, 2, 21–29.

Bird, S., Sapp, S.G. and Lee, M.Y. (2001). "Small Business Success in Rural Communities: Explaining the Sex Gap". *Rural Sociology*, 66, 4, 507–531.

Blau, F.D. (1998). "Trends in the Well-Being of American Women, 1970–1995". *Journal of Economic Literature*, 36, 1, 112–165.

Block, J. (1995). "A Contrarian View of the Five-Factor Approach to Personality Description". *Psychological Bulletin*, 117, 2, 187–215.

Block, J. (2001). "Millennial Contrarianism: The Five-Factor Approach to Personality Description 5 Years Later". *Journal of Research in Personality*, 35, 1, 98–107.

Borna, S. and White, G. (2003). " 'Sex' and 'Gender': Two Confused and Confusing Concepts in the 'Women in Corporate Management' Literature". *Journal of Business Ethics*, 47, 2, 89–99.

Boudreau, J.W., Boswell, W.R., Judge, T.A. and Bretz, R.D. Jr (2001). "Personality and Cognitive Ability as Predictors of Job Search Among Employed Managers". *Personnel Psychology*, 4, 1, 25–50.

Brodie, S. and Stanworth, J. (1998). "Independent Contractors in Direct Selling: Self-employed but Missing from Official Records". *International Small Business Journal*, 16, 3, 95–101.

Brush, C.G. (1992). "Research on Women Business Owners: Past Trends, a New Perspective and Future Directions". *Entrepreneurship Theory and Practice*, 16, 4, 5–30.

Busenitz, L.W. and Barney, J.B. (1997). "Differences Between Entrepreneurs and Managers in Large Organisations: Biases and Heuristics in Strategic Decision-Making". *Journal of Business Venturing*, 12, 1, 9–30.

Buttner, E.H. and Moore, D.P. (1997). "Women's Organisational Exodus to Entrepreneurship: Self-Reported Motivations and Correlates with Success". *Journal of Small Business Management*, 35, 1, 34–46.

Cannella, A.A. Jr and Monroe, M.J. (1997). "Contrasting Perspectives on Strategic Leaders: Toward a More Realistic View of Top Managers". *Journal of Management*, 23, 3, 213–237.

Carland, J.A.C. and Carland, J.W. (1991). "An Empirical Investigation into the Distinctions Between Male and Female Entrepreneurs and Managers". *International Small Business Journal*, 9, 3, 62–72.

Carland, J.W., Hoy, F., Boulton, W.R. and Carland, J.C. (1984). "Differentiating Entrepreneurs from Small Business Owners: A Conceptualization". *Academy of Management Review*, 9, 3, 354–359.

Cattell, R.B. (1966). "The Meaning and Strategies of Factor Analysis". In Cattell, R.B. (ed.), *Handbook of Multivariate Experimental Psychology*. Chicago, IL: Rand McNally.

Cejka, M.A. and Eagly, A.H. (1999). "Gender-Stereotypic Imagers of Occupations Correspond to the Sex Segregation of Employment". *Personality and Social Psychology Bulletin*, 25, 4, 413–423.

Chaganti, R. and Greene, P.G. (2002). "Who Are Ethnic Entrepreneurs? A Study of Entrepreneurs' Ethnic Involvement and Business Characteristics". *Journal of Small Business Management*, 40, 2, 126–143.

Cliff, J.E. (1998). "Does One Size Fit All? Exploring the Relationship Between Attitudes

Towards Growth, Gender, and Business Size". *Journal of Business Venturing*, 13, 6, 523–542.

Collins, C.J., Hanges, P.J. and Locke, E.A. (2004). "The Relationship of Achievement Motivation to Entrepreneurial Behavior: A Meta-Analysis". *Human Performance*, 17, 1, 95–117.

Constantinople, A. (1973). "Masculinity–Femininity: An Exception to a Famous Dictum". *Psychological Bulletin*, 80, 5, 389–407.

Cooper, A.C., Gimeno-Gascon, F.J. and Woo, C.Y. (1994). "Initial Human and Financial Capital as Predictors of New Venture Performance". *Journal of Business Venturing*, 9, 5, 371–395.

Costa, P.T. and McCrae, R.R. (1992). *Revised NEO Personality Inventory Manual*, Odessa, FL, Psychological Assessment Resources, Inc.

Cromie, S. (1987). "Motivations of Aspiring Male and Female Entrepreneurs". *Journal of Organisational Behaviour*, 8, 3, 251–261.

Cromie, S. (2000). "Assessing Entrepreneurial Inclinations: Some Approaches and Empirical Evidence". *European Journal of Work and Organisational Psychology*, 9, 1, 7–30.

Cromie, S. and O'Donaghue, J. (1992). "Research Note: Assessing Entrepreneurial Intentions". *International Small Business Journal*, 10, 2, 66–73.

Cromie, S., Callaghan, I. and Jansen, M. (1992). "The Entrepreneurial Tendencies of Managers: A Research Note". *British Journal of Management*, 3, 1, 1–5.

Cronbach, L.J. (1951). "Coefficient Alpha and the Internal Structure of Tests". *Psychometrika*, 16, 1, 297–334.

Culkin, N. and Smith, D. (2000). "An Emotional Business: A Guide to Understanding the Motivations of Small Business Decision Takers". *Qualitative Market Research*, 3, 3, 145–157.

Everett, J.E. (1983). "Factor Comparability as a Means of Determining the Number of Factors and Their Rotation". *Multivariate Behavioural Research*, 18, 197–218.

Fagenson, E.A. and Marcus, E.C. (1991). "Perceptions of Sex-Role Stereotypic Characteristics of Entrepreneurs: Women's Evaluations". *Entrepreneurship Theory and Practice*, 15, 4, 33–47.

Fischer, E.M., Reuber, A.R. and Dyke, L.S. (1993). "A Theoretical Overview and Extension of Research on Sex, Gender, and Entrepreneurship". *Journal of Business Venturing*, 8, 2, 151–168.

Friedenberg, L. (1995). *Psychological Testing: Design, Analysis, and Use*, 1st edn. Needham Heights, MA, Allyn & Bacon.

de Fruyt, F. and Merveide, I. (1999). "RIASEC Types and Big Five Traits as Predictors of Employment Status and Nature of Employment". *Personnel Psychology*, 52, 3, 701–727.

Gentile, D.A. (1993). "Just What are Sex and Gender, Anyway?" *Psychological Science*, 4, 2, 120–122.

Geoffee, R. and Scase, R. (1983). "Business Ownership and Women's Subordination: A Preliminary Study of Female Proprietors". *Sociological Review*, 31, 4, 625–648.

Gherardi, S. (1994). "The Gender We Think, the Gender We Do In Our Everyday Organisational Lives". *Human Relations*, 47, 6, 591–610.

Goldberg, S.B. (1994). "Odd Man Out: Does It Help or Hurt to be Male in the Paralegal Profession?" *Legal Assistant Today*, 11, 3, 58–63.

Hair, J.F., Jr, Anderson, R.E., Tatham, R.L. and Black, W.C. (1998). *Multivariate Data Analysis*, 5th edn. Upper Saddle River, NJ, Prentice Hall.

Hankinson, A., Bartlett, D. and Ducheneaut, B. (1997). "The Key Factors in the Small

Profiles of Small–Medium Enterprise Owner–Managers that Influence Business Performance: The UK (REnnes) SME Survey 1995–1997 – An International Research Project UK Survey". *International Journal of Entrepreneurial Behaviour and Research*, 3, 3, 168–175.

Helson, R., Stewart, A.J. and Ostrove, J. (1995). "Identity in Three Cohorts of Midlife Women". *Journal of Personality and Social Psychology*, 69, 3, 544–557.

Henkens, K., Grift, Y. and Siegers, J. (2002). "Changes in the Female Labour Supply in the Netherlands 1989–1998: The Case of Married and Cohabiting Women". *European Journal of Population*, 18, 1, 39–57.

Hofstede, G. (1980). *Culture's Consequences: International Differences in Work-Related Values*, Beverly Hills, CA, Sage.

Hofstede, G. (1983). "The Cultural Relativity of Organisational Practices and Theories". *Journal of International Business Studies*, 14, 2, 75–89.

Hofstede, G. (1991). *Cultures on Organisations: Software of the Mind*, London, McGraw-Hill.

Hofstede, G. (1993). "Cultural Constraints in Management Theories". *Academy of Management Executive*, 7, 1, 81–94.

Hofstede, G. (1998). *The Cultural Construction of Gender. Masculinity and Femininity: The Taboo Dimension of National Culture*, Thousand Oaks, CA, Sage, 75–105.

Humphreys, L.G. (1964). "Number of Cases and Number of Factors: An Example Where N is Very Large". *Educational and Psychological Measurement*, 24, 3, 457–466.

Hurtz, G.M. and Donovan, J.J. (2000). "Personality and Job Performance: The Big Five Revisited". *Journal of Applied Psychology*, 85, 6, 869–879.

Jackson, D.N. (1976). *Personality Inventory Manual*, Goshen, NY, Research Psychologists Press.

Jaumotte, F. (2003). "Female Labour Force Participation: Past Trends and Main Determinants in OECD Countries". *OECD Economics Department Working Papers*. Luxembourg: OECD.

Judge, T.A. and Bono, J.E. (2000). "Five-Factor Model of Personality and Transformational Leadership". *Journal of Applied Psychology*, 85, 5, 751–765.

Judge, T.A. and Ilies, R. (2002). "Relationship of Personality to Performance Motivation: A Meta-Analytic Review". *Journal of Applied Psychology*, 87, 4, 797–807.

Judge, T.A., Heller, D. and Mount, M.K. (2002). "Five-Factor Model of Personality and Job Satisfaction: A Meta-Analysis". *Journal of Applied Psychology*, 87, 3, 530–541.

Kaiser, H.F. (1960). "The Application of Electronic Computers to Factor Analysis". *Educational and Psychological Measurement*, 20, 1, 141–151.

Kalleberg, A.L. and Leicht, K.T. (1991). "Gender and Organisational Performance: Determinants of Small Business Survival and Success". *Academy of Management Journal*, 34, 1, 136–161.

Kanter, R.M. (1989). "The New Managerial Work". *Harvard Business Review*, 67, 6, 85–92.

Kaufmann, P.J., Welsh, D.H.B. and Bushmarin, N.V. (1995). "Locus of Control and Entrepreneurship in the Russian Republic". *Entrepreneurship Theory and Practice*, 20, 1, 43–56.

Keats, B.W. and Bracker, J.S. (1988). "Toward a Theory of Small Firm Performance: A Conceptual Model". *American Journal of Small Business*, 2, 4, 41–58.

Kickul, J. and Neuman, G. (2000). "Emergent Leadership Behaviours: The Function of Personality and Cognitive Ability in Determining Teamwork Performance and KSAs". *Journal of Business and Psychology*, 15, 1, 27–51.

Kirchmeyer, C. (2002). "Gender Differences in Managerial Careers: Yesterday, Today, and Tomorrow". *Journal of Business Ethics*, 37, 1, 5–24.

Kolb, J.A. (1999). "The Effect of Gender Role, Attitude Toward Leadership, and Self-Confidence on Leader Emergence: Implications for Leadership Development". *Human Resource Development Quarterly*, 10, 4, 305–320.

Kolvereid, L. (1995). "Prediction of Employment Status Choice Intentions". *Entrepreneurship Theory and Practice*, 21, 1, 47–57.

Konrad, A.M. and Harris, C. (2002). "Desirability of the Bem Sex-Role Inventory Items for Women and Men: A Comparison Between African Americans and European Americans". *Sex Roles*, 47, 5/6, 259–271.

Korth, B. (1975). *Exploratory Factor Analysis. Introductory Multivariate Analysis*. In Amick, D.J. and Walberg, J.J. Berkeley, CA: McCutchan.

Kuratko, D.F., Hornsby, J.H. and Naffziger, D.W. (1997). "An Examination of Owner's Goals in Sustaining Entrepreneurship". *Journal of Small Business Management*, 35, 1, 24–33.

Lamsa, A.M., Sakkinen, A. and Turjanmaa, P. (2000). "Values and Their Change During the Business Education – a Gender Perspective". *International Journal of Value-based Management*, 13, 3, 203–213.

Lefkowitz, J. (1994). "Sex-Related Differences in Job Attitudes and Dispositional Variables: Now You See Them . . ." *Academy of Management Journal*, 37, 2, 323–349.

LePine, J.A. and Van Dyne, L. (2001). "Voice and Cooperative Behaviour as Contrasting Forms of Contextual Performance: Evidence of Differential Relationships with Big Five Personality Characteristics and Cognitive Ability". *Journal of Applied Psychology*, 86, 2, 326–336.

Levenson, H. (1974). "Activism and Powerful Others: Distinctions Within the Concept of Internal-External Control". *Journal of Personal Assessment*, 38, 1, 377–383.

Levenson, H. (1981). "Differentiating Among Internality, Powerful Others, and Chance". In Lefcourt, H.M. (ed.), *Research With the Locus of Control Construct: Assessment Methods*. New York, NY: Academic Press, 15–63.

Lippa, R. (1991). "Some Psychometric Characteristics of Gender Diagnosticity Measures: Reliability, Validity, Consistency Across Domains, and Relationship to the Big Five". *Journal of Personality and Social Psychology*, 61, 6, 1000–1011.

Loscocco, K.A., Robinson, J., Hall, R.H. and Allen, J.K. (1991). "Gender and Small Business Success: An Inquiry into Women's Relative Disadvantage". *Social Forces*, 70, 1, 65–85.

Lumpkin, J.R. (1988). "Establishing the Validity of an Abbreviated Locus of Control Scale: Is a Brief Levenson's Scale Any Better?" *Psychological Reports*, 63, 2, 519–523.

Mallon, M. and Cohen, L. (2001). "Time for a Change? Women's Accounts of the Move from Organisational Careers to Self-Employment". *British Journal of Management*, 12, 3, 217–230.

McAdams, D.D. (1992). "The Five-Factor Model in Personality: A Critical Appraisal". *Journal of Personality*, 60, 2, 329–361.

McClelland, D.C. (1961). *The Achieving Society*, Princeton, NJ, Van Nostrand.

McClelland, D.C. (1975). *Power: The Inner Experience*, New York, NY, Irvington.

McCrae, R.R. and Costa, P.T. (1987). "Validation of the Five-Factor Model of Personality Across Instruments and Observers". *Journal of Personality and Social Psychology*, 52, 1, 81–90.

McCrae, R.R. and Costa, P.T. (1992). "An Introduction to the Five-Factor Model and Its Applications". *Journal of Personality*, 60, 2, 175–215.

66   *J. Watson and R. Newby*

McDowell, C. (1995). "Small Business Objectives: An Exploratory Study of NSW Retailers". *Small Enterprise Research*, 3, 1/2, 65–83.

McGregor, J. and Tweed, D. (2001). "Gender and Managerial Competence: Support for Theories of Androgyny?" *Women in Management Review*, 16, 5/6, 279–286.

Marusic, I. and Bratko, D. (1998). "Relations of Masculinity and Femininity with Personality Dimensions of the Five-Factor Model". *Sex Roles*, 38, 1/2, 29–44.

Masters, R. and Meier, R. (1988). "Sex Differences and Risk-Taking Propensity of Entrepreneurs". *Journal of Small Business Management*, 26, 1, 31–35.

Milkie, M.A., Bianchi, S.M., Mattingly, M.J. and Robinson, J.P. (2002). "Gendered Division of Childbearing: Ideals, Realities, and the Relationship to Parental Well-being". *Sex Roles*, 47, 1/2, 21–38.

Miner, J.B. (1997). *A Psychological Typology of Successful Entrepreneurs*, Westport, CT, Quorum Books.

Mintzberg, H. (1989). *Mintzberg on Management*, New York, NY, Free Press.

Morrison, K.A. (1996). "An Empirical Test of a Model of Franchisee Job Satisfaction". *Journal of Small Business Management*, 2, 3, 27–41.

Morrison, K.A. (1997). "How Franchise Job Satisfaction and Personality Affects Performance, Organisational Commitment, Franchisor Relations, and Intention to Remain". *Journal of Small Business Management*, 35, 3, 39–67.

Mueller, S.L. and Thomas, A.S. (2001). "Culture and Entrepreneurial Potential: A Nine Country Study of Locus of Control and Innovativeness". *Journal of Business Venturing*, 16, 1, 51–75.

Mukhtar, S.M. (1998). "Business Characteristics of Male and Female Small and Medium Enterprises in the UK: Implications for Gender-Based Entrepreneurialism and Business Competence Development". *British Journal of Management*, 9, 1, 41–51.

Naffziger, D.W., Hornsby, J.S. and Kuratko, D.F. (1994). "A Proposed Research Model of Entrepreneurial Motivation". *Entrepreneurship Theory and Practice*, 18, 3, 29–42.

Newby, R., Watson, J. and Woodliff, D. (2004). "A Scale for Measuring SME Owner-Operator Objectives: Further Development and Validation". In Gillin, L.M., Yencken, J. and La Pira, F. (eds), *Regional Frontiers of Entrepreneurship Research: Refereed Proceedings of the First AGSE-Babson Entrepreneurship Research Conference*. Melbourne, Australia: Swinburne University of Technology, 312–331.

Newby, R.R., Watson, J. and Woodliff, D.R. (2003). "Using Focus Groups in SME Research: The Case of Owner-Operator Objectives". *Journal of Developmental Entrepreneurship*, 8, 3, 237–246.

Norman, W.T. (1963). "Toward an Adequate Taxonomy of Personality Attributes: Replicated Factor Structure in Peer Nomination Personality Ratings". *Journal of Abnormal and Social Psychology*, 66, 6, 574–583.

Nunnally, J.C. (1967). *Psychometric Theory*, New York, NY, McGraw-Hill.

Nunnally, J.C. (1978). *Psychometric Theory*, 2nd edn. New York, NY, McGraw-Hill.

Olson, S.F. and Currie, H.M. (1992). "Female Entrepreneurs: Personal Value Systems and Business Strategies in a Male-Dominated Industry". *Journal of Small Business Management*, 30, 1, 49–57.

Olver, J.M. and Mooradian, T.A. (2003). "Personality Traits and Personal Values: A Conceptual and Empirical Integration". *Personality and Individual Differences*, 35, 1, 109–125.

O'Neill, R.M. and Blake-Beard, S.D. (2002). "Gender Barriers to the Female Mentor–Male Protégé Relationship". *Journal of Business Ethics*, 37, 1, 51–63.

Orser, B. and Hogarth-Scott, S. (2002). "Opting for Growth: Gender Dimensions of

Choosing Enterprise Development". *Canadian Journal of Administrative Sciences*, 19, 3, 284–300.

Parasuraman, S., Purohit, Y.S. and Godshalk, V.M. (1996). "Work and Family Variables, Entrepreneurial Career Success and Psychological Well-Being". *Journal of Vocational Behaviour*, 48, 3, 275–300.

Peters, T.J. (1987). *Thriving on Chaos: Handbook for a Management Revolution*, London, Macmillan.

Poiesz, T.B.C. and von Grumbkow, J. (1988). "Economic Well-Being, Job Satisfaction, Income Evaluation and Consumer Satisfaction: An Integrative Attempt". In van Raaij, W.F., van Veldhoven, G.M. and Wärneryd, K.-E. (eds), *Handbook of Economic Psychology*. Dordrecht: Kluwer Academic Publishers, 570–593.

Powell, G.N. and Butterfield, D.A. (1979). "The 'Good Manager': Masculine or Androgynous?" *Academy of Management Journal*, 22, 2, 395–403.

ProQuest Information and Learning Company (2000). ProQuest 5000 International, Bell and Howell Co., ProQuest Inc. and University Microfilms International, 2004.

du Rietz, A. and Henrekson, M. (2000). "Testing the Female Underperformance Hypothesis". *Small Business Economics*, 14, 1, 1–10.

Roberts, B.W. and Robins, R.W. (2000). "Broad Dispositions, Broad Aspirations: The Intersection of Personality Traits and Major Life Goals". *Personality and Social Psychology Bulletin*, 26, 10, 1284–1296.

Robichaud, Y., McGraw, E. and Roger, A. (2001). "Toward the Development of a Measuring Instrument for Entrepreneurial Motivation". *Journal of Developmental Entrepreneurship*, 6, 2, 89–201.

Rosa, P., Carter, S. and Hamilton, D. (1996). "Gender as a Determinant of Small Business Performance: Insights from a British Study". *Small Business Economics*, 8, 4, 463–478.

Rotter, J.B. (1966). "Generalized Expectancies for Internal Versus External Control of Reinforcement". *Psychological Monographs: General and Applied*, 80, 2, 1–28.

Schein, V.E. (1973). "The Relationship Between Sex Role Stereotypes and Requisite Management Characteristics". *Journal of Applied Psychology*, 57, 1, 95–100.

Schein, V.E. (1975). "The Relationship Between Sex Role Stereotypes and Requisite Management Characteristics Among Female Managers". *Journal of Applied Psychology*, 60, 3, 340–344.

Schmit, M.J. and Ryan, A.M. (1993). "The Big Five in Personnel Selection: Factor Structure in Applicant and Non-Applicant Populations". *Journal of Applied Psychology*, 78, 6, 966–974.

Schumpeter, J.A. (1934). *The Theory of Economic Development*, Cambridge, MA, Harvard University Press.

Scott, C.E. (1986). "Why More Women are Becoming Entrepreneurs". *Journal of Small Business Management*, 24, 4, 37–44.

Sexton, D.L. and Bowman, N. (1985). "The Entrepreneur: A Capable Executive and More". *Journal of Business Venturing*, 1, 1, 129–140.

Shane, S., Kolvereid, L. and Westhead, P. (1991). "An Exploratory Examination of the Reasons Leading to New Firm Formation Across Country and Gender". *Journal of Business Venturing*, 6, 6, 431–446.

Shane, S., Locke, E.A. and Collins, C.J. (2003). "Entrepreneurial Motivation". *Human Resource Management Review*, 13, 2, 257–279.

Smith, N.R. and Miner, J.B. (1983). "Type of Entrepreneur, Type of Firm, and Managerial Motivation: Implications for Organisational Life Cycle Theory". *Strategic Management Journal*, 4, 4, 325–340.

Sneed, C.D., McCrae, R.R. and Funder, D.C. (1998). "Lay Conceptions of the Five-Factor Model and Its Indicators". *Personality and Social Psychology Bulletin*, 24, 2, 115–126.

Stanworth, M.K.J. and Curran, J. (1976). "Growth and the Small Firm – An Alternative View". *Journal of Management Studies*, 13, 2, 95–110.

Steers, R.M. and Braunstein, D.N. (1976). "A Behaviourally-based Measure of Manifest Needs in Work Settings". *Journal of Vocational Behaviour*, 9, 2, 251–266.

Stevenson, L.A. (1986). "Against All Odds: The Entrepreneurship of Women". *Journal of Small Business Management*, 24, 4, 30–36.

Stewart, W.H. and Roth, P.L. (2001). "Risk Propensity Differences Between Entrepreneurs and Managers: Meta-Analytic Review". *Journal of Applied Psychology*, 86, 1, 145–153.

Stewart, W.H., Watson, W.E., Carland, J.C. and Carland, J.W. (1999). "A Proclivity for Entrepreneurship: A Comparison of Entrepreneurs, Small Business Owners, and Corporate Managers". *Journal of Business Venturing*, 14, 2, 189–214.

Tharenou, P. (2001). "Going Up? Do Traits and Informal Social Processes Predict Advancing in Management?" *Academy of Management Journal*, 44, 5, 1005–1017.

Thoresen, C.J., Bradley, J.C., Bliese, P.D. and Thoresen, J.D.(2004). "The Big Five Personality Traits and Individual Job Performance Growth Trajectories in Maintenance and Transitional Job Stages". *Journal of Applied Psychology*, 89, 5, 835–853.

Twenge, J.M. (1997). "Changes in Masculine and Feminine Traits Over Time: A Meta-Analysis". *Sex Roles*, 36, 5/6, 305–325.

Vecchio, R.P. (2003). "Entrepreneurship and Leadership: Common Trends and Common Threads". *Human Resource Management Review*, 13, 2, 303–327.

Verheul, I. and Thurik, R. (2001). "Start-up Capital: Does Gender Matter?" *Small Business Economics*, 16, 4, 329–346.

Wärneryd, K.E. (1988). "Introduction to Part III (Business Behavior)". In van Raaij, W.F., van Veldhoven, G.M. and Wärneryd, K.-E. (eds), *Handbook of Economic Psychology*. Dordrecht: Kluwer Academic Publishers, 361–367.

Watson, J. (2002). "Comparing the Performance of Male- and Female-Controlled Businesses: Relating Outputs to Inputs". *Entrepreneurship Theory and Practice*, 26, 3, 91–100.

Watson, J. and Robinson, S. (2003). "Adjusting for Risk in Comparing the Performances of Male- and Female-Controlled SMEs". *Journal of Business Venturing*, 18, 6, 773–788.

Willemsen, T.M. (2002). "Gender Typing of the Successful Manager – a Stereotype Reconsidered". *Sex Roles*, 46, 11/12, 385–391.

Willock, J., Deary, I.J., McGregor, M.M., Sutherland, A., Edward-Jones, G., Morgan, O., Dent, B., Grieve, R., Gibson, G. and Austin, E. (1999). "Farmers' Attitudes, Objectives, Behaviours, and Personality Traits: The Edinburgh Study of Decision Making on Farms". *Journal of Vocational Behaviour*, 54, 1, 5–36.

Woodliff, D., Watson, J., Newby, R. and McDowell, C. (1999). "Improving Survey Instrument Validity and Reliability: The Case of SME Owner Objectives". *Small Enterprise Research*, 7, 2, 55–65.

Zhuplev, A., Kon'kov, A. and Kiesner, F. (1998). "Russian and American Small Business: Motivations and Obstacles". *European Management Journal*, 16, 4, 505–516.

4 Attitudes towards entrepreneurship among female and male undergraduates

A preliminary study

Shirley-Ann Hazlett, Joan Henderson, Frances Hill and Claire Leitch

Introduction

The design of the research discussed in this chapter has been influenced by three main factors. First, in the early 1970s it was considered unusual for a young person to consider entrepreneurship as an option for employment (Greene *et al.*, 2001) and, indeed, as Bechhoffer and Elliott (1976) have noted, entrepreneurs were largely thought of as either being part of the petite bourgeoisie or alternatively considered to be at the margins of society (Stanworth and Curran, 1973). However, in the last couple of decades there has been a change in attitude and, increasingly, entrepreneurs are considered to be important in relation to both wealth creation and economic regeneration. Indeed, the role and importance of entrepreneurship and new business creation to both developed and developing economies have received increased attention from practitioners, academics and policy makers in recent years (Henry *et al.*, 2003).

This growth in interest in the economic contribution of entrepreneurship has been reflected in an increased level and variety of public and private sector policy initiatives at local, regional, national and supranational levels to stimulate and support the development of the sector. For example, in Europe, the European Commission 'is committed to boosting entrepreneurship as part of its strategy to transform its economy and build its future economic and competitive strength' (Commission of the European Communities, 2004). While the importance of entrepreneurship to the European economy as a driver of innovation, competitiveness and growth is clearly acknowledged, it is also recognised that the European Union is not fully exploiting its entrepreneurial potential, with only 17 per cent of Europeans opting for self-employment, and only a small proportion of these generating substantial growth. As a result of these and other factors, the productivity gap and the gap in per capita GDP between Europe and the US, is widening. Furthermore, if these issues are not addressed, it is feared that Europe's economic position will be threatened by the emerging Asian economies (Commission of the European Communities, 2004).

Second, within the UK, enterprise is central to the government's approach to economic policy both nationally and locally. This is premised on the belief that not only does entrepreneurship contribute to productivity, innovation, competition and wealth creation, but also it has a (social) role to play in addressing disadvantage across marginalised groups and communities (O'Reilly and Hart, 2002). Accordingly, in recent years a range of policy initiatives has been introduced directed at increasing levels of entrepreneurial activity and business formation. These include the Phoenix Development Fund established by the Department for Trade and Industry (DTI) in 1999, aimed at generating entrepreneurship activity among under-represented and disadvantaged groups. More recently, the Department's Small Business Service launched the Strategic Framework for Women's Enterprise which aims to provide a collaborative and long-term approach to the development of women's enterprise in the UK (DTI, 2003). At regional level, these have translated into a range of support programmes and regional initiatives tailored to the needs of specific localities. For example, in the Northern Ireland context there has been particular focus on raising awareness of new business creation amongst women and young people who are under-represented in entrepreneurial activity (www.investni.com). One aspect of this is a gap between women's self-assessment of their ability to start up in business and that of men (O'Reilly and Hart, 2003). This potentially reflects a number of differences between men and women with respect to the creation of a new venture, including differences in business and industry choices, financing strategies, growth patterns and governance structures (Carter *et al.*, 2001; Greene *et al.*, 2003).

Third, the work of Kourilsky and Walstad (1998) has provided evidence in support of the need to improve the entrepreneurship education of students, in both secondary and tertiary education, and especially of young women. In particular, they note that, while projections indicate that females will play an increasingly important role in the entrepreneurial development of economies, little is known about what young women either understand or think about entrepreneurship. From the findings of a survey of high school students, both male and female, Kourilsky and Walstad discovered that, while both men and women exhibited low levels of entrepreneurship knowledge, females were more aware of their deficiencies in this area than their male counterparts. In addition, they also discovered that, although interested in starting a business, females were significantly less likely than males to want to start a business of their own. Furthermore, they found that while the majority of students may aspire to new venture creation, many, especially women, held views which could be detrimental to entrepreneurial success. There is a need, therefore, to explore these issues more fully and to investigate the understanding and perceptions of new venture creation among this group.

This chapter reports upon the first year of a three-year longitudinal survey which involved undergraduate students within the School of Management and Economics at Queen's University, Belfast, in an attempt to assess their understanding and perceptions of, as well as their attitudes towards, self-employment and new venture creation. The main elements of the chapter are as follows. First, we consider trends in female entrepreneurship at an international level. Second, the economic context of Northern Ireland is presented. Third, we discuss the low levels of enterprise among females in Northern Ireland. Fourth, we summarise the methodology adopted in this research and report baseline findings. Fifth, based on an analysis of the data gathered to date, we explore the extent to which there are discernable differences in the understanding and perceptions of, as well as attitudes towards, entrepreneurship between female and male undergraduate students. Finally, a selection of findings are mapped onto the literature and some conclusions drawn.

Trends in female entrepreneurship

Although female entrepreneurship is a relatively minor constituent of the academic literature that focuses on new venture creation and entrepreneurial activity, research investigating the influence of gender has developed considerably over the past fifteen years. Despite the fact that 'there is no real shortage of academic research in the area … there is, however, a clear lack of cumulative knowledge and a failure to date to adequately conceptualise and build explanatory theories' (Carter *et al.*, 2003:72). The growth in presence, size and contribution of women-owned businesses worldwide has attracted significant attention over the past ten years. For example, in the last two decades in the US, not only have women-owned businesses outpaced the overall growth of businesses by nearly two to one, they have also made a more significant impact upon the economy in terms of employment and revenues generated, than the growth in the number of such firms would indicate (Greene *et al.*, 2001). Furthermore, predictions have suggested that by 2005, there will be 4.7 million self-employed women which is an increase of 77 per cent since 1983 – this in comparison to the 6 per cent increase in the number of self-employed men (United States Small Business Association, 1998).

In Europe, while there has been an increase in female entrepreneurial activity, the rate of growth has not been so rapid (Carter *et al.*, 2003). For example, in the Netherlands, females comprise 34 per cent of all those who are self-employed, while in Finland, Denmark, Spain, Belgium and the UK the percentage is somewhat lower, with average figures of around 25 per cent (Duchenaut, 1997; Nilsson, 1997). However, within these European countries the ratio of female/male new ventures varies between countries. For instance, based on the data generated as a result of the GEM (Global Entrepreneurship Monitor) studies in 2003, the UK was found to rank sixteenth out of a possible thirty-four countries in terms of this ratio (Minniti *et al.*, 2005). In turn, within the UK itself, differences between the levels of entrepreneurial activity amongst the female population in comparison to the male population also exist. Regionally, the TEA (Total Entrepreneurial Activity) index of females was highest in the South West (5.8 per cent) and in Wales (4.8 per cent) (O'Reilly and Hart, 2004), while in Northern Ireland the figure was 2.3 per cent in comparison with a figure of 7.8 per cent for male entrepreneurial activity (O'Reilly and Hart, 2004). When compared with the data for the previous year this seems to suggest a decrease in female TEA (from 3.5 per cent); however, it may actually be the result of the change in sample size between the two years (3,000 in 2002, and 5,000 in 2003).

The Northern Ireland economic context

Northern Ireland is the most westerly region of the UK, with a population of around 1.6 million. As such, it is part of the European Union (EU) and, until 2000, had Objective One status since its GDP was less than 75 per cent of European GDP. In relative terms, the economic position of Northern Ireland is particularly weak, as it continues to lag behind its European counterparts in relation to economic performance. The per capita GDP for Northern Ireland is one of the lowest in the UK, at only 77 per cent of the UK average (Ulster Society of Chartered Accountants, 2001:2). This economic gap is partly attributable to political instability, reliance on public sector employment and the decline of the region's traditional industries. In addition, there are very few public limited companies (only five compared with almost 270 in Scotland) and the private sector is dominated by small businesses employing fewer than twelve people, many of which are family owned. In light of this, it is acknowledged that growth in the SME sector is a critical stimulant to overall economic growth in the region. However, in Northern Ireland the level of business start-ups is lower than in the rest of the UK (6.9 per cent of business registrations against current businesses, compared with 11.5 per cent in the UK as a whole). In addition, the level of fast growing businesses is also low, with only 7 per cent of start-up companies being classified as such (Ulster Society of Chartered Accountants, 2001:22). Moreover, despite the assistance provided by government agencies such as Invest Northern Ireland (InvestNI), the region's SMEs appear to have difficulty progressing from start-up to high growth companies (Harding, 2003a; O'Reilly and Hart, 2003). This may be due to the dominant role that the public sector plays in the Northern Ireland economy, leading to a reduction in the level of individual risk-taking, as well as the emphasis placed on pursuing a career in the professions, such as medicine, accountancy and law, for the most able (O'Reilly and Hart, 2003). All of these are perceived as contributory factors to the region's low levels of entrepreneurial activity.

The main economic development organisation in Northern Ireland is InvestNI, the aim of which is to 'add value to the economy and create wealth' (www.investni.com). It seeks to achieve this by encouraging more people to start a business and by helping companies grow and compete in global markets. Accordingly, it offers a range of start-up programmes contributing, on average, 20 per cent of set-up costs. However, their aims also include achieving higher levels for growth by indigenous and externally owned businesses. To this end, a 'Global Start Team' was recently established and is currently determining its remit. It will target businesses which seek to develop leading edge technologies with the potential to trade internationally. With particular respect to increasing levels of female entrepreneurship within the economy, InvestNI has embarked upon the widely publicised 'Go for It' and 'Investing in Women' initiatives, which seek to improve not only the low levels of female entrepreneurship in the region, but also the quality of start-ups by women. The agency aims to achieve this by attempting to alter the structural and cultural obstacles that traditionally limit female entrepreneurial activity. In addition, it aims to boost the perform-ance of those already in business by providing initiatives targeted directly at this group, such as the development of business networks and the promotion of role models to offer support and encouragement to entrepreneurial women.

Women's entrepreneurship in Northern Ireland

As O'Reilly and Hart (2002:11) have noted, 'Northern Ireland is a lagging region in terms of entrepreneurial activity' and indeed, it ranks alongside the poorest performing regions in the UK. For instance, in comparison with the north east of England, Northern Ireland has roughly similar proportions of potential entrepreneurs and a slightly higher proportion of entrepreneurs. Both regions, when measured in terms of per capita GDP, are among the poorest areas of the UK (O'Reilly and Hart, 2002). The TEA index for Northern Ireland is 5 per cent (2.3 per cent for women and 7.8 per cent for men) (O'Reilly and Hart, 2004), indicating that women in the region are less than one-third as likely as men to be entrepreneurs. Indeed, in comparison with their peers in England and Ireland, females in Northern Ireland are much less likely to be engaged in, or thinking about, starting an enterprise. Interestingly, female necessity entrepreneurship, where women enter self-employment because they perceive that they have no better choices for work, is lower in Northern Ireland for women than men, and lower than women in the UK generally (O'Reilly and Hart, 2004).

While there is good information available on the start-up process, a reason-able degree of financial support, as well as an awareness of equity funding and a strong banking sector (Harding, 2003a), it has also been noted that there are low levels of take up of support by females, young people and older entrepreneurs (O'Reilly and Hart, 2002). One reason for this might be the fact that women in Northern Ireland are more likely than women in any other region of the UK, to report fear of failure as preventing them from starting a new business venture (O'Reilly and Hart, 2003). It should be noted, however, that generally a higher fear of failure exists in Northern Ireland among potential entrepreneurs of both sexes (43 per cent in Northern Ireland compared with 32.9 per cent in the UK) (O'Reilly and Hart, 2004). Moreover, fewer women in Northern Ireland, com-pared to the majority of regions elsewhere in the UK, believe they have the skills to start a business, while similar proportions indicate that they personally know an entrepreneur and that the opportunities for start-up are good. These beliefs are in contrast to those held by males. For example, just over half of men, compared to less than one-third of women, believed that they had the necessary skills to start a business and were less likely to fear failure. Furthermore, more men than women were likely to have personally known an entrepreneur in the past two years, as well as believing that the opportunities for initiating new venture creation within the next six months were good (O'Reilly and Hart, 2004).

These findings are consistent with the findings of the GEM study conducted in the UK, where Harding *et al.* (2004) found that, irrespective of educational qualifications, men are more likely than women to know an entrepreneur, which means that women are less likely than men to have role models with whom they can identify. Furthermore, they also discovered that men, irrespective of the level of educational attainment they achieve, are significantly more likely to believe that they have the skills to establish a business and are less likely to fear failure than women. However, among the student population this trend was somewhat different, as male respondents from this group indicated that they are more likely than women to fear failure (31.1 per cent compared to 24.8 per cent). On the other hand, 44 per cent of male students compared to 28.6 per cent of female students believed that they have the skills to start a new venture. Indeed, it was found that men with degrees are twice as likely as women with degrees to be actively involved in the start-up process and that the only level of qualification for which female entrepreneurship is higher than male entrepreneurship is to be found among the post-doctoral population.

In Northern Ireland the propensity of the female graduate population to engage in entrepreneurial activity is also low, with female graduates only one-third as likely as male graduates to be involved in entrepreneurial activity. Indeed, as O'Reilly and Hart (2004) note, female graduates in Northern Ireland record one of the lowest TEA rates of all the UK regions, even when age is controlled for. Both male and female student respondents in the UK indicated that they were unlikely either to know an entrepreneur or be able to identify an opportunity to exploit. This contrasts with the situation in the Republic of Ireland, where it was found that men and women in all response categories were more likely to have known an entrepreneur. While both men and women in Ireland were more likely than their counterparts in Northern Ireland to report that they had the necessary skills to start a business, there was no difference between women in Northern Ireland and Ireland concerning their attitude to risk, with two-fifths claiming that fear of failure would prevent them from starting a business venture (O'Reilly and Hart, 2003). The fact that more women than men report that they consider themselves to be risk averse with respect to new venture creation is not surprising, and corresponds to the findings of other research. For instance, in a study commissioned by the Gender Equality Unit in the Republic of Ireland, fewer women than men described themselves as having 'high esteem', being 'self-confident' and 'likely to take risks' (NDP Gender Equality Unit, 2003). In light of this, it is somewhat surprising to note that more women in Northern Ireland than in the UK as a whole regard setting up a new business venture as a good career choice and consider that successful entrepreneurs have a high social status. Clearly, therefore, there would seem to be a disconnect between women's perceptions and their behaviours, and/or a disconnect between their perceptions and aspirations.

Methodology

Reported in the next section are some baseline findings from a survey of undergraduate students in the School of Management and Economics at Queen's University, Belfast. The survey was conducted in the academic year 2002/2003 and was funded by the Development of Learning and Teaching Funds administered by the Centre for the Enhancement of Learning and Teaching at the University. The School comprises five subject areas, namely Management, Economics, Finance, Accounting and Information Systems. Students participating in the study are drawn from all of these areas, thus it is possible to disaggregate and analyse data by subject when appropriate. Timetabled educational provision of entrepreneurship, at present, is limited to one elective module at final year level (level three) which may only be taken by Management students.

The majority of the undergraduate body are from Northern Ireland, with approximately 10 per cent from overseas; around 65 per cent are female and 35 per cent are male and so the data may also be disaggregated and analysed by domicile/nationality and sex when required. Information was gathered from students at each of the three undergraduate levels by means of self-complete questionnaires made up of structured and unstructured questions and administered during scheduled classes, thus ensuring relatively high response rates. (It should be noted that 'levels one, two and three' referred to below, equate to years one, two and three of the degree programmes in question.) The design of questions was informed by previous research in which two of the authors were involved (see Henry *et al.*, 2003), findings of the GEM surveys conducted in the UK and Northern Ireland (Harding, 2003a, b), and the Household Entrepreneurship Survey which was carried out in Northern Ireland (O'Reilly and Hart, 2002). The questionnaire had a total of twenty-six questions divided into six main sections, namely, personal details (seven questions), understanding and prior experience of entrepreneurship (eight questions), attitudes towards and perceptions of entrepreneurship (three questions), perceived barriers to entrepreneurship (two questions), getting started (four questions) and entrepreneurship education (two questions). Seven questions had multiple parts. Similar questionnaires will be administered over a three-year period, so that, ultimately, longitudinal data will have been generated.

This chapter reports a subset of the baseline findings relating to one of the objectives of the study, namely that of conducting a longitudinal investigation, over a three-year period, of undergraduate students taking Management and related degree courses at the School of Management and Economics to examine their understanding and perceptions of, as well as attitudes towards, entrepreneurship. A total of 596 undergraduates completed the questionnaires. Table 4.1 provides some categorical data relating to this cohort of students. At the time of questionnaire completion, none of the students surveyed had undertaken the entrepreneurship elective module. However, Management students would have been exposed to a very small amount of entrepreneurship teaching (around two hours) at level one.

Table 4.1 Categorical data

	Level 1	Level 2	Level 3	Totals
Females	115	96	108	319 (54%)
Males	126	77	74	277 (46%)
Totals	241 (40%)	173 (29%)	182 (31%)	596 (100%)

Findings

Data were analysed using the SPSS statistical package (version 10). As the scales on the questionnaire are mainly ordinal scales, non-parametric statistical tests have been carried out in relation to the data reported below. Regarding Tables 4.2 to 4.5, the statistical tests employed to determine significant differences were two-tailed Mann-Whitney U Tests:

> When at least ordinal measurement has been achieved the Mann-Whitney U Test may be used to test whether two independent groups have been drawn from the same population. This is one of the most powerful nonparametric tests, and it is a most useful alternative to the parametric *t* test when the researcher wishes to avoid the *t* test's assumptions or when the measurement in the research is weaker than interval scaling.
>
> (Siegal, 1956:116)

In relation to Tables 4.6 and 4.7, which relate to dichotomous data (yes/no responses) the test employed to determine statistical significance was the chi-square test. This is used to establish whether there are statistically significant differences between the observed (actual) frequencies and the expected (hypothesised) frequencies of two variables. The larger the observed frequency, the larger the chi-square statistic and the more likely the difference is statistically significant (Vogt, 1993:34).

Attributes and characteristics associated with entrepreneurs

Question 9 on the questionnaire required students to indicate the extent to which they associated a number of characteristics and attributes (eighteen in total) with entrepreneurs. Each characteristic/attribute was rated on a six-point, Likert-type scale where zero equals not at all, and five equals to a very high extent. The responses have been analysed for males and females at each of the three levels; frequencies and medians have been calculated, and tests for statistically significant differences between male and female responses at each of the three levels have also been carried out. In relation to those who responded, the statistically significant differences ($p \leq 0.05$) are given in Table 4.2.

Given the findings of recent surveys it is interesting to examine the

Table 4.2 Attributes and characteristics associated with entrepreneurs

Variable	Level 1	Level 2	Level 3
Enjoys a challenge	$p \leq 0.941$	$p \leq 0.899$	$\mathbf{p \leq 0.001}$
Is well educated	$\mathbf{p \leq 0.002}$	$\mathbf{p \leq 0.018}$	$p \leq 0.165$
Can tolerate ambiguity and uncertainty	$\mathbf{p \leq 0.012}$	$\mathbf{p \leq 0.002}$	$p \leq 0.134$
Seeks good interpersonal relationships	$\mathbf{p \leq 0.017}$	$\mathbf{p \leq 0.006}$	$p \leq 0.507$

Note
Values significant at $p \leq 0.05$ level are in bold.

responses to a number of the parts of this question in a little more detail. In particular: 'has a good network of contacts'; 'is confident in their own abilities'; 'is willing to take risks'; 'wants to be in control'; 'desires power'; 'can tolerate ambiguity and uncertainty'; 'seeks good interpersonal relationships'. In all cases, the proportions cited relate to students associating the particular characteristic/attribute with entrepreneurs either to a high or very high extent.

High proportions of students of both sexes and at all levels associated the variable 'has a good network of contacts' with entrepreneurs. The category of respondent who associated this descriptor with entrepreneurs most were level three females (79.7 per cent). Even higher proportions of students of both sexes associated the characteristic 'being confident in their own abilities' with entrepreneurs, and the category recording the highest level of association was level one males (92.8 per cent). It is interesting to note that the equivalent proportions for female students are 81.7 per cent (level one), 83.4 per cent (level two) and 86.2 per cent (level three). Once again, high proportions of all students associated the characteristic 'willingness to take risks' with entrepreneurs, the category recording the highest level of association being level one males (89.7 per cent). The characteristic of 'wanting to be in control' was also associated with entrepreneurs by all categories of students, with slightly higher proportions of males than females at levels one and two making this association, while at level three, the situation was reversed (75.9 per cent of females against 74.3 per cent of males).

With respect to the attribute 'desires power', the association was less strong. Again, at levels one and two higher proportions of males than females made the association, while at level three, the opposite was the case (56.4 per cent of females and 48.6 per cent of males). As can be seen above, there are significant differences between the associations made by males and females at levels one and two with regard to the variable 'tolerating ambiguity and uncertainty'. At those levels, considerably higher proportions of females than males associated toleration of ambiguity and uncertainty with entrepreneurs. The proportions of students of both sexes making this association at level three are higher than at either levels one or two, and more level three females (50 per cent) than males (41.9 per cent) made the association. Again, as can be seen above, there

were significant differences between males and females at levels one and two
with regard to associating entrepreneurs with 'seeking good interpersonal
relationships'. At those levels higher proportions of females than males associated the search for good interpersonal relationships with entrepreneurs.
However, at level three, there is little difference in the proportions of students of
the two sexes making the association (43.2 per cent males, 45.4 per cent
females).

Importance attributed to tasks performed by entrepreneurs

Question 12 on the questionnaire required students to indicate the extent to
which they believe a range of tasks (thirteen in total) performed by entrepreneurs are important. Each task was rated on a five-point, Likert-type scale
where one equals completely unimportant, and five equals very important. The
responses were analysed for males and females at each of the three levels; frequencies and medians were calculated and tests for statistically significant differences between male and female responses at each of the three levels were also
conducted. In relation to those who responded, the statistically significant differences ($p \leq 0.05$) are indicated in Table 4.3.

As can be seen from Table 4.3, in relation to the importance attributed to a
range of tasks performed by entrepreneurs, there are a considerable number of
statistically significant differences between the responses of males and females
at the various levels. It is interesting to note that in relation to all of the tasks
listed above, the proportion of females rating each task as either important or
very important is higher at all three levels than the equivalent proportion of
males.

Table 4.3 Importance attributed to tasks performed by entrepreneurs

Variable	Level 1	Level 2	Level 3
Development of a business plan	$p \leq 0.061$	$p \leq \mathbf{0.002}$	$p \leq \mathbf{0.011}$
Market research	$p \leq \mathbf{0.018}$	$p \leq \mathbf{0.009}$	$p \leq \mathbf{0.002}$
Feasibility study	$p \leq 0.103$	$p \leq 0.066$	$p \leq \mathbf{0.035}$
Development of marketing strategy/plan	$p \leq \mathbf{0.039}$	$p \leq \mathbf{0.008}$	$p \leq 0.191$
Networking	$p \leq \mathbf{0.013}$	$p \leq 0.692$	$p \leq \mathbf{0.006}$
Planning and managing the business operation	$p \leq 0.411$	$p \leq \mathbf{0.003}$	$p \leq 0.974$
Planning and managing human resource development	$p \leq \mathbf{0.038}$	$p \leq \mathbf{0.023}$	$p \leq \mathbf{0.005}$
Determining legal requirements and constraints	$p \leq \mathbf{0.024}$	$p \leq 0.088$	$p \leq \mathbf{0.000}$

Note
Values significant at $p \leq 0.05$ level are in bold.

Influences on students' understanding of entrepreneurship

Question 13 offered students eight factors that might have informed their under-standing of entrepreneurship. The factor reported by most students, and male students in particular, as being most influential in this respect, was the media (i.e. television, newspapers and items on radio programmes) – more than one response was permitted. This was followed by students' experiences of working for a small business; the experiences of family members of running a business which was reported by slightly higher proportions of females than males at all three levels; students' contact with small businesses either as customers or sup-pliers; and modules at university (levels two and three). Although cited by relat-ively small proportions of students overall, at all three levels a higher proportion of males than females cited friends' experiences of running a business.

With regard to question 14, which asked whether any family or friends have ever owned a business, relatives cited by the highest proportions of students overall were parents and relatives other than parents, partner/spouse or brother/sister. The highest proportion was for level two males (36.5 per cent) and the lowest was for level three females (26.9 per cent). Higher proportions of males than females at all three levels cited friends owning businesses, although in all cases the proportions fell below 30 per cent, and in the case of level two and level three females, below 20 per cent.

Self-perception

Question 18 comprised sixteen statements which questions how respondents perceive themselves. Each statement was scored on a five-point Likert-type scale where one equals strongly disagree, and five equals strongly agree. The responses have been analysed for males and females at each of the three levels; frequencies and medians were calculated, and tests for statistically significant differences between male and female responses at each of the three levels were carried out. In relation to those who responded, the statistically significant differences ($p \le 0.05$) are presented in Table 4.4.

Table 4.4 Self-perception

Variable	Level 1	Level 2	Level 3
When the going gets tough I hate to give up	$p \le 0.072$	$\boldsymbol{p \le 0.036}$	$p \le 0.713$
I do not shy away from hard decisions	$\boldsymbol{p \le 0.019}$	$\boldsymbol{p \le 0.000}$	$p \le 0.063$
I enjoy the challenge of situations that many consider risky	$\boldsymbol{p \le 0.005}$	$p \le 0.182$	$\boldsymbol{p \le 0.001}$
When working in groups I prefer that someone else takes the leading role	$p \le 0.115$	$p \le 0.615$	$\boldsymbol{p \le 0.042}$
I am the sort of person who handles uncertainty well	$p \le 0.061$	$p \le 0.073$	$\boldsymbol{p \le 0.045}$
I usually trust my own judgement even if others don't agree with me	$\boldsymbol{p \le 0.000}$	$p \le 0.066$	$p \le 0.066$

Note
Values significant at $p \le 0.05$ level are in bold.

With respect to the statement 'when the going gets tough I hate to give up' similar proportions of males and females agreed or strongly agreed with the statement, except at level two, where the differences in responses are significant, with 78 per cent of males either agreeing or strongly agreeing with the statement, compared with only 67 per cent of females. At all three levels, the proportions of males who agreed or strongly agreed with the statement 'I do not shy away from hard decisions' were higher than the proportions of females, and the differences in responses were significant at levels one and two (70.5 per cent, 64 per cent and 69.8 per cent, 48.8 per cent respectively – proportions of males are cited first in each case). Again, at all three levels the proportions of males who agreed or strongly agreed with the statement 'I enjoy the challenge of situations that many consider risky' were higher than the proportions of females, and the differences in responses were significant at levels one and three.

In relation to levels one and two, the proportions of males and females agreeing or strongly agreeing with the statement 'when working in groups I prefer that someone else takes the leading role' are very similar. However, regarding level three, the responses are significantly different – only 19.2 per cent of males agreed or strongly agreed, while the equivalent proportion of females is 32.7 per cent – the highest of all six categories of students.

Interestingly, at all three levels the proportions of females either agreeing or strongly agreeing with the statement 'when I have plans I am almost certain to make them happen', are higher than the proportions of males. The differences in responses are noteworthy at level three (males, 48.6 per cent; females, 63.4 per cent). The converse is apparent with respect to the statement 'I'm the sort of person who handles uncertainty well'. For all three levels higher proportions of males than females agreed or strongly agreed with this statement, and the differences in responses are significant for level three. A similar pattern of responses is evident for the statement 'I usually trust my own judgment even if those around me don't agree with me', and the differences are significant at level one.

Perceived barriers to setting up a business

Question 19 requires respondents to indicate the extent to which they believe a range of fourteen factors to be potential barriers to setting up a business. Each factor is rated on a six-point, Likert-type scale where zero equals 'not at all' and five equals 'to a very high extent'. In relation to those who responded, Table 4.5 shows the statistically significant differences ($p \leq 0.05$).

With regard to the above, it is possible to make the following observations. As far as not knowing how to start a business is concerned, at level one a smaller proportion of males (29.4 per cent) than females (46.1 per cent) perceived this as a potential barrier to a high or very high extent. A similar situation applies to not having the necessary skills to start a business, as this was perceived as a potential barrier to a high or very high extent by 27.7 per cent of males compared with 41.8 per cent of females. At level three, not knowing how to get hold of premises, equipment or staff was perceived as a potential barrier

Table 4.5 Perceived barriers to setting up a business

Variable	Level 1	Level 2	Level 3
Not knowing how to start a business	**$p \leq 0.047$**	$p \leq 0.250$	$p \leq 0.702$
Not having the necessary skills to start a business	**$p \leq 0.025$**	$p \leq 0.342$	$p \leq 0.670$
Not knowing how to get hold of premises, equipment or staff	$p \leq 0.319$	$p \leq 0.540$	**$p \leq 0.013$**
The risk involved	$p \leq 0.054$	$p \leq 0.729$	$p \leq 0.264$

Note
Values significant at $p \leq 0.05$ level are in bold.

to a high or very high extent by 42.5 per cent of males compared with only 21.1 per cent of females. Concerning not having an idea for a business, at levels one and three the proportions of males and females perceiving this as a potential barrier to a high or very high extent are fairly similar (49.2 per cent, 46.9 per cent and 55.4 per cent, 53.7 per cent respectively – the proportion of males is cited first in each case). However, there are greater differences in responses at level two (61.1 per cent, 42.7 per cent – proportion of males cited first).

Regarding the risk involved in setting up a business and the chance the business might fail, the pattern that emerges is not quite as clear as one might expect, with the proportions of males and females perceiving the risk involved as a potential barrier to a high or very high extent being (the proportion of males is cited first in each case): level one (27.7 per cent, 33.9 per cent); level two (33.8 per cent, 28.1 per cent); level three (43.3 per cent, 55.6 per cent). As far as the chance the business might fail is concerned, the proportions perceiving this as a potential barrier to a high or very high extent are fairly similar at all three levels. These are (the proportion of males is cited first in each case): level one (34.1 per cent, 39.1 per cent); level two (39 per cent, 38.6 per cent); level three (47.3 per cent, 51.8 per cent). It is interesting that the students recording the highest levels of fear of business failure are those at level three. The proportions of males and females perceiving fear of getting into debt as a potential barrier are as follows (the proportion of males is cited first in each case): level one (39.7 per cent, 42.6 per cent); level two (53.3 per cent, 41.7 per cent); level three (47.3 per cent, 48.1 per cent).

In relation to getting finance for the business, the findings reveal little evidence that females perceive this as a potential barrier to a significantly greater extent than males. Indeed, as far as both levels two and three are concerned, the proportions of females responding 'to a high' or 'very high extent' are lower than the proportions of males, as follows (proportion of females cited first in each case): level two (46.9 per cent, 63.7 per cent); level three (54.7 per cent, 59.5 per cent) – at none of the levels is the difference in responses significant.

With respect to the statement 'not knowing how to start a business' it is interesting to observe that, in relation to levels one and three, higher proportions of males than females believed this to be a potential barrier to a high or very high extent (48.1 per cent, 27.1 per cent and 41.9 per cent, 32.4 per cent respectively – proportion of males cited first in each case).

Consideration of self-employment as an alternative to employment

As can be seen from Table 4.6, at levels one and three, significantly higher proportions of males than females have considered self-employment as an alternative to employment. The lowest proportion of individuals at all three levels who have considered self-employment as an alternative to employment is 54.2 per cent of females at level three. This figure is somewhat disconcerting given that these students are at the final stage of a degree course related to management and business.

Considered setting up a business

Table 4.7 reveals that at levels one and three, significantly higher proportions of males have considered setting up a business than females. However, this is not the case at level two, where a higher proportion of females than males have considered setting up a business, though the difference in responses is not significant. The lowest proportion of individuals at all levels who have considered setting up a business is 49.5 per cent of females at level three. Again, this figure is somewhat disconcerting, given that these students are at the final stage of a management/business degree course.

Discussion

As is evident, the findings of this study resonate with many of the issues raised in the literature and highlighted in the early sections of the chapter. One of the purposes of asking questions relating to attributes and characteristics associated with entrepreneurs was to determine if males and females perceived these differently. Furthermore, in relation to females specifically, this study sought to determine whether or not they associated attributes and characteristics with entrepreneurs which, research suggests, many women in the general population do not believe they possess themselves. This in turn may have a negative impact

Table 4.6 Consideration of self-employment as an alternative to employment: answered yes

	Male	*Female*	*Chi-Square*
Level 1	96 (76.8%)	70 (60.9%)	0.008
Level 2	59 (58.4%)	70 (70.6%)	0.837
Level 3	60 (82.2%)	58 (54.2%)	0.000

Note
Figures in parenthesis = % within gender.

Table 4.7 Considered setting up a business: answered yes

	Male	Female	Chi-Square
Level 1	93 (74.4%)	69 (60.5%)	0.022
Level 2	48 (62.3%)	62 (66.7%)	0.557
Level 3	53 (72.6%)	53 (49.5%)	0.002

Note
Figures in parenthesis = % within gender.

upon their propensity to consider self-employment as a viable career option. High proportions of students of both sexes associated entrepreneurs with a willingness to take risks, confidence in their own abilities and wanting to be in control. These are characteristics which, research suggests, many women may not perceive themselves to possess (O'Reilly and Hart, 2004). In relation to risk, it is noteworthy that higher proportions of males than females at all levels either agreed or strongly agreed with the statement 'I enjoy the challenge of situations that many consider risky'. Moreover, regarding the statement 'I am the sort of person who handles uncertainty well', higher proportions of males than females agreed or strongly agreed.

A similar pattern of responses is evident for the statement 'I usually trust my own judgment even if those around me don't agree with me', which suggests that male respondents have more self-confidence than females. Regarding control, the results were less clear-cut, because at levels one and two the proportions of males and females agreeing or strongly agreeing with the statement 'when working in groups I prefer that someone else takes the leading role', are similar. However, the category of respondents in which the highest proportion agreed or strongly agreed with the statement was level three females. Given that the respondents are all undergraduate university students, these findings are consistent with those of the GEM study conducted in the UK (Harding and Cowling, 2003). It is difficult to interpret these findings without entering into a discussion of 'gender as a basic organizing principle in society' which 'holds that women have experiences and interests that are different from men's, based on their socializing and their subordinated position' (Ahl, 2004:19). Such a discussion is beyond the scope of this chapter.

Concerning perceived barriers to setting up a business and attitude to risk in this context, the patterns observed in other studies are largely replicated here. However, it is noteworthy that the students most likely to perceive risk as a potential barrier are level three students of both sexes, but again particularly females. Given that these students are following Management and business-related degree programmes, this is disquieting but perhaps not surprising, especially since none of these students had been exposed to a dedicated module in entrepreneurship.

As stated above, some research findings suggest that men are less likely than women to fear failure and the findings of this study are consistent with this.

Again, the students most likely to perceive fear of business failure as a barrier to setting up a new venture are those at level three. Also referred to above is the fact that, to a greater extent than women, men perceive themselves as possessing the necessary skills to establish a business. However, the findings of this study are equivocal on this matter.

As shown above in relation to the importance attributed to entrepreneurial tasks, significantly higher proportions of females than males at all three levels considered planning and managing human resource development to be either important or very important. This is consistent with the observation of Verheul *et al.* (2002:465) that a 'distinguishing feature of female entrepreneurship is that business and personal aspects are intertwined'. Moreover, Brush (1992) asserts that women tend to see their businesses as cooperative networks of relationships. A related issue is networking, which is considered to be a vital aspect in the survival and success of firms (Aldrich *et al.*, 1997). Some commentators have suggested that there are gender differences in the way networks are created and used, particularly in respect of access to finance (Rosa and Carter, 1998). However, others have disputed this view and Carter *et al.* (2001) identify this as an under-researched area and highly contentious. It emerged from this study that at all levels, higher proportions of women than men believed networking to be an important entrepreneurial task and the differences are significant at levels one and three.

Concerning influences on students' understanding of entrepreneurship, perhaps not surprisingly given the age group, the biggest influence on all, but especially males, is the media. At a general level, in Northern Ireland both sexes perceive that there is better media coverage than their counterparts in the UK, but the perceptions are even more positive in Ireland (O'Reilly and Hart, 2003). This may reflect that the extensive media campaigns conducted by InvestNI and Enterprise Ireland to raise awareness of entrepreneurship as a career option have been successful. As stated above, another potentially important influence is role models, and research to date would indicate that women in particular require more exposure to successful female entrepreneurs (McMurray, 2001). As far as this study is concerned, there is little appreciable evidence of role models having greater impact on male students' understanding of entrepreneurship than is the case for females.

In relation to self-perception, what was particularly noticeable was the fact that, regarding the statement 'I usually trust my own judgment even if others do not agree with me', considerably higher proportions of males than females agreed with it. This supports the findings of the study commissioned by the Gender Equality Unit in Ireland (2003), regarding gender differences in levels of self-confidence. However, it is mitigated by the fact that females in this study had higher beliefs in their own self-efficacy than males. This is perhaps not surprising as the respondents are university undergraduates who would have considerable experience of achievement, especially in the academic context.

With respect to potential barriers to new venture creation, considerably smaller proportions of males than females perceived not having the necessary skills to start a business as a potential barrier to a high or very high extent. This is very similar to the GEM (UK) findings discussed above. It is interesting to note that the respondents least likely to have considered self-employment or setting up a business as an alternative to employment are level three females. Such a finding is concerning given that one function of universities is to educate and train undergraduates to play meaningful roles in society and especially in this instance, as these respondents are at the final stage of an applied Management or business-related degree programme. However, in the absence of longitudinal data it would be premature to draw strong negative inferences.

Conclusions

As the reports of the Northern Ireland GEM studies conducted in the years 2002–2004 have highlighted, there is a need to tailor educational curricula to raise the TEA for Northern Ireland students at tertiary level (Kourilsky and Walstad, 1998). This is particularly necessary in relation to female students, as women are currently only one-third as likely as men to start a business. Accordingly, another of the objectives of this research project is to design (in due course, and once all of the relevant data have been gathered) a suite of activities to address some of these issues, to develop appropriate entrepreneurial skills at each level of study, and in light of Brush *et al.*'s (1995) recommendation, to incorporate a variety of pedagogies to meet the needs of both female and male students.

References

Ahl, H. (2004). *The Scientific Reproduction of Gender Inequality: A Discourse Analysis of Research Texts on Women's Entrepreneurship*, Copenhagen, Copenhagen Business School Press.

Aldrich, H.E., Elam, A.B. and Reece, P.R. (1997). 'Strong Ties, Weak Ties and Strangers: Do Women Owners Differ from Men in their Use of Networking to Obtain Assistance?' In Birley, S. and MacMillan, I.C. (eds), *Entrepreneurship in a Global Context*. London: Routledge.

Bechhoffer, F. and Elliott, D. (1976). 'Persistence and Change: The Petite Bourgeoise in Industrial Society'. In Curran, J., Stanworth, J. and Watkins, D. (eds), *The Survival of the Small Firm: The Economics of Survival and Enterpreneurship*. Aldershot: Gower, 139–155.

Brush, C.G. (1992). 'Research on Women Business Owners: Past Trends, a New Perspective and Future Directions'. *Entrepreneurship Theory and Practice*, 16, 5–30.

Brush, C., Griffin, J. and Smith, C. (1995). 'Perceived Value of Entrepreneurship Course Content and Pedagogy'. Available: www.sbaer.uca.edu/research/sbida/1995/pdf/10.pdf (accessed 25 April 2005).

Carter, S., Anderson, S. and Shaw, E. (2001) 'Women's Business Ownership: A Review of the Academic, Popular and Internet Literature', Report to the Small Business Service, Sheffield.

Carter, S., Anderson, S. and Shaw, E. (2003). 'Women's Business Ownership: A Review of the Academic, Popular and Internet Literature with a UK Policy Focus'. In Watkins,

D. (ed), *ARPENT: Annual Review of Progress in Entrepreneurship*. Brussels: The European Foundation for Management Development, 66–157.

Commission of the European Communities (2004). *Action Plan: The European Agenda for Entrepreneurship*. Communication from the Commission to the Council, the European Parliament, the European Economic and Social Committee and the Committee of the Regions, COM.

Department of Trade and Industry (1999). 'Phoenix Development Fund'. Available: www.sbs.gov.uk/phoenix/women.php (accessed 25 April 2005).

Department of Trade and Industry Small Business Service (2003). 'A Strategic Framework for Women's Enterprises: Sharing the Vision' *A Collaborative Approach to Increasing Female Entrepreneurship*, London, Department of Trade and Industry Small Business Service.

Duchenaut, B. (1997). 'Women Entrepreneurs in SMEs'. Report prepared for the OECD Conference on Women Entrepreneurs in Small and Medium Sized Enterprises: A Major Force for Innovation and Job Creation, Paris: OECD.

Greene, F.J. (2002). 'An Investigation into Enterprise Support for Younger People, 1975–2000'. *International Small Business Journal*, 20, 3, 315–336.

Greene, P.G., Brush, C.G., Hart, M.M. and Saparito, P. (2001). 'Patterns of Venture Capital Funding: Is Gender a Factor?' *Venture Capital: An International Journal of Entrepreneurial Finance*, 3, 1, 63–83.

Greene, P.G., Hart, M.M., Gatewood, E.J., Brush, C.G. and Carter, N.M. (2003). *Women Entrepreneurs: Moving Front and Center: An Overview of Research and Theory*. Coleman White Paper Series.

Harding, R. (2003a). *Global Entrepreneurship Monitor: Northern Ireland*, London, London Business School.

Harding, R. (2003b). *Global Entrepreneurship Monitor: UK*, London, London Business School.

Harding, R. and Cowling, M. (2003). *Global Entrepreneurship Monitor: London*, London, London Business School and The Work Foundation.

Harding, R., Cowling, M. and Ream, M. (2004) *Achieving the Vision: Female Entrepreneurship*, London, The British Chamber of Commerce.

Henry, C., Hill, F. and Leitch, C. (2003). *Entrepreneurship Education and Training*, Aldershot, Ashgate Publishing Ltd.

Kourilsky, M. and Walstad, W.B. (1998). 'Executive Forum: Entrepreneurship and Female Youth: Knowledge, Attitudes, Gender Differences, and Educational Practices'. *Journal of Business Venturing*, 13, 77–88.

McMurray, A. (2001). 'Mapping of Support Provision for Women in Enterprise in N. Ireland and A Strategic Framework for the Future', Belfast, Anne McMurray Consulting Ltd.

Minniti, M., Arenius, P. and Langowitz, N. (2005). 'GEM 2004 Report on Women and Entrepreneurship', London, Babson College and London Business School.

NDP Gender Equality Unit (2003). *Women and Men in Ireland as Entrepreneurs and as Business Managers*, Department of Justice, Equality and Law Reform, Ireland.

Nilsson P. (1997). 'Business Counseling Directed Towards Female Entrepreneurs – Some Legitimacy Dilemmas'. *Entrepreneurship and Regional Development*, 9, 3, 239–257.

O'Reilly, M. and Hart, M. (2002). *The Household Entrepreneurship Survey: Northern Ireland*, Belfast, InvestNI.

O'Reilly, M. and Hart, M. (2003). *Global Entrepreneurship Monitor, Northern Ireland*, Belfast and London, InvestNI and London Business School.

O'Reilly, M. and Hart, M. (2004). *Global Entrepreneurship Monitor, Northern Ireland*, Belfast and London, InvestNI and London Business School.

Rosa, P. and Carter, S. (1998). 'The Financing of Male and Female-Owned Businesses'. *Entrepreneurship and Regional Development*, 10, 225–241.

Siegal, S. (1956). *Nonparametric Statistics for the Behavioral Sciences*, New York, McGraw-Hill.

Stanworth, M.J.K. and Curran, J. (1973). *Management Motivation in the Smaller Business*, Aldershot, Gower.

Ulster Society of Chartered Accountants (2001). *Financing for Growth*, Northern Ireland, Industrial Development Board and Local Enterprise Development Unit.

United States Small Business Administration (1998). *The State of the Small Business*, Washington, DC, United States Small Business Administration.

Verheul, I., Risseeuw, P. and Bartelse, G. (2002). 'Gender Differences in Strategy and Human Resource Management'. *International Small Business Journal*, 20, 4, 443–476.

Vogt, W.P. (1993). *Dictionary of Statistics and Methodology: A Non-Technical Guide for the Social Sciences*, Newbury Park, CA, Sage.

5 Media expressions of entrepreneurs

Presentations and discourses of male and female entrepreneurs in Norway

Elisabet Ljunggren and Gry Agnete Alsos

Introduction

In the twenty-first century, entrepreneurship is still a male-dominated activity. In spite of growing rates of participation in new venture creation among women, particularly in North America, women are even now substantially under-represented among entrepreneurs in Western countries (Reynolds *et al.*, 2003). In the Nordic countries, the share of women entrepreneurs is especially low. In Norway, for example, about one-quarter of new business founders are women, a share that has been remarkably stable over the last ten years (Ljunggren, 1998; Kolvereid and Alsos, 2005). As the Scandinavian countries are frequently portrayed as leaders regarding equality between the genders, the low number of women entrepreneurs makes one particularly curious. When formal gender discrimination is essentially removed, gender equality has become politically correct, and there is an apparent push towards creating a gender-equal society amongst politicians and authorities, as well as the "man in the street". However, this does not seem to be the case with regard to women's entrepreneurship.

During the last twenty years, a number of studies have focused on the gender issues of entrepreneurship resulting in studies on women entrepreneurs, as well as some comparative studies on entrepreneurship and gender. In 1992, Brush reviewed articles in this field from the 1980s and concluded that there seemed to be more similarities than differences between the genders when it comes to geographic factors, problems and business characteristics, but that men and women differ in experiences, goals and motivations. Ten years later, Ahl reviewed articles on entrepreneurship and gender from a feminist perspective. She concluded that most research in this area looks for differences between male and female entrepreneurs, but that "contrary to expectations, few such differences were found. Within-group variation was typically larger than between-groups variation" (Ahl, 2002:114).

More recently, some criticism has been raised concerning research on entrepreneurship and gender. Carter and Weeks (2002), for example, argued that, while there is no real shortage of research in this area, it is still underdeveloped. They claimed that there is a lack of cumulative knowledge, conceptualization and explanatory theories. Marlow (2002) argued that studies on entrepreneurship and gender have largely ignored women's subordination within the broader society both as a conceptual notion and as an empirical explanation. Hence, in this respect, the earlier studies are only partial. Adopting a social-constructionist and feminist perspective, Ahl (2002) showed how even research texts on gender and entrepreneurship are themselves gendered. The manner in which these texts raise questions, and argue and explain their findings, serves to recreate women's subordinate role in society.

Consistent with this, Holmquist (2002) suggested two approaches or perspectives concerning the theoretical approach to gender and entrepreneurship. First, that some researchers maintain that gender theory and feminist perspectives are necessary in order to understand the phenomenon. Second, that others argue that differences and similarities between women and men should be considered within conventional theories relating to the entrepreneurship research field. Holmquist concluded that contributions from both perspectives are needed. Studies focusing on differences between women and men concerning entrepreneurship contribute to our understanding of an interesting imbalance in society, which demands attention and requires action. However, there is also a need for studies which provide an insight into the "mechanisms" behind this imbalance. How can the gender aspects of entrepreneurship be studied without implicitly holding men as the norm, as often found in the comparative studies (Haavind, 2000)? What alternative perspectives can be applied in order to obtain an understanding of the imbalance?

In this chapter we use an understanding of entrepreneurship and gender as social constructions to explore how images of men and women as entrepreneurs are created in Norwegian society. The empirical data comprises newspaper articles on entrepreneurs in the leading Norwegian commerce and trade newspaper *Dagens Næringsliv*. These articles not only create (male and female) entrepreneurship through their description of entrepreneurs and their actions; they also reflect the social construction of (male and female) entrepreneurship in the wider society. Consequently, they constitute an interesting and suitable basis for the study of such constructions. Parallel to the societal perceptions or discourses of entrepreneurs there also exist discourses of gender and gender differences. Hence, these discourses represent understandings of women and men which can be claimed to be social constructions (see for example, Alvesson and Billing, 1999; Haavind, 2000).

The chapter investigates the discourses created and expressed by the *Dagens Næringsliv* newspaper about entrepreneurs, and in particular, the extent to which there are differences in the descriptions of female and male entrepreneurs. Newspaper presentation of phenomena such as entrepreneurship can be comprehended as an expression of general attitudes and understandings in society about a phenomenon – one can interpret current discourses from the written texts in the media. As such, studying a newspaper representation of entrepreneurs makes it possible to interpret societal attitudes towards entrepreneurs by analysing the newspaper's expression of them.

The study presented in this chapter consists of two parts: part one commences with a quantitative account of the exposure of entrepreneurs in the articles in the newspaper, providing us with an overview of the frequency with which entre-preneurs appear in articles featured in the paper. In part two we analyse how the newspaper describes male and female entrepreneurs, and what may be under-stood and interpreted concerning entrepreneurship and gender from the news-paper texts. Among the questions explored are; what subjects are discussed in the articles on female and male entrepreneurs, how female and male entre-preneurs are presented, and whether certain characteristics are emphasized.

The chapter proceeds as follows: first, as social constructions of entrepreneur-ship and gender are clearly embedded in the processes, discourses and other aspects of the society of which they are a part, the Norwegian context is exam-ined. Second, a brief review of the literature within the area of gender and entre-preneurship is presented. This review serves two purposes. First, as research is affected by, as well as affects, the discourses and social constructions of phe-nomena, the literature review reflects what input entrepreneurship research has made to the social constructions of entrepreneurship and gender, and vice versa. Second, this research is the basis upon which we, as entrepreneurship researchers, depart and, as such, impacts our perspective of entrepreneurship as it is presented in newspaper texts. In addition, the method applied for this study is briefly described prior to the analysis of the newspaper texts. Finally, conclu-sions and suggestions for further research are given.

The Norwegian context

Norway is a country perceived by many as one where equality between the genders is highly developed. A consideration of the Norwegian welfare state and initiatives for families reveals, for example, generous maternity leave, i.e. one person in the family is entitled to one year's leave with 80 per cent of their salary paid,[1] and four weeks of leave are mandatory for the male partner. If the male partner is unable to take advantage of this, the family loses these weeks. Norway also has generous health insurance, even for shorter sick leave, with full-payment entitlements from day one. In addition, parents can stay home for twenty days annually when a child is ill without income reduction. The demand for kindergarten places is almost fully satisfied, and families with children up to three years not availing of such places are entitled to a cash benefit. In addition, within politics, gender (women) quotas are common and relatively accepted as a means to get more women into the field; such quotas often requiring 40 per cent female participation in the government sector.

In spite of this, Norway has very gender-segregated educational and labour markets, and is ranked as having the fifth most gender-segregated labour force among the OECD countries (OECD, 2000). Women constitute 94 per cent of preschool teachers, 90 per cent of nurses and 70 per cent of teachers; while men constitute 82 per cent of engineers and 78 per cent of chartered engineers (Statistics Norway, 2001). Even though 63 per cent of individuals in higher edu-cation are women (www.likestilling.no), women are largely educated for jobs in the public sector, while men are educated for work in the private sector.

Norwegian women's participation in the labour force is high (84 per cent) compared to other countries (34 per cent), compared with 75 per cent in EU/EFTA countries, but this participation is marked by a high degree of part-time involvement (32 per cent in EU/EFTA countries) (www.ssb.no/vis/sam-funnsspeilet).

The gender skewness is also very visible when economic activity is scrutinized. For example, the share of Norwegian women in management positions and in boardrooms is almost insignificant, and has actually decreased over the last five years. With regard to management positions, 6 per cent of senior executives in the private sector are women, as opposed to 16 per cent in the USA and 9 per cent in the UK (Catalyst, 2002; Fortune 500). A recent study (AFF, 2002) showed that the proportion of women managers had declined from 23.8 per cent in 1999, to 21.4 per cent in 2002. Similarly, women's participation in boardrooms is seemingly limited to 5.9 per cent of a total of 1,164 board positions (*Økonomisk Rapport*, 1999). When the employees' representatives are subtracted, women hold 3.4 per cent of the board positions. The debate on women's participation in the private sector has been particularly intense in recent years, with a 40 per cent women's quota on board membership in private companies now being suggested.[2]

It is argued that one reason for the generous Norwegian welfare state is the national income derived from the oil and gas industry.[3] However, Norway has now started to prepare for the post-oil era, and entrepreneurship and innovation are fast becoming key concepts. As already highlighted, few women become entrepreneurs. It is, therefore, agreed that there is high potential among women for entrepreneurship, and this societal resource has yet to be utilized.

Interestingly, factors such as role models, cultural variables and attitudes towards entrepreneurship have been shown to affect the number of business start-ups in general. The media plays an important role in the creation of attitudes, as well as making potential role models visible. Studies of nascent women entrepreneurs and entrepreneurial intentions among women indicate that the gender dimension of such factors may be an important explanation for the low propensity to establish businesses among women (Alsos and Ljunggren, 1998; Alsos *et al.*, 2000; Ljunggren, 2002). The Scandinavians have the highest level of purchase and readership of newspapers in the world and, in this regard, Norway ranks second with 600 issues per 1,000 inhabitants, compared to France which has 160 issues per 1,000 inhabitants (ranked twenty-third) (*Dagbladet*, 18 October 2004).

Entrepreneurship and gender in the literature

Virtually all research conducted on entrepreneurs and business start-ups until the early or mid-1980s was gender "blind", implicating either that women were not thought to start new businesses, or that those who did acted no differently from men (Marlow and Strange, 1994). During the last two decades researchers have platformed the gender issues of entrepreneurship, resulting in a number of studies on women entrepreneurs and others that compare the genders. These vary largely, both regarding the variables measured and the methods used, resulting in few conclusive results being generated (Brush, 1992; Fisher *et al.*, 1993). Using Gartner's (1985) new venture creation framework to organize the studies, we summarize some of the findings to date. This framework, suggested by Brush (1992), distinguishes four categories of entrepreneurship studies: studies focusing on individual characteristics, studies focusing on the entrepreneur's environment, studies focusing on the organizations created and those focusing on the entrepreneurial process.

The individual

The largest number of studies of gender differences has concentrated on the individual entrepreneur, reflecting variables such as demographic background, psychological characteristics, motivation, and educational and occupational experiences. This is consistent with most research into entrepreneurship (Gartner, 1988; Aldrich, 1999). According to Brush's (1992) review of the literature, this research has shown that there are more similarities than differences between men and women entrepreneurs across individual characteristics such as demography, business skills and some psychological traits. Some differences have been found in educational and occupational background, motivation for business start-ups, business goals and approaches to business creation (Brush, 1992; Fisher *et al.*, 1993). Studies have also identified different age distributions between the genders and different marital status (Watkins and Watkins, 1984; Stevenson, 1986). Contrary to this, Brush (1992) noted several studies which found demographic characteristics, such as marital status, age, birth order and having a self-employed father, were similar for both genders.

The gender-segregated labour market, which is especially obvious in Scandinavia, leads to differences in work experience between the genders. Several studies found, not surprisingly, that these differences also applied to entrepreneurs (Brush, 1992). Further, compared to female entrepreneurs, male entrepreneurs seem to have more experience in managing employees and working in similar firms (Fisher *et al.*, 1993), and tend to be more likely to have previous entrepreneurial experience (Kalleberg and Leicht, 1991; Rosa and Hamilton, 1994; Alsos and Kolvereid, 1998). In their study, Birley *et al.* (1987) found no significant differences in the education *level* between men and women who had enrolled in small business training courses. However, differences were found with regard to the *kind* of education they had received (Brush, 1992). For example, while Fisher *et al.* (1993) found that male entrepreneurs had a more production-related business education than their female counterparts, they did not find statistically significant differences between the genders with regard to marketing, finance, personnel, accounting, strategy or general education. In their study of Norwegian entrepreneurs, Ljunggren and Kolvereid (1996) found that women perceived themselves as possessing more entrepreneurial abilities than men.

Interestingly, Hisrich (1986) claimed that there are strong similarities between male and female entrepreneurs when it comes to measuring personality. For example, entrepreneurs tend to be energetic, goal-oriented and independent, regardless of gender. Similarly, Birley (1989:33) concluded that it is "clear from the literature that the motivation of female entrepreneurs is similar in most respects to those of their male counterparts". In a study of male and female entrepreneurs versus managers, Fagenson (1993) found that gender had very little impact on personal value systems. In a similar vein, Bellu (1993) also found that female entrepreneurs did not differ from male entrepreneurs in values and attributional style (typically related to success or failure). However, it is notable that many of the instruments used to measure personality and entrepreneurial traits are derived from research on samples of male entrepreneurs, and may, therefore, be inappropriate for measuring gender differences (Brush, 1992).

In terms of motivational attributes, Shane *et al.* (1991) found no gender differences regarding independence as a form of start-up motivation. Male and female entrepreneurs both reported controlling their own time, flexibility in personal and family life, and freedom to adapt one's own approach to their work as the most important reasons for a business start-up. However, they found that achieving a higher position in society, together with more status and prestige for the family, were more important for men than for women. On the other hand, women, more so than men, valued acquiring recognition and achieving something higher. Ljunggren and Kolvereid (1996) found that female entrepreneurs placed stronger emphasis on independence as an expected outcome of starting a business than male entrepreneurs. However, no statistically significant gender differences were reported in expectations related to risk, profitability or the personal challenge the new business might offer. Likewise, Gatewood *et al.* (1995) found that men and women had different reasons for going into business, and that these appeared to be significant indicators of their future ability to successfully start a business.

Environment

A few studies have concentrated on the impact of environmental factors on male and female entrepreneurs and their enterprises. In particular, there has been a focus on the issue of discrimination in access to capital and credit. Buttner and Rosen (1992), for example, found no evidence of gender discrimination in bank loan considerations, and similarly, Fabowale *et al.* (1995) found that, when structural factors were taken into account, no evidence of gender discrimination by banks' loan officers was evident. However, women still perceived that they were discriminated against. Contrary to this, Fay and Williams (1993) found indications of gender discrimination. Identical loan applications were sent to bank officers in New Zealand, with only education and gender varying. Interestingly, they found that education was judged to be significantly more important for female than for male applicants. Further, women were significantly more frequently judged to have insufficient equity/security, and that loans were granted more frequently to male than to female applicants. Riding and Swift (1990) concluded that, while the terms of loans granted to male and female business owners did not vary significantly, there were gender differences in the banking relationship. This was further supported by a recent Norwegian study which indicated that ownership of capital and property is unevenly distributed among men and women (Jensen, 2005a). Consequently, women do not have the possibility to obtain a mortgage and thereby acquire equity for the business. This situation is, more than likely, not unique to Norway, as indicated by an EU report (Jensen, 2005b).

Organization

International studies have indicated that businesses started by women are more often in the service sectors (Johnson and Storey, 1993; Miskin and Rose, 1990), are smaller in terms of revenue and employment (Fisher *et al.*, 1993; Rosa *et al.*, 1994), are more likely to employ women (Johnson and Storey, 1993), tend to grow less (Cliff and Cash, 2006; Cliff, 1998; Fisher *et al.*, 1993; Kalleberg and Leicht, 1991) and are less profitable (Fisher *et al.*, 1993; Rosa *et al.*, 1994) than businesses started by men. Some of these differences can be explained by the sector within which most women-owned businesses are found, namely the service sector where businesses are smaller and less profitable.

Process

Some studies have explored gender differences in the process of creating a business, reflecting how male and female entrepreneurs behave in opportunity identification, resource acquisition, organization building, managing the business and responding to the environment (Brush, 1992). One area of research which would appear to be particularly important is networking as a means of obtaining information or resources. In this regard, Aldrich *et al.* (1989) did not find any gender differences in the process of building network contacts. In a later study, Aldrich *et al.* (1996) concluded that women entrepreneurs are as active as men in networking in order to obtain assistance, and as successful as men in obtaining high-quality assistance. With regard to support systems, some studies indicate that women entrepreneurs tend to have strong supporters, particularly a spouse or a "significant other" (Brush, 1992). For example, Ljunggren and Kolvereid (1996) found that women perceived a higher degree of social support during the business gestation process than men. In contrast, Alsos and Ljunggren (1998), who studied the business start-up process among nascent entrepreneurs, found few differences between men and women with regard to the various activities undertaken to start a business. Moreover, the propensity to succeed in starting a new business as a result of this process was similar for women and men.

Gender and entrepreneurship as social constructions

In spite of the relatively broad range of studies on gender and entrepreneurship, it seems that the understanding of *gender* is defective or simple. Using Harding's (1987) three categories on feminist research:

1   Empirical feminism implies "that sexism and androcentrism are social biases correctable by stricter adherence to the existing methodological norms of scientific inquiry" (p. 24). This has led to a focus on the methodologies one applies within entrepreneurship and gender research to avoid criticism from other researchers that feminist research is political and, as such, value-loaded, hence "non-scientific".
2   Standpoint feminism implies "that men's dominating position in social life results in partial and perverse understandings, whereas women's subjugated position provides the possibility of more complete and less perverse understandings" (p. 26).
3   Postmodern feminism challenges the two prior perspectives and claims that "feminists share a profound scepticism regarding universal (or universalising) claims about the existence nature and powers of reasons, progress, science, language and the subject/self" (pp. 27–28).

There seems to be an understanding of gender in the above-mentioned studies, consistent with either empirical feminism, standpoint feminism or a mixture of both, although this is not usually stated explicitly.

A further development and adaptation of Harding's categories of entrepreneurship research was made by Berg (2002), who introduced: (1) gender as a variable, (2) gender as relations and (3) gender as a process. This implies that, by understanding gender as a variable, one analyses differences between men and women entrepreneurs. The intention is to describe and make gender differences visible. Behind this is a notion of gender as static and biologically determined. Understanding gender as a relation implies seeing gender as a result of social actions and a necessity to see men and women in relation to each other. The intention is to upgrade women's values and women's ways of conducting entrepreneurship instead of comparing it with men's entrepreneurship as the norm. A perspective on gender as a process implies a further development of the notion of gender as socially constructed in social relations – hence, changeable in time and space. Here, it is possible to question the categories "male and female entrepreneurs" and also to deconstruct them. This deconstruction of categories may give new insight into the social constructions of gender and entrepreneurship.

According to this overview, gender is most frequently understood as a variable in entrepreneurship studies. Some gender differences are illustrated, but there are still more similarities than differences between the genders. Thus, we believe that the concept of examining gender differences by "counting bodies" (Alvesson, 1997) is incomplete, and suggest the need for a perspective which, in a constructivist way, reveals the meaning of gender in entrepreneurship. This calls for a perspective that does not regard gender solely as a variable, but which also includes gender as a relation and as a process. In this study, our understanding of gender is consistent with a mixture of gender as a relation and a process. This enables a broader discussion of the gendered discourses of entrepreneurship in society.

Methodology and analysis

In this study, we are applying Alvesson and Sköldberg's (1994:281) understanding of a discourse as "a social text". We are also inspired by a Faircloughian critical discourse analysis limiting the discursive concept to text, speech and other semi-logic systems (Jørgensen and Phillips, 1999). In this respect, we claim that our understanding of discourse is somewhat more towards an analysis of discourse practices, where people's written expressions are focused, and where we as researchers have to be reflexive when it comes to our role. This is especially important, as we perceive ourselves as entrepreneurship researchers and, hence, as a part of the discursive field. Written texts are perceived as expressions of discourses on entrepreneurship, business life and gender in the field we are approaching, here defined as the community of business (wo)men and individuals in empowered positions reading this kind of newspaper. We acknowledge the importance of context. We have, therefore, accounted for the Norwegian context in which the newspaper articles analysed are embedded. Further, it is necessary to describe the newspaper from which these articles are taken.

The newspaper Dagens Næringsliv[4]

The analysed texts are all articles in the leading industry and commerce newspaper in Norway – *Dagens Næringsliv*. This has a circulation of about 70,515 and is published six days a week. Reader inquiries suggest the number of daily readers to be about 292,000. The paper covers all parts of the country, though most readers are found in urban areas. The target readers of the newspaper define the discursive field under investigation, and the large bulk of readers represent the business community and other people in decision-making positions in Norwegian society. The newspaper's profile, as expressed in advertisements (e.g. "Modern business hotels serve you *Dagens Næringsliv* for breakfast" and "Norway's leading business newspaper with morning deliveries in the whole country"), supports its image as the leading business and commerce newspaper, as does its slogan: "A free newspaper", its tradition as an offspring of *Norges Handels-og Sjøfartstidende* (the former conservative newspaper on shipping and trade), its many pages with reports from stock exchanges in Norway and other countries, and the colour of the paper (which is pink, similar to the *Financial Times* in the UK, *Dagens Industri* in Sweden and *Børsen* in Denmark). Moreover, those taking part in chronicles and debates are first and foremost politicians, business representatives and researchers.

The empirical material reviewed for this study included 117 issues of the newspaper, equivalent to five months of publishing. During this period, some entrepreneurs were much exposed due to a conflict of ownership in the large firms Orkla and Kværner which dominated the news for a while. This resulted in a slightly heavier exposure of a number of entrepreneurs involved in these conflicts than one might expect in other periods. Still, these are typically the sort of topics that receive attention in *Dagens Næringsliv*. All in all, the 117 issues included in this analysis can be regarded as fairly representative of the newspaper.

Definition of entrepreneur

When identifying articles on entrepreneurs to use as our empirical data, we wanted to include all articles which dealt with entrepreneurs, whether or not the journalist found it necessary to mention that this person is an entrepreneur. As the concept is little used in Norwegian everyday speech, we decided it was not sufficient to include the Norwegian words for entrepreneur (*entreprenør, gründer, etablerer*). We, therefore, decided to identify the articles more qualitatively, reading through the newspapers. For this purpose, we first had to find a suitable definition of the concept "entrepreneur".

When studying entrepreneurs and entrepreneurship the question of "what is an entrepreneur?" is frequently discussed (Gartner, 1988; Carland *et al.*, 1988). Acknowledging this discussion, a definition is still required when studying entrepreneurs empirically. In this regard, the options are vast. According to Bruyat and Julien (2000), for example, two perceptions of entrepreneurship have been predominant within entrepreneurship research: (1) either to perceive the entrepreneur as an individual who creates and develops new businesses or (2) to perceive the entrepreneur as an innovative individual who, by his/her actions, impacts the economy. Landström (2000) gives an historical retrospective of the concept "entrepreneur". The common denominators he identified were the terms risktaker, innovator, organizer and capitalist. Bygrave and Hofer (1991:14) define an entrepreneur as "someone who perceives an opportunity and creates an organisation to pursue it". The concept of an entrepreneur is also related to that of "self-employed". Evans and Leighton (1989:520) defined self-employed to "include all sole proprietors, partners and sole owners of incorporated businesses". However, to own and manage a business does not necessarily mean that one must have created it oneself. A business can be bought, inherited or received as a gift. Thus, a business owner–manager needs to be either an entrepreneur or self-employed. Goeffe and Scase (1985:33) presented a categorization based upon four roles of business owners which, to some extent, overlaps some of the above.

1 Self-employed: an individual who works for him/herself and employs no labour.
2 Small employer: an individual who works in production together with his/her employees but also undertakes managerial tasks.

3   Owner–controllers: individuals who "are solely and singularly responsible for the administration and management of their enterprises".
4   Owner–director: an individual who owns and controls companies with hierarchies of decision making and who delegates power within the hierarchy.

For the purposes of this study we adopted a broad definition of "entrepreneur", including most of the common understandings of the concept. Included in our definition are self-employed, business owner–managers and business founders. We include both persons who create and develop new business activities in the context of new organizations, as well as those who do this within existing organizations.

Stages in data analysis

The data analysis was carried out in four stages. First, all articles on entrepreneurs in the 117 issues of *Dagens Næringsliv* were identified based on the broad definition adopted above. The identification was undertaken by the two researchers who, separately and independently, went through all 117 newspaper issues and registered all articles considered to be about entrepreneurs. Second, the researchers' lists of articles were compared. Articles registered on only one of the lists were discussed according to the utilized definition of an entrepreneur, and a decision was made regarding inclusion in the study. A broad definition of entrepreneur resulted in a heterogeneous group of entrepreneurs represented in the articles.

Stage three was to categorize the articles. A taxonomy of entrepreneurial roles was developed from the empirical material based on the kind of entrepreneurial activities to which individuals were linked in the articles. Three broad entrepreneurial roles were identified: founder, business owner–director and investor. An individual who possesses the *founder* role is described in the media as having established a new business recently, or as going to start a new business. The *business owner–director* role implies having started, inherited or bought a business and still being actively involved in both the ownership and management of the business(es). Individuals with an *investor* role were described as investing their own capital in existing and new businesses established by others, and also being actively involved in the management of these businesses, at least as a board member. Finally, the articles were then sorted into these categories. Again, each of the researchers made the categorization separately and then compared the results. There was a high extent of agreement between the authors. In the few cases with different categorization, an agreement was reached after discussion. Some entrepreneurs were referred to in several different articles, and sometimes they represented different entrepreneurial roles in different articles. The articles were sorted according to the entrepreneurial role specified in the article in question, and different articles on the same entrepreneur may, therefore, be sorted into different categories.

Inspired by Fairclough (1992) and his three-dimensional model for critical discourse analysis,[5] we next analysed the texts (dimension one) with regard to the use of specific words in the articles describing the entrepreneurs and their actions. Further, we investigated whether men and women were described using different words. Moreover, the pictures (if present) were analysed. They told us for instance whether the entrepreneurs were presented as active or passive. Based on the text and picture analysis, we accounted for the content of the entrepreneur articles, as well as how (male and female) entrepreneurs are presented. In this sense, the discursive practices were uncovered. For illustrative purposes, we then identified six articles, representing the typical article within each category (female owner–manager, male owner–manager, women owner–director, etc.). These six articles are given a broader description in the chapter.

Frequency of appearance

In total, there were references to 276 entrepreneurs in the articles, of which 251 were men and twenty-five were women. They were distributed among the three entrepreneurial roles as reported in Table 5.1. As shown in Table 5.1, 14.6 per cent of the references to founders, 13.6 per cent of the references to business owner–directors and 1.8 per cent of the references to investors relate to women. This is low compared to the proportion of female entrepreneurs in Norway which is about 25 per cent (Ljunggren, 2002; Alsos and Kolvereid, 2004). This gives an indication of the under-reporting of women entrepreneurs in this newspaper. It also gives an indication that the topic of entrepreneurs generally receives a low level of coverage in the newspaper.

Discourses of male and female entrepreneurs

Content

The subjects mentioned in the articles on the entrepreneurs are dependent on the role presented. In spite of this, there are clear gender differences in the content. References to male entrepreneurs, for example, are made more frequently in terms of financial results, in figures and in share prices. Articles on male entrepreneurs also present negative financial results and show more critical journalism revealing possible violations of business ethics and law. Further, the image of entrepreneurs as profit-seekers and financial risk-takers are enhanced by the content of the articles on male entrepreneurs. Conversely, references to female

Table 5.1 Frequencies of entrepreneurs, by gender and entrepreneurial roles

	Founders		*Business owner–directors*		*Investors*	
Men	35	85.4%	108	86.4%	108	98.2%
Women	6	14.6%	17	13.6%	2	1.8%
Total	41	100%	125	100%	110	100%

entrepreneurs are less specific on business issues, and more frequently present the business and/or the entrepreneur in general terms. Financial results are referred to less frequently, and more often these references concern strategic actions and business development. The understanding of women entrepreneurs is affected by the more general understanding of women as possessing more compassionate values, including diversified goals, such as not only seeking profit but also self-realization.

Presentation

There appears to be differences concerning the presentation of the entrepreneurs. Although the presentations vary according to the central issue in the article, the nature of the business ideas, as well as the size of the business, there also seems to be gender differences. These differences are particularly evident when it comes to the individual characteristics and the additional information on the entrepreneur. Subjects which do not directly relate to the issue discussed but are presented to make the article more "spicy" – often referred to as "the human touch" – occur more frequently when female entrepreneurs are presented. Female entrepreneurs are described and characterized in a slightly different manner from male entrepreneurs. This is evident throughout most of the articles in the empirical material, although there are also large variations in the description of female entrepreneurs as well as those of men. For instance, in several cases when referring to female entrepreneurs the journalist also presents her spouse as well as the number of children. This kind of information is very seldom added to articles presenting male entrepreneurs. Also, presentations of female entrepreneurs more frequently include how she personally views her own business and the returns she acquires (e.g. self-realization), while presentations of male entrepreneurs include this type of information more seldom. They are more often presented by facts, such as financial figures, the size of the business, financial goals, etc.

To illustrate our findings we present in more detail six articles typical of the different categories. These six articles provide us with some examples of the differences according to the gender of the entrepreneur referred to. However, they also show that there are huge differences in the presentations within gender, not least depending on the financial power possessed by the entrepreneur.

Case one – female founder (AnnBeth Berg)

This article was found on the last page of the newspaper where "soft" or "happy" news is often presented. The female founder is referred to in an article describing how her company is partly sold to a large stakeholder in the market (Tine), allowing further development and growth of the firm. The firm's history is described, telling us the background of the business idea which concerns baby food based on Norwegian raw materials without additives. The founder was "frightened of the animal health in Europe", and we learn that the prototype was developed in her kitchen. She started her business by emptying a Nestlé glass of baby food, attaching her own label, filling up the glass with her baby food, and knocking on the doors of large commodity trade companies in a "hunt for customers". The founder is also described as being a mother of young children. In a text box, her age, address, income, assets and ownership are accounted for. The title of the article is "Small people to Tine", and "Small people" (*Småfolk*) is the name of the brand. The photo illustration shows us three happy and smiling people, and the man in the middle – the representative for the new owner – embracing the two women.

Case two – female business owner–director (Anna S. Bye)

This article was also found on the last page. The female business owner–director is presented in an article describing the delivery of a cruise ship from the shipyard she controls. The article also has the character of a portrait interview. We are told that she inherited the shipyard from her father when he died some years ago, and that she used to work as a principal at the local elementary school. She is referred to as Anna several times, and among other things, the article mentions that she "likes to entertain her business partners by reading poems and telling histories during their meetings". The shipyard has made her one of the most wealthy women in Mid-Norway. We get to know her assets and wages, but it is clearly stressed in the article that: "As she keeps the whole village and more in employment, and doesn't show off her wealth, there is little envy within the village." The title is "Milliards in dock". The picture shows Anna Synnøve Bye *en face*, looking into the camera.

Case three – female investor (Celina Middelfart)

Celina Middelfart is known in Norway from several media appearances, including TV and weekly gossip magazines. She inherited the firm (together with her sister and her step-mother) after her father died. The young female investor is referred to in an article describing an acquisition made by the family firm which she controls, making her the chairman of board in another company. In the article she is neutrally described, and the focus is on her as a business investor and strategic decision maker in the company. This is an example of a female entrepreneur with relatively large financial power. In other articles in the same newspaper she was often referred to as Kjell Inge Røkkes' girlfriend, although, in comparable articles, he was never presented as her boyfriend.[6] Also, her access to money, as an inheritor, was mentioned in some articles. The picture of her is quite neutral and composed the same way as most of the pictures of men; she is gesturing, wearing a white shirt and a masculine watch. The title of the article is "Taking over the new Sunshine-board".

Case four – male founder (Svein Mathiasen)

Two male founders are referred to in an article describing an annual shareholders' meeting which resulted in the entrepreneurs losing their influence over the company. The business idea of the company is described (the development of technology to use fingerprints as passwords in mobile phones and PCs), and the founders are referred to, but no information about the founders other than commercial details is presented. The point of view of one of the founders was portrayed using statements such as "the founder strongly goes for", "he heavily attacked" and "he maintains that". The title of the article is "Overrun Entrepreneur" and the photo illustrating the article shows the CEO and the largest shareholder apparently discussing the matter. The founding entrepreneurs themselves are not depicted.

Case five – male business owner–director (Jens Petter Ekornes)

In a portrait interview we get to know a lot about the male business owner–director for a large furniture manufacturer. He inherited the business from his uncle, and it is located in a part of Norway (Sunnmøre) which is known to be entrepreneurial. We are told of his opinions about other industry managers and their actions. We learn about how he has had a business talent since he was ten years old, how he never has been afraid of being distinctive from others and how he never enjoyed losing. He is also presented as a dropout from school who was not able to adapt to the rigid system, and with a need to assert himself. We also learn how he has been the driving force behind the company's success, partly through phrases such as "work harder", "talent of sales" and "wins every time". Concerning his personal life, only his marital status and number of children are very briefly mentioned, although the relationship with his uncle is further explained:

> Ekornes tampers with his glasses. "Except for my parents, there is no one in the world with whom I have had a closer relationship. It will follow me the rest of my life. Almost every day I measure my decisions to what I think he would have done".

This article is a double-page spread in the Saturday edition, and the illustration is a caricature, which is typical of the Saturday portraits. The title of the article is "The Chair Game".

Case six – male investor (Christen Sveaas)

Christen Sveaas is quite well known in Norway, and has an image of a food and wine connoisseur with an interest for fine arts. In other articles he is presented as a guy who was motivated to become rich from adolescence in order to get back some of the fortune his grandfather had made but which was unfortunately lost. In this regard, he has succeeded. In this article his personal income for the past year is presented, referring to him as the Norwegian in Oslo with the highest income in 1999. We learn that his income has increased to ten times the level of 1998, and that his personal wealth has also been heavily increased. He is described as "bringing home victories from all battles". However, the article mostly presents the "cold" financial facts. The title of the article is "Cycling All the Way to the Top", and the photo shows a smiling Sveaas cycling in the rain. Apart from his income and wealth, the only thing we get to know about him as a person is that he rides a bicycle, a fact that is used and stressed in other articles about him. He was often mentioned in the many articles about Kværner and Orkla, and here, emotive terms such as "hits back" are used to describe his actions.

Discussion

A general observation from our study is that entrepreneurs, particularly small and new entrepreneurs, are seldom covered in the newspaper. A small group of male entrepreneurs (four to five men) have most of the media exposure, representing "big business". Female entrepreneurs are even more seldom referred to. What does this tell us about the discourses that are produced and presented in *Dagens Næringsliv*? We claim that these discourses reflect Norwegian society's ideas regarding entrepreneurs and gender.

We appreciate that we are dealing with several discourses and discursive fields which partly overlap. We suggest that there is not just one discourse on entrepreneurs in *Dagens Næringsliv*, but that the main discourse is supplemented with another, completely different discourse on female entrepreneurs. This discourse is strongly influenced by the general discourse on gender in society, as documented by Harding (1987) and Berg (2002). The main discourse describes entrepreneurs as men with distinct risk-taking behaviour, heavy involvement in the stock market, using power to achieve their ambitious goals, and representative of strong, high growth firms. In contrast, the female entrepreneurs presented in the newspaper are not described in accordance with this discourse. Rather, the separate discourse on female entrepreneurs represents different entrepreneurial characteristics, such as being motivated by lifestyle or other "soft" goals, being creative, having a caring attitude (e.g. for employees and/or customers) and as individuals who have a life outside that of an entrepreneur (i.e. family). In this way, *Dagens Næringsliv*, through its articles on entrepreneurs, presents female entrepreneurs as something different from (male) entrepreneurs, i.e. not "real" entrepreneurs.

We have argued that the newspaper articles in our study reflect more than the journalists' perceptions of male and female entrepreneurs. More importantly, these articles, through the voices of the journalists, reflect the discourses in the greater society of which both the journalists and their readers are members. Hence, the discourses on entrepreneurs found in the newspaper articles are also discourses of this society. Therefore, these findings inform us about how entrepreneurship and gender are socially constructed in Norwegian society.

First, these findings illustrate that the main discourse on entrepreneurs is highly masculine. This has earlier been referred to as the hegemonic masculinity of entrepreneurship (Ljunggren, 2002). In fact, our understanding of "entrepreneur" is so masculine that we find it hard to describe female entrepreneurs along the same dimensions as the male "norm". This also shows how strongly our understanding of women entrepreneurs is influenced by discourses on gender. The impact of the gender discourses is so strong that the "conflict" between the masculine construction of "entrepreneur" and the fact that women hold this position, results in a separate, more feminized discourse on the "female entrepreneur". This relates to Beauvoir's (1949/2000) description of women as "the other". The female entrepreneur is presented as "the other" – something different from "entrepreneur". When the main discourse of entrepreneur is presented as the "norm", the construction of "female entrepreneur" becomes the deviation. In this way the media presentations of female entrepreneurs are confirming the subordinated role of women in society.

Second, it is apparent that even the discourse on female entrepreneurs changes according to the particular context in which it is discussed. The more different the entrepreneur presented is from the traditional image of an entrepreneur, the more feminized the presentation becomes. Furthermore, when the woman presented is more equal to the image of risk-taking behaviour, use of power and large financial resources, the description is also less feminized than those of other female entrepreneurs. This is apparent in the example of the female investor Celina Middelfart. However, the impression of female entrepreneur being something different is still present.

Third, it is easy to show that the main discourse on the entrepreneur is truly reflective of the population of entrepreneurs, including male entrepreneurs. Most people starting up, owning or investing in businesses in Norway do not fit the description of risk-taking, powerful, high-flying entrepreneurs, as presented in *Dagens Næringsliv*. Obviously, the readers are interested in the news on powerful entrepreneurs. Further, it is the role of the press to monitor more closely the entrepreneurs representing "big business". It, therefore, makes sense that these kinds of entrepreneurs attract the most space in the newspaper. On the other hand, the large stock of entrepreneurs, small business owners and investors that represent the large mass of business life also represent power, albeit not as concentrated as the "norm entrepreneurs". Moreover, in sum, these entrepreneurs are even more important for value creation and economic growth. In addition to an understanding of critical discourse, the issue of power is also apparent in this discursive field. In this regard, we claim that the more money involved (hence, the more (financial) power an entrepreneur possesses), the more the media coverage afforded to the individual entrepreneur. Such coverage will mirror the language of power and, as we have shown earlier, this has implications on the gendered entrepreneur discourse, such that the more money (power) a woman possesses, the more equal to a man she is perceived to be (e.g. Celina Middelfart).

Fourth, *Dagens Næringsliv* is completely failing to present female entrepreneurial role models. Female entrepreneurs are featured so seldom that they are more or less invisible in the newspaper. This finding is in accordance with prior studies pointing at the invisibility of women as entrepreneurs (see, for example, Sundin and Holmquist, 1989). If we acknowledge that attitudes, norms and role models are important when explaining why some people start a career as an entrepreneur while others do not (Ajzen, 1991; Kolvereid, 1996; Ljunggren and Kolvereid, 1996), then our findings may help us to better understand the recruitment process of entrepreneurs. It might be argued that media representations contribute to women's alienation from entrepreneurship.

Conclusions

This study has investigated how men and women entrepreneurs are presented in one particular newspaper in Norway. We suggest that this particular empirical setting can tell us something about the more general discourses in the discursive field represented by Norwegian business life and other readers of *Dagens Næringsliv*. Nevertheless, we recognize that our study merely scratches the surface with regard to discourses on gender and entrepreneurship in society. Further studies, exploring different manifestations of discourses on entrepreneurship and gender in different countries and in different economic, social and political climates, are clearly needed. We believe our understanding would be fruitfully developed through discourse analyses of, for instance, policy documents, political speeches, regional and local newspapers, television and so forth, on both a national and international basis. Furthermore, studies are also needed on how media expressions of entrepreneurs influence and are influenced by such discourses.

One practical implication of our findings is the need to raise journalists' consciousness about their role as creators and mediators of images/understandings of entrepreneurs, especially with regard to the gender dimension. This may be gained by offering on-the-job training.

Notes

1 The mother is required to have six months' waged employment for the last ten months before birth.
2 This rule is applied to government-owned businesses.
3 Apart from a relatively high tax pressure (i.e. 40 per cent for personal wage income and 27 per cent for limited companies).
4 Translates as Business Today.
5 The dimensions are: text, discursive practice (production and consumption of text, highly interwoven with the text) and social practice.
6 Røkkes is famous in Norway for being a self-made man with an extravagant lifestyle.

References

AFF (Administrativt Forskningsfonds lederundersøkelse) (2002). "ARF Management Study", Bergen, Administrativt Forskningsfond.

Ahl, H.J. (2002). "The Making of the Female Entrepreneur. A Discourse Analysis of Research Texts on Women's Entrepreneurship". JIBS Dissertation series no. 15, Jönköping International Business School, Jönköping.

Ajzen, I. (1991). "The Theory of Planned Behaviour". *Organisational Behavior and Human Decision Processes*, 50, 179–211.

Aldrich, H.E. (1999). *Organisations Evolving*, London, Sage.

Aldrich, H.E., Elam, A.B. and Reece, P.R. (1996). "Strong Ties, Weak Ties, and Strangers: Do Women Business Owners Differ from Men in their Use of Networking to Obtain Assistance?" In Birley, S. and MacMillan, I.C. (eds), *Entrepreneurship in a Global Context*. London: Routledge, 1–25.

Aldrich, H.E., Reece, P.R. and Dubini, P. (1989). "Women on the Verge of a Breakthrough? Networking Among Entrepreneurs in the US and Italy". *Entrepreneurship and Regional Development*, 1, 4, 339–356.

Alsos, G.A. and Kolvereid, L. (1998). The Business Gestation Process of Novice, Serial and Parallel Business Founders". *Entrepreneurship Theory and Practice*, 22, 4, 101–114.

Alsos, G.A. and Kolvereid, L. (2004). "Entrepreneurship among Women in Norway". In Hauge, E.S. and Havnes, P.A. (eds), *Women Entrepreneurs. Theory, Research and Policy Implications*. Kristiansand: Fagbokforlaget.

Alsos, G.A. and Ljunggren, G. (1998). "Does the Business Start-Up Differ by Gender? A Longitudinal Study of Nascent Entrepreneurs". *Journal of Enterprising Culture*, 6, 4, 347–367.

Alsos, G.A., Ljunggren, E. and Rotefoss, B. (2000). "Who Makes it Through the Business Formation Process? A Longitudinal Study of Entrepreneurs". Paper presented at the Babson Conference on Entrepreneurship at Babson College USA, June 2000.

Alvesson, M. (1997). *Kroppsräkning, Konstruktion av kön och Offentliga Organisationer*, Stockholm, Statens offentliga utredningar.

Alvesson, M. and Billing, Y.D. (1999). *Kön och Organisation* (Understanding Gender and Organisation), Lund, Studentlitteratur.

Alvesson, M. and Sköldberg, K. (1994). *Tolkning och Reflektion Vitenskapsfilosofi och Kvalitativ Metod*, Lund, Studentlitteratur.

Beauvoir, S.D. (1949/2000). *Det Annet Kjonn* (The Second Sex), Oslo, Bokklubben dagens boker.

Bellu, R. (1993). "Task Role Motivation and Attributional Styles as Predictors of Entrepreneurial Performance: Female Sample Findings". *Entrepreneurship and Regional Development*, 5, 4, 331–344.

Berg, N.G. (2002). "Kjønn, Livsløp, Sted og Entreprenørskap en Teoretisk Diskusjon". In Berg, N.G. and Foss, L. (eds), *Entreprenørskap Kjønn,Llivsløp og Sted*. Oslo: Abstrakt forlag.

Birley, S. (1989). "Female Entrepreneurs: Are they Really any Different?" *Journal of Small Business Management*, 27, 1, 7–31.

Birley, S., Moss, C. and Sanders, P. (1987). "Do Women Entrepreneurs Require Different Training?" *American Journal of Small Business*, Summer, 27–35.

Brush, C.G. (1992). "Research on Women Business Owners: Past Trends, a New

Perspective and Future Directions". *Entrepreneurship Theory and Practice*, 16, 4, 5–29.

Bruyat, C. and Julien, P.-A. (2000). "Defining the Field of Research in Entrepreneurship". *Journal of Business Venturing*, 16, 165–180.

Buttner, H. and Rosen, B. (1992). "Rejection in the Loan Application Process: Male and Female Entrepreneurs: Perceptions and Subsequent Intentions". *Journal of Small Business Management*, 30, 1, 59–65.

Bygrave, W.D. and Hofer, C.H. (1991). "Theorizing About Entrepreneurship". *Entrepreneurship Theory and Practice*, 16, 2, 13–22.

Carland, J.W., Hoy, F. and Carland, J.A.C. (1988). " 'Who is an Entrepreneur?' Is a Question Worth Asking". *American Journal of Small Business*, Spring, 33–39.

Carter, S. and Weeks, J. (2002). "Gender and Business Ownership – International Perspectives on Theory and Practice". *Entrepreneurship and Innovation*, May, 81–82.

Catalyst, Inc. (2002). "Census of Women Corporate Top Officers and Top Earners". Available: www.catalystwomen.org/knowledge/titles/title.php?page=cen_WOTE02.

Cliff, J. (1998). "Does One Size Fit All? Exploring the Relationship Between Attitudes Towards Growth, Gender, and Business Size". *Journal of Business Venturing*, 13, 523–542.

Cliff, J. and Cash, M.P. (2006). "Women's Entrepreneurship in Canada: Progress, Puzzles and Priorities". In Green, P.G., Brush, C.G., Carter, N.M., Gatewood, E.J. and Hart, M.M. (eds), *Growth Orientated Women Entrepreneurs and their Business – A Global Research Perspective*. Northampton, MA: Edward Elgar.

Evans, D.S and Leigthon, L.S. (1989). "Some Empirical Aspects of Entrepreneurship". *American Economic Review*, 79, 3, 519–535.

Fabowale, L., Orser, B. and Riding, A. (1995). "Gender, Structural Factors, and Credit Terms Between Canadian Small Businesses and Financial Institutions". *Entrepreneurship Theory and Practice*, 19, 4, 41–65.

Fairclough, N. (1992). *Discourse and Social Change*, Cambridge, Polity Press.

Fagenson, E. (1993). "Personal Value Systems of Men and Women: Entrepreneurs Versus Managers". *Journal of Business Venturing*, 8, 5, 409–430.

Fay, M. and Williams, L. (1993). "Gender Bias and the Availability of Business Loans". *Journal of Business Venturing*, 8, 4, 363–376.

Fisher, E., Reuber, R. and Dyke, L. (1993). "A Theoretical Overview and Extension of Research on Sex, Gender and Entrepreneurship". *Journal of Business Venturing*, 8, 2, 151–168.

Fortune 500. List of the Fortune 500. Available: www.fortune.com/fortune/.

Gartner, W.B. (1985). "A Conceptual Framework for Describing the Phenomenon of New Venture Creation". *Academy of Management Review*, 10, 4, 696–706.

Gartner, W.B. (1988). "Who is an Entrepreneur? is the Wrong Question". *American Journal of Small business*, Spring, 11–31.

Gatewood, E.J., Shaver, K.G. and Gartner, W.B. (1995). "A Longitudinal Study of Cognitive Factors Influencing Start-Up Behaviours and Success at Venture Creation". *Journal of Business Venturing*, 10, 11–31.

Goeffe, R. and Scase, R. (1985). *Women in Charge: the Experience of Female Entrepreneurs*, London, Allen and Unwin.

Haavind, H. (2000). *Kjønn og Fortolkende Metode. Metodiske Muligheter i Kvalitativforskning* (Gender and Interpreting Methodology), Oslo, Gyldendal Akademisk.

Harding, S. (1987). "Conclusion Epistemological Questions'. In Harding, S. (ed.), *Feminism and Methodology – Social Science Issues*. Bloomington: Indiana University Press.

Hisrich, R. (1986). "The Woman Entrepreneur: Characteristics, Skills, Problems, and Prescriptions for Success". In Sexton, D.L. and Smilor, R.W. (eds), *The Art and Science of Entrepreneurship*. Cambridge, MA: Ballinger.

Holmquist, C. (2002). "Kvinnors Företagande – Genus och Företagande Tydligt Integrerade i Praktiken". In Holmquist, C., og Sundin, E. (eds), *Företagerskan – om Kvinnors Entreprenörskap*. Stockholm: SNS Förlag.

Jensen, R.S. (2005a). "Women Towards Ownership, in Business and Agriculture". National Report. Oslo: ISF.

Jensen, R.S. (2005b). "Women Towards Ownership, in Business and Agriculture". International Report, Andre rapporter 2005/2006. Oslo: Innovation Norway.

Johnson, S. and Storey, D. (1993). "Male and Female Entrepreneurs and Their Businesses: a Comparative Study". In Allen, S. and Truman, C. (eds), *Women in Business: Perspectives on Women Entrepreneurs*. London: Routledge.

Jørgensen, M.W. and Phillips, L. (1999). *Diskursanalyse som Teori og Metode* (Discourse Analysis as Theory and Method), Roskilde, Roskilde Universitetsforlag.

Kalleberg, A. and Leicht, K.T. (1991). "Gender and Organisational Performance: Determinants of Small Business Survival and Success". *Academy of Management Journal*, 34, 1, 136–161.

Kolvereid, L. (1996). "Prediction of Employment Status Choice Intentions". *Entrepreneurship Theory and Practice*, 21, 1, 47–57.

Kolvereid, L. and Alsos, G.A. (2005). "Entrepreneurship Among Women in Norway". In Hauge, E.S. and Havnes, P.A. (eds), *Women Entrepreneurs: Theory, Research and Policy Implications*. Kristiansand: Høyskoleforlaget.

Kolvereid, L., Alsos, G.A. and Åmo, B.W. (2004). *Entreprenørskap i Norge 2004, Global Entrepreneurship Monitor*, Bodø, Handelshøgskolen i Bodø.

Landström, H. (2000). *Entreprenörskapets Rötter*, 2nd edn, Lund, Studentlitteratur.

Ljunggren, E. (1998). *The New Business Formation Process: Why are there so Few Female Entrepreneurs?* Licentiate dissertation, Umeå, Sweden, Umeå University.

Ljunggren, E. (2002). *Entreprenørskap og Kjønn* (Entrepreneurship and Gender). PhD thesis, Studier i företagsekonomi, serie B, no. 48, Sweden, Umeå University.

Ljunggren, E. and Kolvereid, L. (1996). "New Business Formation: Does Gender Make a Difference?" *Women in Management Review*, 11, 4, 3–12.

Marlow, S. (2002). "Women and Self-Employment. A Part of or Apart from Theoretical Construct?" *Entrepreneurship and Innovation*, May, 83–91.

Marlow, S. and Strange, A. (1994). "Female Entrepreneurs – Success by Whose Standards?" In Tanton, M. (ed.), *Women in Management: A Developing Presence*. London: Routledge, 172–184.

Miskin, V. and Rose, J. (1990). "Women Entrepreneurs: Factors Related to Success". In Churchill, N.C., Bygrave, W.D., Hornaday, J.A., Muzyka, D.F., Vesper, K.H. and Wetzel, W.E. Jr (eds), *Frontiers of Entrepreneurship Research*. Wellesley, MA: Babson College, 27–38.

OECD (2000). *OECD Employment Outlook*, Paris, OECD.

Økonomisk Rapport (1999). Farmand: Økonomisk Rapport Oslo. Available: www.orapp.no/oversikt.

Reynolds, P.D., Bygrave, W., Autio, E., Cox, L. and Hay, M. (2003) *Global Entrepreneurship Monitor 2003 Executive Report*. Wellesley, MA: Babson College and London: London Business School.

Riding, A.L. and Swift, C.S. (1990). "Women Business Owners and Terms of Credit:

Some Empirical Findings of the Canadian Experience". *Journal of Business Venturing*, 5, 5, 327–340.

Rosa, P. and Hamilton, D. (1994). "Gender and Ownership in UK Small Firms". *Entrepreneurship Theory and Practice*, 18, 3, 11–27.

Rosa, P., Hamilton, D., Carter, S. and Burns, H. (1994). "The Impact of Gender on Small Business Management: Preliminary Findings of a British study". *International Small Business Journal*, 12, 3, 25–32.

Shane, S., Kolvereid, L. and Westhead, P. (1991). "An Exploratory Examination of the Reasons Leading to New Firm Formation Across Country and Gender". *Journal of Business Venturing*, 6, 6, 431–446.

Statistics Norway (2001). "Antall Fullførte Utdanninger, Etter Kjønn, Studiåret 1999/2000". Available: www.ssb.no/emner/04/utdanning_as/200108/vedltabper cent203.html.

Stevenson, L.A. (1986). "Against all Odds: The Entrepreneurship of Women". *Journal of Small Business Management*, 24, 4, 30–36.

Sundin, E. and Holmquist, C. (1989). *Kvinnor som Företagare – Osynlighet, Mångfald och Anpassning, en Studie*, Malmö, Liber.

Watkins, D.S. and Watkins, J. (1984). "The Female Entrepreneur: Her Background and Determinants of Business Choice, Some British Data". *International Small Business Journal*, 2, 4, 21–31.

6 An exploration of networking practices of female entrepreneurs

Pauric McGowan and Alison Hampton

Introduction

In recent government publications, women have been recognised as a significant, yet relatively untapped, source of entrepreneurial potential (Sundridge Park Management Centre, 1995; CEEDR, 2001; O'Reilly and Hart, 2003). This is particularly true in the area of new venturing and enterprise development (Carter and Anderson, 2001; McMurray, 2001; Orhan and Scott, 2001; Henry and Kennedy, 2003). Indeed, as areas of research, female entrepreneurship and the efforts of women to establish and develop growth-oriented business ventures are largely underdeveloped (Brush, 1992; Rosa and Hamilton, 1994). Often, it is claimed that research in this area, particularly that conducted by male researchers, is presented in a manner that suggests that women operate businesses in ways that are similar to male entrepreneurs (Buttner, 1993; Davis and Long, 1999). Yet, one key difference identified between men and women in business is in the area of network development (Aldrich, 1989). Networking, as an area of research, continues to offer potential for greater development (O'Donnell and Cummins, 1999) and, with reference to female entrepreneurial networking practices, this is particularly true. Shaw *et al.* (2001), for example, suggest that, although there exists a substantial amount of anecdotal evidence to indicate that gender differences are evident in building and utilising networks, the subject has received little by way of rigorous academic research attention. There is a need, therefore, first to acknowledge that, when it comes to managing networks, women may not do business in the same way as men and second, to show that there is real potential in examining how women create and manage networks in order to establish new ventures and grow existing businesses.

The aim of this chapter, therefore, is to build on existing research by providing further insights into the networking practices of both new and established female entrepreneurs. In this regard, we present the findings of our pilot study which focuses on two groups of female entrepreneurs: one group engaged in new venture start-up, and the second in the development of their existing ventures. As part of a wider, longitudinal study, the aim of this research was to determine the extent to which a model of the networking behaviour of female entrepreneurs could be developed for subsequent testing with a larger sample.

Sectoral issues, while relatively unimportant at this stage of the research, will be addressed in the wider study. However, an important dimension, even at this initial pilot stage, is the exploration of the contribution of other females to the networking activities of female entrepreneurs. The chapter is structured as follows: first, the authors discuss the research context for their study by reviewing the pertinent literature on entrepreneurial networking and female networking so that the key issues can be distilled. Second, details of the methodology adopted for the study are presented, and, given the pilot nature of the research, this section includes a discussion on the limitations of the methodology and sample size. Following this, the analysis of the research data is presented. The penultimate part of the chapter provides a discussion of the key issues arising, and presents a tentative model of female networking behaviour. Finally, by way of conclusion, the authors consider important areas for further research.

Research context

Entrepreneurial networking defined

An entrepreneurial individual is described as one who combines particular traits and behaviours with appropriate managerial skills in order to establish a new venture or to develop an existing one (Adams and Chell, 1993). The entrepreneurial process, which challenges the entrepreneurial individual to obtain and maintain a fit between an opportunity in the marketplace and the resources needed to exploit it, is recognised in research to be a particularly dynamic one (Timmons, 1994). A key resource in managing this dynamic process, and in making decisions on how to progress a venture speedily and accurately in an often rapidly changing environment, is the entrepreneur's network of contacts. Indeed, as Johanisson (1986:20) suggests, 'the personal network of the entrepreneur should be regarded as his/her major asset'.

Entrepreneurial networks are defined as those relationships that an individual develops and utilises, consciously or subconsciously, to progress a particular enterprise, whether it is to establish a new venture, for example, or to develop an existing one. They can be highly personal, reflecting relationships that are deeply embedded in the life of the individual. Such contacts are characterised by high levels of mutual trust and commitment that have been developed over time and through shared experiences (Cromie and Birley, 1992). They can be highly formal, also reflecting a more deliberate and controlled approach to managing relationship building. They include network brokers, Enterprise Centre personnel and other professionals who seek to provide support to the entrepreneurial individual in his or her efforts to establish or develop their business ventures (Aldrich and Zimmer, 1986; Blois, 1996).

The value of an entrepreneur's network of relationships in making decisions about how to progress an enterprise depends, however, on a number of quality factors (Aldrich and Zimmer, 1986; Hunt and Morgan, 1995). Research suggests that any network needs to have 'density', reflecting the degree to which those in the individual's network know each other and can share ideas and opinions, even in the absence of the entrepreneur him or herself. 'Diversity' in an individual's network means that there is a sufficient variety of skills and experiences in the network to provide the individual with rich feedback. 'Reachability' in a network addresses the issue of the individual being able to make contacts through the existing network with people outside it. This raises a final quality factor in terms of the 'strength of weak ties', where the value of being able to access the contributions of people with whom the individual entrepreneur is unacquainted becomes apparent. Strong ties, made up of people who know the entrepreneur almost too well, may cease to be able to provide objective guidance and advice. A weak tie, on the other hand, has no other agenda than to make an objective contribution to a decision to be made or a problem to be resolved (Granovetter, 1973, 1982; Hoang and Antoncic, 2003).

A further point is the need to recognise that networks change over time. For example, the network of relationships that the new venture founder has initially when establishing the venture will necessarily develop and change as the venture begins to develop and grow. Butler and Hansen (1991), indeed, suggest that, for the lead entrepreneur in any enterprise, the development and management of networks of relationships over the life cycle of the firm amounted to a strategic imperative.

Networking behaviour of female entrepreneurs

Female entrepreneurs, similar to their male counterparts, need to be effective networkers. Indeed, Brush (1997) suggests that networking is crucial for female entrepreneurs seeking to grow their firms or to establish new ventures. Other research suggests that clear gender differences exist in the networking practices of females, for example, with respect to building and maintaining networks (Carter, 2000), defining the role of networks (Aldrich, 1989), in the composition of networks (Aldrich *et al.*, 1997) and in the determination of quality in female networks (Ibarra, 1993; Knouse and Webb, 2001).

It is clearly important to understand what constitutes effective female networking and, indeed, to gain insights into how females develop quality in their network of relationships, which is deemed so essential for any successful business formation and expansion (Carter and Allen, 1997; Carter and Anderson, 2001; Shaw *et al.*, 2001). From the literature, it would appear that the networking practices of female entrepreneurs are heavily influenced by family responsibilities in the decisions they make with respect to entrepreneurship practice (Martin, 2001). Other factors that have a bearing on their decision-making process appear to be the limited nature of their educational qualifications and the lack of appropriate business experience beyond middle management (Aldrich, 1989). In order to further our understanding of the networking practices of female entrepreneurs we turn now to consider the role of female entrepreneurial networks.

The role of female entrepreneurs' networks

Networked relationships are a critical resource for female entrepreneurs seeking to establish or grow their enterprises (Rosa and Hamiliton, 1994). The benefits of networking for the female entrepreneur seeking to establish a new venture or to develop an existing business include, but are not limited to, providing information on a dynamic environment (Birley, 1985), offering support and confirmation in decision making (Johannisson *et al.*, 1994), identifying new product ideas (Carson *et al.*, 1995) and developing new contacts, particularly with new customers (Dodd, 1997). Research by Moult (2000), for example, indicates that networking also plays a critical key role for female entrepreneurs. Networks emerge as being of particular importance to females in providing strong emotional support; in building confidence and in providing motivation and high levels of stability in circumstances of change that often characterise the roller-coaster ride of entrepreneurial new venturing (Smeltzer and Fann, 1989; Butler and Hansen, 1991).

Research by Okanlawon (1994) develops an aspect of this theme by suggesting that, within mixed groups, women tend to articulate their viewpoints less often than when they are within the perceived 'safe environment' of an all-female group. It seems that females are reluctant to become involved in formal networks, which they perceive as being largely male-dominated. As such, they fear being seen as less competent than their male counterparts (Smeltzer and Fann, 1989). This appears crucial in affecting the level of confidence of the female entrepreneur in conducting business. More recently, however, it is believed that female entrepreneurs have learned to utilise networking for the purposes of confidence building and to gain reassurance by building networks with females (McGregor and Tweed, 2001). According to Moore (2000), women entrepreneurs rely on other women they trust and in whom they can confide to provide both support and encouragement for achieving their business dreams and ambitions. Also highlighted in this research is the increasingly important role of accessing appropriate network brokers and mentors who are also female. This is addressed in the next section.

Types of networks utilised by female entrepreneurs

Informal networking

Research by Hill and McGowan (1996) suggests that personal contact networking is increasingly viewed as an essential entrepreneurial competence, the mastery of which is a core determinant of the potential of any enterprise. Interestingly, research by Buttner (1993) suggests that, while men's motives for forming informal relationships with others are largely based on issues of personal gain, women's motives to network informally tend to be driven by a need to achieve and maintain strong social affiliations (Moore, 1998; Buttner, 2001). Thus, gaining information and resources through people known to the female entrepreneur, i.e. either directly or through friends and family, is consistent with her particular approach to doing business. Even though females tend to network informally, they appear to approach networking in a conscious, deliberate way in which they seek to actively connect themselves with other females in business and, through them, to find ways of expanding their existing network of contacts (Smeltzer and Fann, 1989). This emphasis on maintaining strong social networks made up largely of family and friends, combined with an interest in building relationships with other females, suggests an inherent weakness in female networking practices. Such an approach, while addressing an individual's need for emotional support and providing motivation and stability, may be detrimental to the development of quality factors, such as density, diversity and reachability. However, it must be recognised that female entrepreneurs have faced great difficulty in gaining access to many of the informal, well-established networking groups, managed for the most part, if not exclusively, by males (Aldrich, 1989; Okanlawsom, 1994). Female entrepreneurship is a relatively new phenomenon. Thus, women's representation in these informal networks is only beginning. Nevertheless, formal networking events and activities, initially involving women only, have gone some way to respond to this challenge to build the networking competencies of female entrepreneurs and to widen their circle of contacts (Davis and Long, 1999). We consider formal networking and female entrepreneurship in the next section.

Formal networking

Extant research suggests that formal networking for women is predominately based on gender rather than permeating gender lines (Buttner, 1993, 2001). The current trend towards all-female formalised networking activities has attempted to provide female entrepreneurs with a forum for developing their competencies as networkers. Research by Strauss (2000), for example, suggests that females tend consequently to become involved in all-female formalised networks in order to gain the advantages they perceive available from informal 'old boy' type networks. As such, these all-female forums can provide a useful opportunity for discussions on overcoming and tackling the challenges of establishing and developing a business. Crucial to effectiveness in this area, particularly for new venturers, are other female mentors. They play a special key role for these new female entrepreneurs. Their experienced guidance and emotional support can be crucial in determining the likelihood of future success, providing the aspiring new venturer with a role model whom they might aspire to emulate (Addison Reid, 1994). This concept is dealt with further below.

Increasing the effectiveness of networking by female entrepreneurs

An understanding of effective networked relationships is essential in gaining access to quality networks, deemed vital for business formation and expansion

(Carter and Allen, 1997; Carter and Anderson, 2001; Shaw *et al.*, 2001). Research suggests, however, that women face real challenges in introducing and developing appropriate quality factors into their networking activities, such as density, diversity, reachability and appropriate ties (Aldrich, 1989; McMurray, 2001; Shaw *et al.*, 2001). Strauss (2000), for example, suggests that, if women are to become more effective at networking, they need to enhance networking competencies in order to build in such quality factors to their networking efforts. To do this, Strauss suggests that they need to access, at least initially, other female entrepreneurs who can act as role models as well as mentors. The suggestion is that other female business owners and women professionals are better placed to provide the help and insights required by aspiring female entrepreneurs seeking to establish and grow business ventures.

In a similar vein, Sullivan (2000) also expresses the view that there is a need to match mentors and clients on the basis of gender. The suggestion is that a key factor in helping women to engage in self-employment and entrepreneurial new venturing is the availability of role models with whom they can identify (Carsrud and Olm, 1987; Bygrave and Minniti, 2000). The difficulty in this regard, however, is the dearth of female network brokers in the enterprise support system, such as female bankers or female venture capitalists, as well as female mentors with the available time to commit. There would appear to be recognition that the availability of other females to provide support and guidance for female new venturers in the entrepreneurial network is essential, if not critical, at the initial stages of venture creation and beyond. The challenge, however, is ensuring that such resources are available in sufficient numbers to make a difference.

By way of summarising the pertinent literature on female entrepreneurial networking to date, we have identified the following key themes.

- Networks are a key entrepreneurial resource in determining how an entrepreneurial female does business, whether in starting a new venture or developing an existing one.
- Some networking practices of female new venturers are particular to them, as a group, placing an emphasis on the social network, and on female specific networks.
- Quality in networks is determined by factors such as density, diversity, reachability and issues of ties. Thus, female networking activities may have limited quality aspects, particularly in the start-up stages.
- Entrepreneurial networks evolve throughout the life cycle of the enterprise, which may have implications for the way that female entrepreneurs network as well as the distinctiveness of that activity.

Given the above, and in view of the importance of networking to female entrepreneurial business creation and development, there is a need for further research to be undertaken. In the following section we outline the nature of our research and describe the particular methodology employed.

The study

As already indicated, our study was designed as part of a larger research project in which a tentative model of female entrepreneurial networking behaviour would be applied. The aim, therefore, of this pilot study was to determine the extent to which such a model could be developed. Hence a qualitative research methodology was considered appropriate for this study, given the infancy of the research topic and the exploratory nature of the research itself (Hirschman, 1986; Miles and Huberman, 1994; Hill *et al.*, 1999; Carson *et al.*, 2001). The empirical study involved a team of two researchers, undertaking a series of unstructured, in-depth interviews. The emphasis by both researchers was on an informal, exploratory discussion, rather than asking a series of specific, rigid questions. However, prior to the collection of any data for the study, an interview guide was formulated on the basis of themes distilled from a review of the pertinent literature.

The themes allowed the researchers to explore the wider issues that surround the key area of female entrepreneurial networking during the interviews, without explicitly referring to the research agenda. Due to the informal nature of the interview structure, the participants were able to discuss their individual experiences, as well as any issues they felt to be pertinent, in an open manner, allowing the issue of networking to emerge naturally. Probing the respondent was only conducted in order to develop the discussion and to keep a focus on the research themes. With particular focus on the networking practices of female entrepreneurs, the core themes that require further research include:

- how the female entrepreneurs started their business ventures;
- the crucial decisions made at different stages of business development and the basis for such decisions;
- how these decisions were validated;
- the critical challenges in maintaining and developing the business.

In-depth interviews were conducted with twelve female entrepreneurs. The focus on in-depth interviews allowed the researchers to gather reliable and valid data (Saunders *et al.*, 2000) in order to explore female entrepreneurial networking practices. Eight of the female entrepreneurs were defined as 'new venturers' and four were the owners of 'established companies'. For the purpose of this research, 'new venturers' are those female entrepreneurs who are involved in the initial start-up phase of company development. In other words, they have been operating the business for a short period of time, perhaps under five years; subsequently, they have a limited market and product range (Carson and Cromie, 1989). The companies which have been in business for over five years were classified by this research as 'established companies'. These enterprises have a greater number of employees, greater market penetration and an extended product range, in comparison with new venture firms, which have developed as a result of their increasing number of years in business.

Participants in the research were drawn from women's networking organisations in Northern Ireland, university innovation centres and the researchers' personal contacts. The sample selection was based on a purposive sample. According to Neuman (1997), this type of research lends itself to purposive sampling, in that the researchers can select cases that will be particularly informative. Given that the findings from this research will essentially inform the direction of the extended study, it was imperative to select female entrepreneurs who would assist the researchers in distilling the key themes that emanated from the literature review. Hence, exploratory in-depth research was core to the pilot research's development and further expansion to include subsequent cases.

Participants, who were selected to form a possible purposive sample list, were then invited to partake primarily on the basis of three criteria. First, they were selected because they were female entrepreneurs, second, they were either seeking to establish a new venture or sought to achieve growth in their existing venture, and third, they reflected those characteristics which are recognised by extant literature as 'entrepreneurial'. In other words, they were individuals who are widely recognised in the literature as obsessively opportunity-focused, continuously innovative and tolerant of risk, and possess the ability to adapt and are comfortable with change (Kao, 1991; Timmons, 1994; Carson *et al.*, 1995; Hill and McGowan, 1996). According to Kao (1989), such individuals are easy to recognise but hard to define. Details of those engaged in the research are provided in Table 6.1.

Table 6.1 Interviewee profiles

Respondent	Business type	Length of time in business	Age of female entrepreneur	No. of employees	Highest level of education attained
One	Internet café	6 months	26 years	1	A-level
Two	Dry cleaning	12 months	55 years	1	O-level
Three	Florist	12 months	38 years	0	A-level
Four	Children's party organiser	6 months	33 years	0	A-level
Five	Dog obedience training	6 months	35 years	0	A-level
Six	IT training	12 months	28 years	1	A-level
Seven	Educational/nature trail	12 months	36 years	0	A-level
Eight	Web designer	2½ years	40 years	3	Degree level
Nine	Software design	6½ years	38 years	14	Degree level
Ten	Data cabling	11 years	45 years	27	Degree level
Eleven	Software design	12 years	54 years	6	Degree level
Twelve	IT systems design	15 years	41 years	20	HND level

Note
O-level exams now currently referred to as GCSEs.

All of the businesses involved were located in Northern Ireland, and none of the female entrepreneurs involved in the study had received formal business training prior to start-up. However, most of them had some level of professional training in relation to their specific area of expertise. All of the companies in the new venture category sourced their clients from a local client base, while two of the businesses in the established category had international clients, and the other two had sourced and gained work at national level. The concentration of business varied from service-based to high-technology companies. The interviews were conducted over a period of three months. Each participant in the research was interviewed for an average period of one hour at her place of work. All interviews were tape recorded and transcribed and, as a consequence, a substantial amount of data was generated. Following recognised practice, a coding protocol or framework for analysis was developed. This sought to reduce the large volume of data generated into a more manageable and structured format (Tesch, 1990; Creswell, 1994).

The value of the research was established by using approaches outlined in the literature for the use of qualitative research methodologies (Hirschman, 1986; Miles and Huberman, 1994). The 'credibility' was established by re-presenting the issues from transcribed interviews on an incremental basis for corroboration. 'Transferability' was established through the continuous reflection and feedback within the research team. 'Confirmability' was established through public exposure and dissemination among research and practitioner audiences.

The authors fully recognise the limitations of the study presented in this chapter. Despite the in-depth, qualitative interviewing approach used, the relatively small sample size (twelve cases) means that the findings cannot be generalised for all female entrepreneurs. However, the findings from this study provide an initial basis on which to extend the research to include additional findings from a greater number of cases. As such, this may include scope for analysis of additional cross-sector entrepreneurial female cases.

Findings

Networking practices of female entrepreneurs

The findings of this research highlight networking as being of key importance to how female entrepreneurs conduct business. Within the more established ventures, the focus for networking was in gaining further business by promoting the company and in providing information for decision-making purposes. A typical comment to reflect this came from one of the established practitioners interviewed:

> It's important that you get your name known and recognised for what your business does. After all, who you network with can get you work, and indeed, a lot of business in this sector gets done on the basis of who you know and how they can help you.

However, within the new venture case examples, the general consensus was that networking, especially within personal networks, was vital to prevent isolation and provide support in the early stages, as evidenced by the following comment: 'My husband and family are a great support ... I couldn't do without them.'

Female entrepreneurial networking behaviour

New-venture start-up networking

For seven of the eight new venture firms involved in this research, networking activities were largely informal, based on consultation with family members and friends, particularly with husbands or life partners. The eighth new venture company failed to utilise networking activities and will be discussed in a later section.

Most of the female entrepreneurs at the start-up stage, who were involved with informal or semi-formal networking activities, claimed that networking was a chance to share their experiences in business and to tell their 'own story'. It also allowed them to hear of other people's experiences, enabling them to learn and obtain guidance from others in a similar business position.

In the early start-up stages, the opportunity for the female entrepreneurs to access advice for decision making, with respect to venture development, provided a means by which they could increase their personal sense of self-confidence. Hence, the expectation was that this would eventually, over time, increase their potential for entrepreneurial success.

Of particular interest is the way that such experiences reinforced and highlighted the importance of networking in the future development and growth of the business. As the following quote indicates: 'I know that if I want to grow the business, then I will have to get to know more people who can help me with that.' Fundamental to this concept is that networking in the initial start-up phases appeared to provide the female entrepreneurs with an appreciation that both existing networked individuals and the extension of their networks could provide their fledgling enterprises with the essential information that, as suggested by the literature, emanates from the development of a quality and diversified network. A typical comment that reflects this view, i.e. that the quality of networks must be developed if any new venture is to enjoy future growth, was: 'You can't go around with blinkers on all your life. I tell other women I know that they can't stick to women's groups all the time because that's going to be a disaster.'

The evidence from the research suggests that, in the initial stages of new venture development, female-only networks were appropriate. For example, such female groups were effective in developing new venture females' levels of confidence. However, the women recognised that any plans for growth would inevitably mean an extension of and a commitment towards the use of a mixed gender network.

Established firm networking

Networking for the established firms engaged in this research, however, appeared to have acquired a higher level of sophistication. Such networking activities had both informal and formal dimensions, with the networks mainly used for gaining information and knowledge, both internally from the management team and externally from the marketplace. Female entrepreneurs in this established stage utilised networks with a view to maintaining the entrepreneurial effort of their enterprise, and in securing its continued growth and development. It seemed that the gender issue had become less important or had less relevance at this stage in the businesses life cycle. Indeed, any female contacts within the female entrepreneurs' networks were evidently part of the network because they were personal friends, ex-work colleagues or old university friends. Thus, networking in established firms appeared to be largely informal. A typical comment reflecting this was: 'I would still ask questions about stuff from my friends, some of whom I have worked with in previous jobs.'

However, in addition, there also existed the formal side of the network, which included professional business advisors or formal network brokers. The following typical quote illustrates this need for access to information from the formal network: 'I now can afford to buy in expert advice, from accountants, lawyers and consultants, for certain aspects of the business.' These individuals were 'tapped' for information and resources because of their knowledge and expertise, not specifically with regard to their gender. In other words, individuals were sought who could address the topic or requirement in question. Therefore, the following comment supports the view that networking, both informal and formal, at this established level of business development, was non-gender specific:

> I would ask questions from anyone that I knew would have the knowledge in that particular area ... regardless of whether they were male or female. Really, it is amazing who you meet ... and you can come away thinking to yourself, yes, that's the answer to that question.

A critical part of female networks was also the networking activities that were undertaken internally with those working within the enterprise. Core to this was also the networks of those internal members of staff who could assist in the development and the growth of the company. An important issue to emerge from this research was the high level of importance that female entrepreneurs within the established businesses placed on their 'internal team'. There was a need to maintain high levels of informal communication within the firm in order to develop this resource. In this regard, the following is a typical quote from one of the four established female entrepreneurs interviewed: 'I tend to rely on the knowledge and expertise of my team and their contacts ... they are vital for my firm's success, and I include them in gathering the information I need to make good decisions.' This quote, so typical of the established female entrepreneur, also exemplifies the issue of reachability within the networks, illustrating the women's reachability to other individuals not directly linked to their own network. This appears to suggest that they have sought to develop quality factors in their networks, by sourcing information through indirect relationships. This quote also supports the fact that diversity and density are apparent within an established female entrepreneur's network of contacts, in that she seeks to lever-age advantages from accessing a wider range and variety of information via her employees. Therefore, it is not only the entrepreneur's networks but also the net-works and networking activities of her team that inform and help her to validate the decisions in developing the business.

New venturer and non-networker

Only one of the twelve respondents in this study was not actively involved in networking practices, particularly formal/semi-formal activities. The female in question was within the new venture category and, to date, had not felt the need to network in order to extend her business. For this individual the potential gain for the business from networking had not yet been fully recognised. She indi-cated that she had started the venture out of her desire to obtain a greater work–life balance, and sought to separate what she saw as quality time at home with her children from time she spent at work. As such, she was unprepared to invest the time and effort in developing a network of contacts, viewing such an investment as inappropriate in the light of her determination to spend time with her children. This quotation conveys this attitude: 'Being involved in activities like that doesn't suit me because I have kids and I'm already away from them all day, so I don't like to be away from them in the evening as well.' It was clear during the interview that this particular female 'new venturer' had no ambition to develop her enterprise much beyond a lifestyle venture. Hence, business growth was not a priority. Therefore, in many respects, this female entrepreneur was an exception to the rule, an outlier to the findings. It could, perhaps, be questionable if she is really entrepreneurial in nature. Furthermore, it may be more appropriate to refer to her as a female operating a 'lifestyle business', as opposed to categorising her as a true entrepreneur.

Types of female entrepreneurial networks

The findings from this study indicated that the majority of women entrepreneurs valued their network of contacts as a key resource and sought to utilise their network to its full potential. In the following section, we consider the different types of networks utilised by the females surveyed.

Informal/semi-formal networks

Informal networking was highlighted by the research as being a vital entrepre-neurial resource. As such, informal networking was undertaken on a very casual basis and, to a certain extent, it was natural and subconscious. The nature of the informal network focused on the importance of social contacts comprising of friends and family. This appeared to be the case in the informal networks of both new venture and established businesses. Yet, it was apparent that the new venture companies were, to date, relying extensively on personal networks. While at the established business level, the personal social networks were integrated with utilisation of business and strategic networks.

The following typical quote attempts to illustrate the importance of the personal informal networking dimension to the female entrepreneurs in this study: 'Often I will have decisions to make. This is where my husband is vital to what I do ... not in making the decision but in helping me form an opinion on the amount of information I will have collected previously.'

With respect to the new venturing females, the study showed support in favour of networking in all female networking groups. This supports the view of Strauss (2000), for example, regarding the bonding element of all-female networking groups. Within these networks, the ability to relax and relate to other females, as well as expressing empathy for the challenges faced by other females in business, was seen as crucial. The degree to which female new venturers and those within established businesses utilised all female networks, however, greatly differed. For some of the women new venturers, the actual and too often negative experience of dealing with men, or more often, the perception that men would not be helpful, persuaded most of the women new venturers to consciously seek to build informal networks with female advisors who were either entrepreneurial practitioners or enterprise support staff. This research indicated that negative attitudes were evident from the banking sector towards female entrepreneurs, a sector which, at least until recent times, has been dominated at managerial levels by men. A new venture female typically stated that her presence at a meeting with the bank manager had gone unnoticed because: 'When I introduced myself and showed him my accounts, he immediately turned, looked at and spoke to my husband as if I was deaf and dumb.'

However, with reference to informal networks or semi-formal networks, our study suggests that it was crucial for the female entrepreneurs to be able to express their views openly in a non-judgemental environment, which was both encouraging and empathic to their needs. The following typical comments support this view: 'Being a part of a women's group allows me to develop my confidence, people will say, thank God only women are here' and 'It's all women there and you know that you won't be laughed at.' This research appeared to support the view identified in extant research that self-confidence is a key issue in determining the likelihood of women pursuing and being successful in an entrepreneurial career. The evidence suggests that informal networking activities play a key role in developing self-confidence in female entrepreneurs, which will, in turn, encourage them to extend their networking activities and to work towards building quality factors into their networks.

Formal networks

The women new venturers, while acknowledging the dangers of being overly short-sighted, considered the support that they had received from other female entrepreneurs as invaluable. They acknowledged the importance of having female agency staff, and they actively sought to develop these types of networks. The following typical quotes provide useful insights into the mindset of the female new venturers surveyed: 'If I need anything, I know I can lift the phone and call Joanne in the enterprise centre, she's always there to help' and

> There are a lot of people out there who can help, but the real trick is knowing who to ask in the first place ... Kelly, the manager in the enterprise agency is very good because even if you don't know who to call, you can contact her and she will send you in the right direction.

A key finding from this research is the relative importance, in the start-up stage of network brokers, of individual 'signposting' and direction. While the new venture female entrepreneurs seemed to recognise the benefits of formally organised/semi-formal, all-female networking groups, this was a view that did not appear to be supported by female entrepreneurs in established companies. For example, in direct comparison with the start-up ventures, the four established female entrepreneurs were asked in the research about their views on the role of formal networks and the value of specific networking activities for their particular industries. The research findings suggest that specific industry-based networking activities were held in high value as a source of crucial information for those owners of established firms. In addition, and in contrast to the interest expressed by the new venturers in developing largely predominantly female networks, female entrepreneurs in the more established enterprises appeared to be less impressed with the idea of all 'women only' networks for their stage in business. The two constituencies in this research appeared to hold positions at either end of a continuum, reflecting their different outlooks, circumstances and levels of confidence. The women entrepreneurs within the established firms expressed negative views and attitudes about the value of such networks for female entrepreneurs seeking to establish and grow a business venture. Their views are expressed and summarised in the following typical quotes: (focus on all-female networks) 'It just wouldn't do much for me in getting business' (focus on all-female networks) 'I never really bothered with them ... I didn't feel they could give me anything or that I could give much value back' and 'I just don't see why it should be any different for women ... if a man's group was started there would be uproar with the women.'

Typically the owners of these relatively mature enterprises indicated that it was vital in business to network with men. This was especially so within traditionally non-female business sectors because of the relatively few women involved. Notwithstanding this, one established entrepreneur commented on the negative reaction she had experienced from men: 'I don't personally notice it now that I have been in business longer, but initially there was a lot of this "wee girl" stuff from men I came in contact with.'

For the most part, the females within the established businesses nurtured key contacts that included males. One female entrepreneur within an established firm commented that she had mainly all-male businesses relationships. She indicated that she had experienced no difficulty on the basis of gender throughout her eleven years in business. Furthermore, her view appeared to reflect those of other women within the more established businesses:

> They're dreadful (all-female networks), I just don't go there. I have tried them and I find they're just unconstructive whingeing and I haven't been to one where I've had any advantages or learned anything. I have worked in a mixed environment and hopefully managed to maintain my femininity, and got by successfully with my abilities and experiences. These groupings (all-female networks) are not the answer for females in business.

Interestingly, the established female entrepreneurs had already gained extensive experience in the industries in which they had subsequently established their own enterprise. What appears to emerge from this research is that, as part of their own entrepreneurial apprenticeship, the women entrepreneurs had already been working in the industry, consciously and subconsciously, to build and develop their network of contacts prior to setting up their own venture, as evidence by this typical comment: 'When I set up I had already been in the industry for years, had made contacts previously, both male and female, and had extensive experience in the field. . ... I had made friends previously which now are very useful to me.'

This further highlights the importance of networking in doing business, and the idea that it is as much 'who' you know in business as 'what' you know that makes a difference. This pilot research appears to suggest that all-female formalised networks have a role to play in the early stages of new venturing: in assisting female entrepreneurs in addressing the demands of the entrepreneurial process, building competencies in network management and nurturing the female entrepreneur's personal confidence. However, it also suggests that a dedication to all-female networks would be a myopic strategy and one to be avoided, certainly in the intermediate and long term. Such an approach is untenable because of the limited number of females involved in entrepreneurship, despite those numbers increasing in recent times (Gundry *et al.*, 2002). There is a clear need for a commitment by female entrepreneurs to building quality into their networking efforts if their enterprises are to grow, especially on a continuous, and indeed deliberate, basis.

Role of female entrepreneurial networks

Decision making

The findings from this research suggest that females who have developed their enterprises are only too willing to involve other people in the decision-making process of their business: 'I'll ask anyone I know who I think can help me with something if I am not sure ... I'm not afraid to ask questions ... You won't get anywhere in this business if you don't.' Similarly, the research supports the view that networking by female entrepreneurs is key to obtaining information for decision making. Ultimately, the final decision rests with the focal female entrepreneur, but she will certainly be guided and influenced by people within her network, be they members of her personal contact network or from within her formal business network. As such, networking has been identified as essential to validating and confirming decisions within the company: 'There are a number of people that I would ask opinions from ... just to have their view before I finally make a decision.'

The issue of confidence appears to be germane to the way in which the females in this research conduct business and make decisions for achieving growth. Research by Drummond (1992) suggests that women are likely to be more inclusive decision makers and, similarly, the females in this study appeared to adhere to this approach in that they were clearly very comfortable, in a natural way, with involving others, when making choices about how they might develop their enterprises. This typical quote supports this view:

> I would always include my team in formulating information about a change in the marketplace or our product ... that's not something that I would just decide by sticking my finger in the air ... we're a team here and the wrong decision could affect us all.

Evidence of this collaborative role played by the female entrepreneurs in this study was predominant, both among the new venturers and the more established enterprises. This was particularly observable with respect to social networks of family and friends in the start-up stage, and with business networks once they became more established. The female entrepreneurs appeared more naturally inclined towards social engagement and to constant communication, including listening, in seeking to build relationships both within and outside their ventures.

Providing support

All respondents appeared to have experienced difficulties in accessing the 'right type' of advisor or network broker in their initial efforts to establish their enterprises. What appeared to be the case was that the agencies established to provide support and guidance in the arena of enterprise development were not themselves sufficiently well informed or networked to support the particular needs of female new venturers and established entrepreneurs. The relative newness of females engaged in entrepreneurship itself posed a challenge to the existing constituency of network brokers; a constituency largely populated by men. A typical comment from one of the female entrepreneurs in this study suggested that, in the start-up stage, any help from the support agencies was disappointing in that:

'they [support agency] failed to understand the nature of our business sector, or the challenges that I (as a women) was facing in trying to set up my business.'

However, what also became apparent from the female entrepreneurs engaged in this study was that they wanted network brokers to be more sensitive to the specific business challenges they were facing. All of the respondents within new venture enterprises spoke of how much they valued the support available from the few women who were working within the support agencies, as well as those few established females entrepreneurs who had acted as role models and potential mentors to other females now embarking on the female entrepreneurial journey.

The findings from this pilot research have sought to gain greater insights in the potential of networks and networking to female entrepreneurs, both in establishing their ventures and in seeking growth. Highlighted by this research was the importance of networking activities in building confidence in the female entrepreneur, and the changing nature of the female network of contacts as the business develops.

In the following section, the authors propose a theoretical model of female entrepreneurial networking behaviour, as derived from this pilot study.

Towards a model of female entrepreneurial networking

Figure 6.1 presents a theoretical model of entrepreneurial networking for female entrepreneurs. This tentative model offers an interpretation of the relative levels of reliance on the network membership of female entrepreneurs. The core constituents of the networking model are the length of time a female entrepreneur is in business, which reflects her level of knowledge (both experiential and learned knowledge), and her personal level of confidence in herself as a business person (which seems to be reflected by her length of time in business and the variety of that experience).

'Early learner'

In the quadrant identified as the 'early learner' approach to networking, the core reliance is, at least initially, solely on all-female networks. At this time confidence is relatively low, particularly in the early stages of the new venture. It seems that reliance is on personal contacts, especially social networks, including husbands, parents and other females. Any competent utilisation of such networks by the female entrepreneur would be expected by her to increase her sense of confidence as an entrepreneurial networker, and to increase her ability to voice her views and opinions in what was perceived as a 'safe' environment. This quadrant, if managed well, will increase the female entrepreneur's prospect of successfully developing mixed relationships of higher quality, in terms of more informed network members and a greater range of contacts. As diversity and density of this network develops in the long term, the female entrepreneur will strive towards the 'high-flyer' quadrant, the optimum-networking quadrant.

Length of time in business

Confidence levels:	Short-time	Long-time
	'Wannabe'	'High-flyer'
High confidence	Less reliance on all-female network members and move towards building and extending their networks towards a mixed gender network	No association with all-female network members: a mixed network approach (non gender-specific)
	'Early learner'	'Myopic'
Low confidence	Initially core reliance on all-female network members (gender-specific)	Extensive dependency on all-female network members with no extension of networks

Figure 6.1 A model of entrepreneurial networking for female entrepreneurs.

Organised, all-female networks appear to play a crucial role for female entrepreneurs at this stage in their development. It permits essential 'signposting' in the initial stages of new venture development and allows access to important business contacts and the widening of existing business practices. As such, this stage is important in building confidence in female entrepreneurs which, in turn, will assist further in developing her networking competencies. Okanlawom (1994) suggests that membership of such a group, where there is a genuine desire to help, acts as an effective solution to address the networking problems faced by women entrepreneurs. Strauss (2000) notes this is the beginning in the initial stages of the female bonding approach.

'Wannabe'

The female entrepreneurs in this quadrant were those, as identified in the study, who had set up a new venture, had been in business for a period of a couple of years, and who were looking to move towards becoming an established firm. In other words, they are 'wannabes', who are seeking to extend their networks beyond female only. They see this as essential if they are to grow their business. Thus, they hope to move to the 'high-flyer' quadrant, they are effectively 'wannabe' high-flyers. These are females who clearly possess the entrepreneurial characteristics alluded to in the literature review. They are keen to utilise networks in a manner that is increasingly conscious and focused on getting advice from other females in order to overcome particular issues, and to access information and advice for decision making. One female entrepreneur who sought to grow her business in the early start-up stage already appeared to have developed quickly towards quadrant two of the model. This individual had begun to recognise the need for wider networking and was taking the initial steps towards developing and expanding networking activities to include male contacts. In this stage of the model, the individual appeared to be developing mixed business relationships, fostering networking with business organisations in the industry and encouraging other women to do likewise. At this level, females become less involved in organised all-female networking activities and recognise the need to source other informed, knowledgeable and experienced people for inclusion in their networks, regardless of gender. The networking activities identified appear to be conducted in a more 'conscious' manner in order to benefit the venture's growth and to increase awareness of the company. In this quadrant there would still be some reliance on accessing all-female network members, but mainly in a supportive mentoring capacity.

'Myopic'

The 'myopic' networking quadrant includes female entrepreneurs who, despite being longer in business, were perceived to have a lower confidence level, and thus, had failed to explore other networking opportunities. Hence, they remain reliant on contacts from their all-female network. Within this quadrant the potential for continued growth and development will be stifled because of the continuing reliance on largely all-female networks and a failure to take action to develop more mixed networks, deemed so crucial for the transition from new venture to established growth-focused firms. The prospects for these 'myopic' female networking types are limited. Thus, their view is relatively myopic or short-sighted with reference to the benefits of networking in order to develop the company. As such, the prospects of continued entrepreneurship in these circum-stances are also seen to be limited. Growth is not a priority for female entre-preneurs in this 'myopic' quadrant and, as such, the quadrant will contain those female entrepreneurs who run 'lifestyle' entrepreneurial businesses. None of the respondents in this research appeared to fit into this category. However, one company in this research within the 'early learner' quadrant appeared to be moving straight towards this quadrant, by failing to recognise the need to network or to attain growth and development of the company.

'High-flyer'

Female entrepreneurs in this quadrant were drawn from the more established businesses. These females appeared to utilise networking for the benefit of growing and developing the company. Thus, the gender issue had become essentially irrelevant. Any female contacts were much less visible and, in one particular case example, were non-existent. However, those females who were involved within the networks of female entrepreneurs in this quadrant were deemed important to the 'high-flyer' female entrepreneur for what they could contribute to their efforts to grow the enterprise and not because they were women. Hence, the individuals who made up the networks of the females in this quadrant were utilised because of the importance they placed on their valuable knowledge, experience and expertise, as opposed to their gender. In other words, individuals were sought who could best assist the entrepreneur in meeting the challenges she faced within her changing environment. Therefore, by this stage of enterprise development, network composition tended to be non-gender specific.

Conclusions

This chapter has sought to explore the networking practices of female entrepreneurs. The literature review conducted by the authors suggested a number of core themes with respect to networking behaviour, addressing the role of networking in the new venture creation process and the types of networking in the context of established female-owned firms. Of key importance to these themes was the evolution of female networking from start-up through to established venture. In fact, the research highlighted the differing roles of networking between the new venture companies and those who were further established.

Those engaged in this study were drawn from two groups of female entrepreneurs: one made up of new venturers and the other of owners of more established enterprises. Both groups were, for the most part, keen to grow and develop their businesses. The authors fully acknowledge the limitations of the study, specifically with regard to sample size and a limited time frame. Hence, further research will be designed to include additional cases, permitting a longer time frame which has scope for second interviews and the verification and clarification of findings.

Although designed essentially as a pilot study and as part of a wider, longitudinal piece of research, this study has led to the development of a tentative model of female entrepreneurial networking behaviour. The model, illustrated in Figure 6.1, identified different categories of networkers and their associated characteristics. The broad thesis emerging from the presentation of this model is that, as a female entrepreneur gains more experience and grows her business, her networking behaviour changes accordingly. Furthermore, it is clear that the character of her networks must also change and become non-gender specific if her business is to successfully grow to its full potential. This pilot study also sought to present insights into this networking process.

Further research, which will be conducted by the authors as part of their wider study, will seek to explore the validity of the networking model presented above by applying it to a much larger sample size across a range of industry sectors. This pilot research has extensively informed the wider research in that it has provided a basis for the development of the tentative interview themes, structure and analysis of any further research. Hence, an additional aim of a further research study will seek to assess the nature and extent of non-gender specific networking in the context of growth-orientated female entrepreneurial firms in continuing to maintain the entrepreneurial process. This pilot research appears to suggest the significance of non-gender specific female networking within the 'high-flyer' category. This appears to strengthen the appropriateness of accessing the 'correct individual' as opposed to the 'correct female'. Therefore, an outcome of any further research will seek to identify and define an 'optimum model of female networking' on the basis of a larger, more diverse study.

There also exists scope for further research to establish the character of female entrepreneurial firms as they grow and develop, as well as considering the practices of female entrepreneurial networking in comparison to those of male entrepreneurs. Further research is also needed to gain insights into the actual networking competencies of female entrepreneurs and to consider how these might be developed. How might, for example, female entrepreneurs in the 'early learner' quadrant, as presented in this research, develop their networking as a key entrepreneurial resource in order to move speedily to the 'high-flyer' quadrant, which essentially epitomises the truly entrepreneurial pursuit of growth and development.

References

Adams, E. and Chell, E. (1993). 'The Successful International Entrepreneur: A Profile'. Proceedings of the European Small Business Seminar on Small Business in Internal Markets, Northern Ireland, EFMD, 147–165.

Addison Reid, B. (1994). 'Mentorships Ensure Equal Opportunity'. *Personnel Journal*, 73, 11, 122–124.

Aldrich, H.E. (1989). 'Networking Among Women Entrepreneurs'. In Hagan, O., Rivchum, C. and Sexton, D. (eds), *Women Owned Businesses*. New York: Praeger, 105–107.

Aldrich, H.E and Zimmer, C. (1986). 'Entrepreneurship Through Social Networks'. In Sexton, D. and Smilor, R.W. (eds), *Art and Science of Entrepreneurship*. Ballinger Publishing Company.

Aldrich, H.E., Elam, A.B. and Reese, P.R. (1997). 'Strong Ties, Weak Ties and Strangers. Do Women Differ from Men in their Use of Networking to Obtain Assistance?' In Birley, S. and McMillan, I.C. (eds), *Entrepreneruship in a Global Context*. London: Routledge, 1–25.

Birley, S. (1985). 'The Role of Networks in the Female Entrepreneurial Process'. *Journal of Business Venturing*, 1, 2, 107–117.

Blois, K.J. (1996). 'Relationship Marketing in Organisational Markets, When is it Appropriate?' *Journal of Marketing Management*, 12, 161–173.

Brush, C.G. (1992). 'Research on Women Business Owners: Past Trends, a New Perspective and Future Directions'. *Entrepreneurship Theory and Practice*, 16, 4, 5–30.

Brush, C.G. (1997). 'Women-Owned Business: Obstacles and Opportunities'. *Journal of Developmental Entrepreneurship*, 2, 1, 1–24.

Butler, J. and Hansen, G. (1991). 'Network Evolution, Entrepreneurial Success and Regional Development'. *Entrepreneurship and Regional Development*, 3, 1–16.

Buttner, E.H. (1993). 'Female Entrepreneurs: How Far have they Come?' *Business Horizons*, 36, 2, 59–65.

Buttner, E.H. (2001). 'Examining Female Entrepreneurs Management Style: An Application of a Relational Frame'. *Journal of Business Ethics*, 29, 3, 253–269.

Bygrave, W. and Minniti, M. (2000). 'The Social Dynamics of Entrepreneurship'. *Entrepreneurship Theory and Practice*, 24, 3, 25.

Carson, D. and Cromie, S. (1989) 'Market Planning in Small Enterprises'. *Journal of Marketing Management*, Summer, 33–50.

Carson, D., Cromie, S., McGowan, P. and Hill, J. (1995). *Marketing and Entrepreneurship in SMEs: An Innovative Approach*, Padstow, Prentice Hall International (UK) Limited.

Carson, D., Gilmore, A., Perry, C. and Gronhaug, K. (2001). *Qualitative Marketing Research*, London, Sage.

Carsrud, A.L. and Olm, W. (1987). 'Entrepreneurs – Mentors, Networks and Successful New Venture Development: An Exploratory Study'. *American Journal of Small Business*, 12, 2, 3–18.

Carter, N.M. and Allen, K.R. (1997). 'Size Determinants of Women-Owned Businesses: Choice or Barriers to Resources?' *Journal of Entrepreneurship and Regional Development*, 9, 3, 211–220.

Carter, S. (2000). 'Improving the Numbers and Performance of Women-Owned Businesses: Some Implications for Training and Advisory Services'. *Education and Training*, 42, 4–5, 326–334.

Carter, S. and Anderson, S. (2001). 'On the Move, Women and Men Business Owners in the United Kingdom', Washington, DC, NFWBO and IBM.

CEEDR (2001). 'Young, Women, Ethnic Minority and Co-Entrepreneurs – Final Report', London, Middlesex University.

Creswell, J.W. (1994). *Research Design: Qualitative and Quantitative Approaches*, London, Sage.

Cromie, S. and Birley, S. (1992). 'Networking by Female Business Owners in Northern Ireland'. *Journal of Business Venturing*, 17, 237–251.

Davis, S.E.M. and Long, D.D. (1999). 'Women Entrepreneurs: What do they Need?' *Business and Economic Review*, 45, 4, 25–26.

Dodd, S.D. (1997). 'Social Network Membership and Activity Rates: Some Comparative Data'. *International Small Business Journal*, 11, 2, 13–25.

Drummond, H. (1992). 'Another Fine Mess: Time for Quality in Decision-Making'. *Journal of General Management*, 18, 1, 1–13.

Granovetter, M. (1973). 'The Strength of Weak Ties'. *American Journal of Sociology*, 78, 6, 1360–1380.

Granovetter, M. (1982). 'The Strength of Weak Ties: A Network Theory Revisited'. In Marsden, P.V. and Lin, N. (eds), *Social Structure and Network Analysis*. Beverley Hills: Sage, 105–130.

Gundry, L.K., Ben-Yoseph, M. and Posig, M. (2002). 'The Status of Women's Entrepreneurship: Pathways to Future Entrepreneurship and Development and Education'. *New England Journal of Entrepreneurship*, 5, 1, 39–50.

Henry, C. and Kennedy, S. (2003). 'In Search of a New Celtic Tiger – Female Entrepreneurship in Ireland'. In Butler, J. (ed.), *New Perspectives on Female Entrepreneurship*. Hong Kong: Information Age Publishing.

Hill, J. and McGowan, P. (1996). 'Developing a Networking Competency for Effective Enterprise Development'. *Journal of Small Business and Enterprise Development*, 3, 3, 148–157.

Hill, J., McGowan, P., Drummond, P. (1999). 'The Development and Application of a Qualitative Approach to Researching the Marketing Networks of Small Firm Entrepreneurs'. *Qualitative Market Research: An International Journal*, 2, 2, 71–81.

Hirschman, E. (1986). 'Humanistic Inquiry in Marketing Research: Philosophy, Method and Criteria'. *Journal of Marketing Research*, 23 August, 237–249.

Hoang, H. and Antoncic, B. (2003). 'Network-Based Research in Entrepreneurship – A Critical Review'. *Journal of Business Venturing*, 18, 165–187.

Hunt, S.D. and Morgan, R.M. (1995). 'Relationship Marketing in the Era of Network Competition'. *Marketing Management*, 3, 1, 19–28.

Ibarra, H. (1993). 'Personal Networks of Women and Minorities in Management: A Conceptual Framework'. *Academy of Management Review*, 18, 56–87.

Johannisson, B. (1986). 'Network Strategies: Management Technology for Entrepreneurship and Change'. *International Small Business Journal*, 5, 1, 19–30.

Johannisson, B., Alexanderson, K.N. and Sennesth, K. (1994). 'Beyond Anarchy and Organisation: Entrepreneurs in Contextual Frameworks'. *Entrepreneurship and Regional Development*, 6, 3, 329–356.

Kao, J.J. (1989). 'Entrepreneurship, Creativity and Organisation', Englewood Cliffs, NJ, Prentice Hall International.

Kao, J.J. (1991). 'The Entrepreneurial Organisation', Englewood Cliffs, NJ, Prentice Hall International.

Knouse, S.B. and Webb, S.C. (2001). 'Virtual Networking for Women and Minorities'. *Career Development International*, 6, 4, 226–229.

McGregor, J.H. and Tweed, D.M. (2001). 'Gender and Managerial Competence: Support for Theories of Androgyny?' *Women in Management Review*, 16, 6, 279–287.

McMurray, A. (2001). 'Mapping of Support Provision for Women in Enterprise in Northern Ireland and a Strategic Framework for the Future'. A report commissioned for the Women in Enterprise Network, Northern Ireland.

Martin, L. (2001). 'Are Women Better at Organisational Learning? An SME Perspective'. *Women in Management Review*, 16, 516, 287–296.

Miles, M.B. and Huberman, A.M. (1994). *Qualitative Data Analysis*, London, Sage.

Moore, D. (1998). 'Networking Keeps Entrepreneurs Afloat'. Published in the *Charleston Post and Couriers Business Major*, business review section, dated 29 June, 1998.

Moore, D.P. (2000). *Careerpreneurs: Lessons from Leading Women Entrepreneurs on Building a Career Without Boundaries*, Palo Alto, CA, Davies Black Publishing.

Moult, S. (2000). 'Is Gender a Key Issue? A Study of Female Entrepreneurs in Grampian'. In the Small Business and Enterprise Development (2000) conference proceedings, European Research Press Ltd, Yorkshire.

Neuman, W.L. (1997). *Social Research Methods* (2nd edn), London, Allyn and Bacon.

O'Donnell, A. and Cummins, D. (1999). 'The Use of Qualitative Methods to Research Networking in SMEs'. *Qualitative Market Research: An International Journal*, 2, 2, 82–91.

O'Reilly, M. and Hart, M. (2003). *Global Entrepreneurship Monitor, Northern Ireland*, Belfast and London, InvestNI and London Business School.

Okanlawon, G. (1994). 'Women as Strategic Decision Makers: a Reflection on Organisational Barriers'. *Women in Management Review*, 9, 4, 25–32.

Orhan, M. and Scott, D. (2001). 'Why Women Enter into Entrepreneurship: an Explanatory Model'. *Women in Management Review*, 16, 5, 232–247.

Rosa, P. and Hamilton, D. (1994). 'Gender and Ownership in UK Small Firms'. *Entrepreneurship Theory and Practice*, 8, 3, 11–27.

Saunders, M., Lewis, P. and Thornhill, A. (2000). *Research Methods for Business Students* (2nd edn), Harlow, Prentice Hall.

Shaw, E., Carter, S. and Brierton, J. (2001). 'Unequal Entrepreneurs: Why Female Enterprise is an Uphill Business'. *The Industrial Society Policy Paper*, 1–19.

Smeltzer, L.R. and Fann, G.L. (1989). 'Gender Differences in External Networks of Small Business Owner Managers'. *Journal of Small Business Management*, 27, 2, 25–32.

Strauss, J. (2000). 'The Establishment of a "New Girls" Network'. *Venture Capital Journal*, 8, 40–42.

Sullivan, R. (2000). 'Entrepreneurial Learning and Mentoring'. *International Journal of Entrepreneurial Behaviour and Research*, 6, 3, 160–175.

Sundridge Park Management Centre (1995). 'UK Women Network Differently – Research Reports'. *Journal of European Industrial Training*, 19, 1, 4–6.

Tesch, R. (1990). *Qualitative Research: Analysis Types and Software Tools*, New York, Falmer.

Timmons, J.A. (1994). *New Venture Creation: Entrepreneurship for the Twenty-First Century* (4th edn), Homewood, IL, Irwin.

Part II

Promoting female entrepreneurship

7 Women and new business creation

Breaking down the risk barriers

Clare Brindley

Introduction

In Schumpeter's (1934) classic text, entrepreneurs are seen as those who reform, revolutionise and reorganise industries. This premise raises two immediate tensions: first, is the term entrepreneur and small business owner interchangeable? Often it appears it is (see, for example, Mirchandani, 2005), and thus, an immediate barrier to entry is created – the individual has not only to contend with all the issues in starting a business but has also got to overthrow the current status quo of the industry. If one then introduces a gender dimension, the second tension arises: are women equipped with the necessary resources to break through into self-employment, and does Schumpeter's premise create a further set of barriers?

This chapter explores the barriers to women's self-employment and favours the term "self-employment" rather than "entrepreneurship" as the most common scenario for those starting out in business. This definition is not intended to curtail ambitions, as indeed, there are examples of women who do conform to Schumpeter's (1934) ideal. Rather, it seeks to avoid a further set of potential barriers. As a woman small business owner reflected at a recent seminar for women business owners (WBOs):[1] "I'm just starting out, I can't relate to these so called role models like Anita Roddick, I want to hear from women just like me."

Research contends that women business owners still face greater hurdles in starting and running their own business (Carter *et al.*, 2001; Coleman, 2002; Fielden *et al.*, 2003). Yet, one might speculate that self-employment in terms of the ownership and management of your own business frees women from many of the encumbrances, barriers and prejudices encountered in a managerial organisational role. The assumption would then be that gender-related differences are not significant within the SME sector, and the problems encountered are not gender specific, but rather related to the risks associated with new business development and growth. This chapter evaluates whether there is a gender impact on the perceptiveness of uncertainty and risks and, consequently, whether there are differences in the preparedness to undertake risky decisions and/or whether contextual factors, both internal and external, may impose gender-related barriers and constraints.

The chapter argues that an understanding of the gender aspects of risk is required if policy measures are to be constructive and help women overcome barriers and achieve their potential. A discussion of the likely policy measures that are required to encourage women into self-employment is also included.

The current position

In spite of the growing number of women business owners, women's self-employment prevalence rates are systematically lower when compared to those of men (Schmidt and Parker, 2003). While Minniti and Arenius's (2003) cross-national study reported that there is no country where women are more active than men in entering self-employment, data from the GEM survey identify that women are still half as likely to move into self-employment as men (GEM, 2004). Recent government initiatives, such as the UK's "Strategic Framework for Women's Enterprise", have demonstrated that self-employment can contribute in various ways to socio-economic development and job creation (Mistick, 1998; McKay, 2001; Minniti and Arenius, 2003). Consequently, encouraging women's business ownership is considered as one of the sources of growth, employment and innovation (Orhan, 2001). Thus, there is an economic imperative to women's self-employment, as Gundry *et al.* (2002) argued. For example, women-owned enterprises in the US employ 23.8 million employees and generate \$2.3 trillion in sales (Carter *et al.*, 2001). Whilst, in Britain WBOs accounted for a turnover of up to £1 million (Barclays Bank Plc, 2000). Women now represent a readily available pool of business activity that countries may leverage to improve their economies. Notwithstanding the above, George Bush's pronouncement: "When it comes to entrepreneurship and job creation, ours is an increasingly women's world" (The Public Forum Institute, 2002:1), seems at best optimistic and, at worst, highly misjudged.

So, if there is still a lag in WBOs despite them being seen as economic saviours, what are the real barriers? The reasons underlying women's foray into the SME sector suggest that a number of inter-related factors are responsible for eliciting this. What is not clear is how these inter-relationships influence women and their decision to become small business owners. Some of the literature proposes that changes in the gendered context influence the needs and behaviour of women. However, in terms of a coherent body of work, the literature is playing catch-up, i.e. whilst acknowledging changes in the decision-making context of women, the literature is not yet focused on the women's self-employment context. It is evident that women may be influenced differently from men by changes in contextual factors. However, for women who are self-employed or thinking of moving into self-employment, a comprehensive testable model of what influences their perception is not forthcoming from the literature. This is problematic, given that studies identify that, in terms of risk propensity, men and women are similar. If their propensity is similar it can be surmised that their risk preparedness and/or risk perception is contingent on the factors that influence these. Furthermore, the literature identifies that perhaps some of the constructs that have been used to study risk may not have taken into account the differing definitional stances taken by men and women.

Women and risk

Risk theories have the potential to embrace several of the main themes of female self-employment, categorised by Carter *et al.* (2001) as motivations, start-up patterns and the management, performance and growth of SMEs. What is more difficult to distil, however, is the gender-specific aspect of entrepreneurial risk, in itself an underdeveloped conceptualisation. It is recognised that for each individual, risk factors and the commercial opportunities they present will be contingent on the other factors and the general context within which the individual operates. The issue may not be that there are differences in risk propensity between individuals, but that the context of the individual decision to become self-employed is contingent on other factors.

Knight's classic definition of risk is the probability of incurring a loss (Knight, 1921). Few, if any, business or investment decisions would be undertaken solely to avoid losses and, in terms of SMEs, decisions are made to try and make gains (Blume, 1971). Risk as a construct maybe subdivided into three parts; risk perception, risk propensity and risk preparedness. Sitkin and Weingart (1995) define risk perception as a subjective interpretation of expected loss. Perception is subjective in that "the internal interpretation of external events and circumstances are the key to risk perception, as each organisation or decision maker may view the same set of events and circumstances with different eyes, resulting in different perceptions" (Ritchie and Brindley, 2001:31). Thus, perceptions may alter as a result of internal and external factors.

The issues of perception and propensity seem then to impact on an individual's preparedness to take risks. An individual's risk preparedness may depend either on the uncertainty of outcomes, because of imperfect knowledge, or on the potential scale of losses or gains. Thus, the importance of risk to self-employment has both an organisational and an individual facet. In this regard, there appears to be some consensus that an appreciation or knowledge of risk is warranted in order that policy makers and, indeed, the potential self-employed themselves, can make objective decisions about the enterprise (see, for example, Busenitz, 1999; Stewart *et al.*, 1999; Forlani and Mullins, 2000). The literature appears to suggest that there are three sets of factors that impact upon entrepreneurial risk; the decision situation context, such as beginning a business during a recession, the personality traits of the individual, where the individual lies on the continuum range of risk seeking to risk averse, and the personal context of the individual, including experience, dependents, income, etc. Whatever the source of the risk, Jover's (1992) premise is that the number of business failures that occur illustrates the considerable risk inherent in business start-up.

Although the literature suggests that business ownership and risk are inextricably linked, it is fair to conclude that there has not been uniformity in the findings from these studies. Busenitz (1999) argued that the higher risk propensity of entrepreneurs has not been supported empirically. He argued that it is not risk propensity that distinguishes the self-employed from managers in large companies, but the differences in the way they think about and perceive risk.

McClelland's (1961) influential work, which adopted a behavioural science approach, identified that successful entrepreneurs were moderate risk takers, which concurs with Brockhaus (1980). Busenitz's (1999:328) premise is that, in an established business, approaches to risk may be different from those at the start-up phase in that "we suspect that entrepreneurs in the founding process tend not to be sensitised to the risk they face". The budding entrepreneurs, therefore, do not view what they are doing as risky. Indeed, entrepreneurs may accept risks in part because they do not expect to have to bear them (Low and MacMillan, 1988).

Self-employment takes place against a backdrop of policies, structures and frameworks which may facilitate or inhibit it, i.e. the contextual setting will differ in terms of previous economic development, regional policies and local support mechanisms. The individual contextual factors include: family history and tradition of self-employment, cultural influences relating to family and friends, family commitments and opportunities, as well as educational opportunities. Furthermore, Amit *et al.* (1995) identified changes in employment status, Dubanin (1989) exposure to role models, and Chrisman *et al.* (1987) access to business start-up advice, as other contextual factors. The individual characteristics influencing the propensity of the individual to engage and develop in self-employment are the personal traits and characteristics, such as attitudes to self-employment, risk-taking behaviour, age, self-confidence and gender. These may be influenced by the individual contextual factors detailed earlier. For example, the individual who originates from a background in which there is a strong tradition of self-employment and family support, may inherit the business or a part of an existing family business automatically. Whilst another individual may need to undertake more of the initial stages of setting up the business, including determining the opportunity, persuading oneself and others about the viability and raising risk capital.

Given the lack of research on women and self-employment, it is not unexpected to find that there are few studies that have specifically focused on self-employed women's risk attributes. It has often been left to other academic disciplines, such as consumer decision making (Ward and Sturrock, 1998), psychology (Fischhoff *et al.*, 1977) or gambling studies (King, 1985; Bruce and Johnson, 1994) to focus on women and risk but, again, these studies often merely include rather than focus on women. The literature has either claimed that men take more risks, that women are risk averse, or that there is little difference between men and women.

Slovic (2000:xxxiv) posits that "almost every study of risk perception has found that men seem to be less concerned about hazards than women". Chung (1998) agrees, arguing that "both the marketing and psychological literature suggest that men tend to make more risky judgements than women". Masters and Meier (1988) on the other hand found no significant difference in risk propensity, which in turn contrasts with Sexton (1989), who found that women were more risk averse. For Chung (1998), this difference is seen as a result of differences in information processing styles, i.e. there is a difference in the approach to risk cues, in that women assigned significantly more weight to risk cues. Indeed, Chung (1998) discovered that women made significantly more risk averse judgements than men.

Becoming self-employed is, undoubtedly, a risky activity. Contextual factors impact upon self-employment and, it could be argued, the social context in which women find themselves could determine their risk perception. Lack of education, family responsibilities and lack of collateral could lead to the decision to become self-employed being inherently more risky. So how can this be changed?

Social support and networks

Brindley and Ritchie (1999) found that choice of business is normally based on one's previous work experience, which may indeed help to minimise the risk of venturing into completely uncharted territory with a new business. During the start-up phase, the main source of support and assistance for WBOs appears to come from family and friends, i.e. trusted sources of help that the women had previously experienced. It would, therefore, appear that by choosing a familiar business activity and by relying on a network of family and friends, women are subconsciously minimising the risk of the new business venture.

However, a major barrier identified by self-employed women is the need for balancing the demands of family and work (Mistick, 1998). According to Barclays' (2000) study, 82 per cent of women, as compared with 27 per cent of men, are mainly responsible for housework. Women business owners with children choose to manage their childcare alongside their work (Barclays Bank Plc, 2000). Nevertheless, self-employed women find it hard to run a business that is fitted with school hours (Fielden *et al.*, 2003). Therefore, the majority of women with children of school age relied heavily on assistance from grandparents, other relatives and friends to look after their children, after school and during the school holidays (Fielden *et al.*, 2003). Self-employed women are having to juggle self-employment and family responsibilities, often with a lack of support (Mistick, 1998; Rouse and Kitching, 2004). The need for networks of support and family friendly tax breaks are, therefore, evident.

Networks can also be a means of enhancing confidence. For example, Fielden *et al.* (2003) found that moral support is more pivotal than financial help to WBOs. In their study, women business owners claimed that they become more confident with emotional support (Fielden *et al.*, 2003). Similarly, Busenitz (1999:331) asserts "individuals with a greater sense of overconfidence are likely to function better in an entrepreneurial setting because they will be less overwhelmed with the multiple hurdles they face". Indeed, Neligan (2003:2) argued that "Confidence is key to business success."

It follows, therefore, that a lack of confidence may perhaps be the greatest obstacle to women's progression to small business ownership (Fielden *et al.*,

2003). As Harding *et al.* (2004:6) found, the low levels of women in self-employment in the UK "rests in the perceptions that women have their own capabilities to set up a business". Men are less likely to fear failure and are more likely to know someone that owns their own business. Studies from other disciplines, such as Bruce and Johnson (1996) and Li and Smith (1976) have suggested that women become less risk averse when they have more confidence. Unless you are able to engender confidence and provide support to self-employed women, based on an understanding of how they view risk and what is influencing their risk perception, such advice will be ill-founded.

Finance

Earlier studies by Grant (2003, 2004) identified that the approach to business start-ups and growth by WBOs dramatically differed from that of their male counterparts, with female start-ups tending to be largely low risk, low investment ventures. This is supported by Drummond (2004), who found that choice of business reflected gender and social background. Indeed, Sexton and Bowman-Upton (1990:34) concluded that women "are less willing to get involved in situations with uncertain outcomes where financial gain is involved".

Financial instability and lack of access to capital are cited as being major barriers to entry and growth (see, for example, Brindley and Ritchie, 1999; Levent *et al.*, 2003; Brindley, 2005), exacerbated by additional barriers subtly applied by funding organisations, often resulting in discrimination against capital-poor inexperienced WBOs. Perceptions of financial risk, growth intentions and access to capital are pivotal in the relationship between self-employed women and those from which they seek financial advice. It is argued that sexual discrimination is overt in banks and financial networks (BBC, 2003). For example, 37 per cent of women reported that they have actually experienced sexual discrimination over the last five years (Barclays Bank Plc, 2000), a position supported by Buttner (1993, as cited in Coleman, 2002).

Grant (2004) argued that policy makers and financiers need to look at smaller "one off", female-friendly financial packages, as well as the inclusion of livelihood sustainability and household well-being, in encouraging female business start-ups and SME growth. However, by their definition many financiers and business angels will not fund such low production, low capital, low risk ventures. Moreover, Buttner (1999) argues that starting with a smaller capital base may disadvantage women SME owners over the longer term, impacting upon subsequent growth opportunities and survival rates. Thus, lack of capital has a negative impact on risk assessment and, thus, on the decision to start a business.

Certainly, most women-owned firms fall into the category of "sole proprietorships" and "small businesses" (Coleman, 2002; Gundry *et al.*, 2002; Levent *et al.*, 2003; Orhan, 2001) and are relatively smaller than those owned by men (Orhan, 2001; Coleman, 2002). The relative smallness of women-owned businesses may again be due to how women view risk. Cliff (1998:526) argues that "women who lack relevant experience may question their ability to manage a quickly growing enterprise and may, therefore, purposely limit the expansion of their firms".

As more women choose to enter into sectors in which they have no relevant experience – turn a hobby into a business pursuit, or start up a business smaller in size and with slower growth rates that do not guarantee large returns (Schmidt and Parker, 2003) – then access to finance becomes more problematic. Thus, WBOs tend to seek internal sources of funding, i.e. their own savings, credit cards and family loans, to start a business instead of applying for bank loans (Gundry *et al.*, 2002). Haynes and Haynes (1999) concluded that women-owned businesses were more likely to borrow from family members and friends as banks may charge higher interest rates than they are supposed to. In the UK, half the number of women compared to men use informal investment (GEM, 2004). Evidently, gender discrimination in the lending processes remains a key issue (Coleman, 2002), with women entrepreneurs still facing difficulties in accessing growth capital (Mistick, 1998).

Growth

Lack of capital and/or access to capital influences risk at the start-up phase. Furthermore, choice of sector and growth aspirations, as well as an over-reliance on family capital, may impact on the future growth and survival ability of the business to cope with external sources of risk. If success in the small business sector is only defined as financial success, the risk preparedness of potential women business owners may be affected. Women may not be prepared to seek financial growth if they risk losing their home–work balance. How growth is phrased and promoted may influence perception and preparedness of women towards self-employment.

Sexton (1989) found that, while there are no psychological reasons that predispose women to keep their enterprises small, there may be contextual factors that account for the relatively smaller size of women-owned businesses. Black (1989) believed that, due to socialisation processes, women have different ways of thinking, different values, etc., which Cliff (1998:527) argues is "a compelling argument for anticipating gender differences in growth intentions".

Growth in itself is, after all, a risk; one which may be financial, or social and which may come from external, or internal sources. Women may perceive growth as a risky option because it would deter them from achieving their goal of developing an "employer–employee relationship based upon trust and mutual respect". Indeed, Taylor and Newcomer (2005) identified that WBOs saw their ethic of care as a measure of success. It may not be a simple choice between growth or no growth but rather in the type of growth women want for their businesses. As Cliff (1998:535) states, women seek "a controlled and manageable rate of growth". However, how these differences are articulated may detract from the actual growth intentions of women-owned businesses.

Conclusions

While it would be wrong to treat women as a homogeneous group, tentative conclusions from the above discussion may be drawn. First, in terms of having the confidence to become self-employed, research has shown that if the individual lacks confidence, then he/she may perceive more barriers and anticipate the decision to be more risky. There is no doubt that self-employment is a risky situation, and lack of confidence can further increase barriers to women considering self-employment. Women tend to become less risk averse as they gain more confidence, thus empowering women is vitally important. Studies, such as Bruce and Johnson (1996) and Li and Smith (1976), support this view. Furthermore, Slovic (2000) and Chung (1998) identified that, although women and men had exhibited similar traits (i.e. in regard to propensity), there were still noticeable differences in risk-taking in practice. If the process by which women view risk and the particular factors influencing their risk perception are not understood, then it is difficult to offer help and advice. A knowledge of risk helps individuals to assess their suitability for self-employment (i.e. their appetite for risk) and to assess the best fit/choice of risk opportunities that the business/individual may face. At the start-up phase the question "Is SME ownership an opportunity for women?" has to be answered. In this regard, support is needed for individuals to help screen themselves as potential WBOs, to recognise the barriers they perceive, to create a dialogue and to influence their own risk perceptions.

Second, assuming confidence can be instilled, then successful women-owned businesses may be developed. However, confidence can only be engendered if accountants and banks understand how women view their engagement with sources of capital and the risks associated with it. For example, if a stereotypical definition of growth is used to promote business ownership, then risk perceptions towards self-employment may increase. It is a false assumption that all women are risk averse or that women-owned businesses are not growth orientated. What has to be acknowledged is that "success" and "growth" may be defined by women in different ways from the usual criteria used to promote these terms. However, this is only possible if business support networks move away from stereotypical definitions, understand that risk perception is not a uniform concept and identify ways in which women can access advice at the screening stage.

Third, as the WBO develops her business from start-up to maturity, banks and financial advisors' obsession with growth increases the number of risk barriers. The definition of success used by outside agencies is more often a financial measure, which may mitigate against women. For self-employed women, their maintenance of a home–work balance may be deemed a success, as they can self-manage their time and collect their children from school. Agencies which choose to promote only financial success may be guilty of promoting a male hegemony that supports a masculine view of self-employment. That women may be more uncomfortable with the traditional interpretations of growth has implications for the advice and support given. There is a need to understand how women want to grow their business, and a subsequent need that they are not castigated if their ambitions are different or if they see fast growth as risky. Currently, it would appear that women have to adapt to equalise, and they may remain disadvantaged if success is only defined in growth terms. Indeed, the raised expectations of an SME's growth potential, or the business inputs/processes required to achieve growth, may not be deliverable by SMEs in certain sectors or those lacking a desire to put into place factors (e.g. time, staffing) to support such growth.

Fourth, access to capital and the attendant issues of financial strategies and growth remain key issues. Business support has the opportunity to widen horizons by reducing barriers to accessing finance and by illustrating how women's skills may be transferred into other business ventures that they may not have considered. Research studies suggest that women self-screen when deciding to begin a business, which often leads them to rely on family capital and to begin businesses based on what they know. During the start-up phase, there needs to be a realisation that women do what they know in order to reduce risk and, hence, they may begin businesses that are located in low growth sectors of the economy. Such a ghettoisation of women-owned start-ups makes them potentially more vulnerable to external risk sources, e.g. new entrants into the market, late payments, etc. Therefore, it has to be recognised that "choice" of business may not be a real choice for women; rather, their choice will be limited by, for example, their education, experience and/or family commitments. Thus, policy measures need to identify and accommodate the contextual factors that impact upon a woman's decision to become self-employed.

Fifth, as the business develops, the WBO may move from being risk averse to risk seeking, and this is when advice and support can help business owners identify/anticipate this oscillation. This would enable the SME owners to recognise their own risk perceptions in managing the business, as well as the influence these may have on the business. Moreover, by managing the sources of risk, sustainability of the business becomes more likely. However, any risk management training must be cognisant of the influence of social structures on women's understanding and attitudes towards risk and self-employment. Interpreting the access barriers to women becoming self-employed and understanding the pertinent influences on their risk profile, can effect a positive change in the SME sector.

What can be done?

What is hindering women becoming self-employed and the impact of the barriers they face are still pertinent questions. Identifying the most effective way of removing or reducing these barriers requires a number of initiatives. It would be naive to assume that one set of measures would be appropriate for all SMEs and for all women. As Orhan (2005:3) found, there is a "complex system of interacting motivations" for women moving into self-employment. Still (2005) supports the view that WBOs are not a homogeneous group in terms of motivations or business type. Factors, such as the changes in social structures (e.g. the family as primary social structure), or changes in the political climate which lead to SME support, will influence attitudes to risk and subsequent behaviour.

Examples of effective support mechanisms for women considering self-employment include Prowess, a UK-based advocacy network which has recently developed a manifesto arguing for women-friendly business support, a welfare benefits overhaul, access to finance, and acknowledgement of women's caring responsibilities. Changes in social structures, for example, in terms of a better social security system to deal with childcare and illness issues have also been advocated by Drummond (2004), as well as Rouse and Kitching (2004). Such developments would help reduce some of the barriers women face in juggling caring commitments with owning a business. Furthermore, education is a key access issue because education is an important determinant of entry into self-employment (Taylor and Newcomer, 2005). In addition, there is a need for initiatives to support lifelong learning (Drummond, 2004), as advice is not only required at the start-up stage but skills development is required throughout the life cycle of the business if WBOs are to capitalise on their strengths and be able to manage their enterprises effectively.

It is heartening that Harding *et al.* (2004) in the UK found there was a 27 per cent increase between 2001 and 2003 in the number of women who felt they had the skills to move into self-employment. However, there are still a number of barriers to be overcome before it is "a woman's world". Certainly, networking and women providing support to each other appears to be gaining strength, as witnessed by the number of groupings that have appeared over the last five years. However, Taylor and Newcomer's (2005) call for successful/established women to assist those in developing countries to enter into self-employment must be contextualised in that there is a need for a diversity of role models. For example, not all self-employed women want to be millionaires. There is also a need for diversity in raising expectations of the particular sectors to which women are attracted with regard to new business creation. For example, women need to be encouraged to create businesses where there is already low participation by women i.e. in the science and engineering sector. Role models, in terms of innovators and inventors, are needed to support women who have innovations that they wish to take to the market. Indeed, the promotion of best practice in its many forms needs to be given space if women are to break through the risk barriers associated with self-employment.

Note

1 February 2005, Manchester Metropolitan University.

References

A Strategic Framework for Women's Enterprise (DTI/SBS 2003).
Amit R., Muller, E. and Cockburn, I. (1995). "Opportunity Costs and Entrepreneurial Activity". *Journal of Business Venturing*, 10, 2, 95–106.

Athayde, R. (1999). "Testing Enterprise Tendency in Women Business Owners". Small Business Research Centre, Kingston University. Available: business.king.ac.uk/research/smbusres.html.

Barclays Bank Plc (2000). "Women in Business – the Barriers Start to Fall". Available: www.smallbusiness.barclays.co.uk.

BBC (2003). "Entrepreneurial Women Failed by 'Sexism' ". *BBC News*, Business. Available: news.bbc.co.uk/1/hi/in_depth/business/2001/womenin_business/ (accessed 18 November 2003).

Black, N. (1989). *Social Feminism*, New York, Cornell University Press.

Blume, M.E. (1971). "On the Assessment of Risk". *Journal of Finance*, 26, 1, 1–10.

Boyd, G. and Vozikis, G.S. (1994). "The Influence of Self-Efficacy on the Development of Entrepreneurial Intentions and Actions". *Entrepreneurship Theory and Practice*, 18, 4, 63–77.

Brindley, C. (2001). "ICT Developments, the Evolution of the Amorphous Supply Chain and Consequences for Corporate Strategies, Risk and Relationships". PhD thesis Manchester Metropolitan University, Manchester.

Brindley, C.S. (2005). "Barriers to Women Achieving their Entrepreneurial Potential: Women and Risk". *International Journal of Entrepreneurial Behaviour and Research*, 11, 2, 144–161.

Brindley, C. and Ritchie, B. (1999). "Female Entrepreneurship: Risk Perceptiveness, Opportunities and Challenges". Twenty-second ISBA National Small Firms Policy and Research Conference, Leeds, November.

Brockhaus, R.H. (1980). "Risk Taking Propensity of Entrepreneurs". *Academy of Management Journal*, 23, 509–520.

Bruce, A.C. and Johnson, J.E.V. (1994). "Male and Female Betting Behaviour: New perspectives'. *Journal of Gambling Studies*, 10, 2, 183–198.

Bruce, A.C. and Johnson, J.E.V. (1996). "Gender Based Differences in Leisure Behaviour: Performance, Risk Taking and Confidence in Off Course Betting". *Leisure Studies*, 15, 65–78.

Brush, C.G. (1998). "A Resource Perspective on Women's Entrepreneurship: Research, Relevance and Recognition". Proceedings of the OECD Conference on Women Entrepreneurs in Small and Medium Enterprises: A Major Force in Innovation and Job Creation, Paris, April, 155–168.

Busenitz, L.W. (1999). "Entrepreneurial Risk and Strategic Decision Making: It's a Matter of Perspective". *Journal of Applied Behavioural Science*, 35, 3, 325–340.

Buttner, E.H. (1993). "Female Entrepreneurs: How Far Have They Come?" *Women in Business – Business Horizons*, 36, 2, 59–65.

Buttner, E.H. (1999). "A Report on Gender Differences in Business Initiation in the US". Proceedings of the Second International Euro PME Conference, Entrepreneurship: Building for the Future, October.

Buttner, E. and Rosen, B. (1988). "Bank Loan Officers' Perceptions of the Characteristics of Men, Women, and Successful Entrepreneurs". *Journal of Business Venturing*, 3, 3, 249–258.

Carter, S., Anderson, S. and Shaw, E. (2001). "Women's Business Ownership: A Review of the Academic, Popular and Internet literature". Report to the Small Business Service, August.

Chrisman, J.J., Hoy, F. and Robinson, R.B. Jr (1987). "New Venture Development: The Costs and Benefits of Public Sector Assistance". *Journal of Business Venturing*, 2, 315–328.

Chung, J.T. (1998). "Risk Reduction in Public Accounting Firms: Are Women More Effective?" *International Review of Women and Leadership*, 4, 1, 39–45.

Cliff, J.E. (1998). "Does One Size Fit All – Exploring the Relationship Between Attitudes Towards Growth, Gender and Business Size". *Journal of Business Venturing*, 13, 6, 523–542.

Coleman, S. (2002) "Constraints Faced by Women Small Business Owners: Evidence from the Data". *Journal of Developmental Entrepreneurship*, 7, 2, 151–174.

Drummond, H. (2004) "See You Next Week? A Study of Entrapment in a Small Business". *International Small Business Journal*, 22, 5, 487–502.

Dubinin, P. (1989). "Which Venture Capital Backed Entrepreneurs Have the Best Chance of Succeeding?" *Journal of Business Venturing*, 4, 123–132.

Fielden, S.L., Davidson, M.J., Dawe, A.J. and Makin, P.J. (2003). "Factors Inhibiting the Economic Growth of Female-Owned Small Businesses in North West England". *Journal of Small Business and Enterprise Development*, 10, 2, 152–166.

Fischhoff, B., Slovic, P. and Lichenstein, S. (1977). "Knowing with Certainty: The Appropriateness of Extreme Confidence". *Journal of Experimental Psychology: Human Perception and Performance*, 3, 552–564.

Forlani, D. and Mullins, J.W. (2000). "Perceived Risks and Choices in Entrepreneurs' New Venture Decisions". *Journal of Business Venturing*, 15, 4, 305–322.

GEM (2004). "UK National Report". Available: www.gemconsortium.org.

Grant, J. (2003). "Growing Rural Female Entrepreneurs: Are They Starved of ICT Skills?" ICSB 48th World Conference Proceedings, June.

Grant, J. (2004). "Farmers' Markets: Are They Growing Female Entrepreneurs?" Third International Conference in Business and Economics, Amsterdam, July.

Gundry, L.K., Ben-Yoseph, M. and Posig, M. (2002). "The Status of Women's Entrepreneurship: Pathways to Future Entrepreneurship Development and Education". *New England Journal of Entrepreneurship*, 5, 1, 39–50.

Harding, R., Cowling, M. and Ream, M. (2004). "Achieving the Vision Female Entrepreneurship". British Chambers of Commerce.

Haynes, G.W. and Haynes, D.C. (1999). "The Debt Structure of Small Businesses Owned by Women in 1987 and 1993". *Journal of Small Business Management*, 37, 2, 1–19.

Jover, M.A. (1992). "Risk-Taking Propensity of Successful and Unsuccessful Hispanic Female Entrepreneurs". Texas Woman's University PhD Dissertation U.M.I. Ann Arbor, MI.

King, K.M. (1985). "Gambling: Three Forms and Three Explanations". *Sociological Focus*, 18, 3, August, 235–248.

Knight, F.H. (1921). *Risk, Uncertainty and Profit*, Boston and New York, Houghton Mifflin Company.

Levent, T.B., Masurel, E. and Nijkamp, P. (2003). "Diversity in Entrepreneurship: Ethnic and Female Roles in Urban Economic Life". *International Journal of Social Economics*, 30, 11, 1131–1161.

Li, W.L. and Smith, M.H. (1976). "The Propensity to Gamble: Some Structural Determinants". In Eadington, W.R. (ed.), *Gambling and Society*. Springfield, IL: Charles C. Thomas.

Ljunggren, E. and Kolvereid, L. (1996). "New Business Formation: Does Gender Make a Difference?" *Women in Management Review*, 1, 4, 3–12.

Low, M.B. and MacMillan, I.C. (1988). "Entrepreneurship: Past Research and Future Challenges". *Journal of Management*, 14, 2, 139–161.

McClelland, D.C. (1961). *The Achieving Society*, Princeton, Van Nostrand.

McKay, R. (2001). "Women Entrepreneurs: Moving Beyond Family and Flexibility". *International Journal of Entrepreneurial Behaviour and Research*, 7, 4, 148–165.

Masters, R. and Meier, R. (1988). "Sex Differences and Risk-Taking Propensity of Entrepreneurs". *Journal of Small Business Management*, 26, 1, 31–35.

Minniti, M. and Arenius, P. (2003). "Women in Entrepreneurship". The Entrepreneurial Advantage of Nations: First Annual Global Entrepreneurship Symposium, 29 April, United Nations Headquarters.

Mirchandani, K. (2005). "Women's Entrepreneurship: Exploring New Avenue". In Fielden, S.L. and Davidson, M.J. (eds), *International Handbook of Women and Small Business Entrepreneurship*. Cheltenham: Edward Elgar, 253–263.

Mistick, B.K. (1998). "The Feminization of Entrepreneurship: A Case for a Women's Model in Fostering Economic Development". Available: www.usas.org/knowledge/proceedings/1998/21.

Neligan, M. (2003). "Business Prizes and the Gender Divide". *BBC News*, Business. Available: news.bbc.co.uk/go/pr/fr/-/1/hi/business/3201445.stm.

Orhan, M. (2001). "Women Business Owners in France: The Issue of Financing Discrimination". *Journal of Small Business Management*, 39, 1, 95–102.

Orhan, M. (2005). "Why Women Enter into Small Business Ownership". In Fielden, S.L. and Davidson, M.J. (eds), *International Handbook of Women and Small Business Entrepreneurship*. Cheltenham: Edward Elgar, 3–16.

Prowess. Available: www.prowess.org.uk.

Ritchie, R.L. and Brindley, C.S. (2001). "The Information–Risk Conundrum". *Marketing Intelligence and Planning*, 19, 1, 209–237.

Rouse, J. and Kitching, J. (2004). "Do Enterprise Support Programmes Leave Women Holding the Baby?" ISBA National Small Firms Policy and Research Conference, Teesside, November.

Schmidt, R.A. and Parker, C. (2003). "Diversity in Independent Retailing: Barriers and Benefits – the Impact of Gender". *International Journal of Retail and Distribution Management*, 31, 8, 428–439.

Schumpeter, J. (1934). *The Theory of Economic Development*, Boston, Harvard University Press.

Sexton, D. and Bowman-Upton, N. (1990). "Female and Male Entrepreneurs: Psychological Characteristics and Their Role in Gender-Related Discrimination". *Journal of Business Venturing*, 5, 1, 29–36.

Sexton, D.L. (1989). "Research on Women-Owned Businesses: Current Status and Future Directions". In Hagen, O., Rivchum, C. and Sexton, D.L. (eds), *Women-owned Businesses*. New York: Praeger, 183–193.

Shaver, K.G. (1995). "The Entrepreneurial Personality Myth". *Business and Economic Review*, 41, 3, 20–23.

Sitkin, S.B. and Weingart, L.R. (1995), "Determinants of Risky Decision-Making Behaviour: A Test of the Mediating Role of Risk Perceptions and Propensity". *Academy of Management Journal*, 33, 6, 1573–1592.

Slovic, P. (2000). *The Perception of Risk*, London, Earthscan Publications Ltd.

Stewart, W.H., Watson, W.E., Carland, J.C. and Carland, J.W. (1999). "A Proclivity for Entrepreneurship – Determinants of Company Success". *Journal of Business Venturing*, 14, 2, 189–214.

Still, L.V. (2005). "The Constraints Facing Women Entering Small Business Ownership". In Fielden, S.L. and Davidson, M.J. (eds), *International Handbook of Women and Small Business Entrepreneurship*. Cheltenham: Edward Elgar, 55–65.

Taylor, S.R. and Newcomer, J.D. (2005). "Characteristics of Women Small Business Owners". In Fielden, S.L. and Davidson, M.J. (eds), *International Handbook of Women and Small Business Entrepreneurship*. Cheltenham: Edward Elgar, 17–31.

The Public Forum Institute (2002). "Women Entrepreneurship in the 21st Century". Publications and Resources, Forum Report. Available: www.publicforuminstitute.org/activities/2002/wes/press.htm.

Ward, P. and Sturrock, F. (1998). "She Knows What she Wants … Towards a Female Consumption Risk-Reducing Strategy Framework". *Marketing Intelligence and Planning*, 16, 5, 327–336.

8 Enhancing women's financial strategies for growth

Candida G. Brush, Nancy M. Carter,
Elizabeth J. Gatewood, Patricia G. Greene
and Myra M. Hart

Introduction

Encouragement and support of new venture start-ups is one of the most important economic and social activities for countries because of the impact on economic growth, innovation, job creation, prosperity and national competitiveness. In many countries entrepreneurship is becoming mainstream, although rates differ significantly by country. The 2003 Global Entrepreneurship Monitor (GEM, Reynolds *et al.*, 2003), for example, reports that the total entrepreneurial activity (TEA) rate for the thirty-one countries surveyed ranged from less than three of every 100 adults in France, to nearly thirty of every 100 adults in Uganda. Research in OECD countries consistently shows that job growth in the entrepreneurial sector is higher than for established (corporate) incumbents (Audretsch and Thurick, 2001).

Clearly, women play an important part in this economic activity. Recent statistics show that women are important drivers of economic growth in many of the world's economies (Minitti *et al.*, 2005). Across all GEM countries, women represent about 33 per cent of those attempting to start a business, with the ratio of men to women being highest in Thailand (1:1.05) and lowest in Israel (1:3.42). The percentage of women-owned businesses also varies by country, with the United States, New Zealand, Finland and Denmark showing higher percentages than Ireland, Slovenia and Canada (Brush *et al.*, 2006).[1] The variation in rates and participation of women as entrepreneurs is due to a variety of factors, including cultural factors, natural resources and industrial bases, as much as to policies, regulations and societal beliefs about women's roles in business (Minnetti *et al.*, 2005; Acs *et al.*, 2005).

For example, in Canada, industry context in combination with motivations influence the potential size of a woman's venture (Cliff and Cash, 2006). In Denmark, women are supported by liberal childcare facilities and state support of maternity, yet few choose to grow their ventures. It is speculated that sociocultural norms and perceptions influence Danish women entrepreneurs' growth patterns (Neergard *et al.*, 2006). In Germany, the growth orientation of women entrepreneurs seems to be tied to education levels, as those with more education tend to be more growth oriented. A variety of financing and credit programmes are available to German women entrepreneurs; however, few seek credit and in relatively small amounts (Welter, 2006).

In this chapter we explore the financing strategies of women-led businesses. We begin with a discussion on the impact of women-led ventures on the economy, and this is followed by a consideration of the challenges facing those attempting to launch high growth businesses. We then pay particular attention to the financing strategies employed by women business owners. The nature of our empirical study is then described, and this is followed by the presentation and discussion of our findings. Specific recommendations concerning the enhancement of women's financial strategies, along with some conclusions, complete the chapter.

The impact of women-owned businesses

Despite the extent of their involvement in new business formation, the economic impact of women-led businesses is frequently downplayed. Women are portrayed as only favouring lifestyle businesses where they can balance work and family, or as seeking opportunities to supplement household income. Researchers find that women's businesses are smaller on average than those of men, both in terms of sales revenues and number of employees (Loscocco *et al.*, 1991; Loscocco and Robinson, 1991; Chaganti and Parasuraman, 1996; Ehlers and Main, 1998; Minnetti *et al.*, 2005). While it is widely recognized that business growth is a choice, and most entrepreneurs choose not to grow, there is increasing evidence that many women aspire to build high growth businesses (Cliff, 1998; Brush *et al.*, 2004a).

Data from the United States show that, since January 2000, more than 3,000 women entrepreneurs in fourteen forums across seven markets applied to participate in Springboard Enterprises (www.springboardenterprises.org/about/default.asp), a programme connecting women-led businesses with the equity providers – clear evidence that a considerable number of women have high growth aspirations for their businesses. It was estimated that there were more than 110,000 women-owned firms with more than a million dollars in sales, and almost 8,500 women-owned firms with more than 100 employees and average revenues of $66 million (Center for Women's Business Research, 2001). While high aspiring, fast growth-oriented women entrepreneurs are less studied in the international arena, emerging work examines women's access to growth capital, the extent to which access is gender biased, and whether or not women are able to successfully finance their businesses (Brush *et al.*, 2006).

The potential impact of fast growth women-led businesses is substantial. The dominant source of new jobs comes as a result of new fast-growth businesses (Birch, 1979; Acs, 1999). GEM researchers (Zacharakis *et al.*, 2001; Acs *et al.*, 2005) found that approximately 11 per cent of "opportunity entrepreneurs", those attempting to create high-potential, high growth businesses, expect to create twenty or more jobs over the next five years, compared to the 2 per cent expected by "necessity entrepreneurs" who are starting new businesses for self-employment. If future wealth creation depends on growth-oriented entrepreneurs, it seems only prudent that an environment be created whereby all entrepreneurs with high growth aspirations – both men and women – can maximize their probability of success.

The challenges for high-growth entrepreneurs

There are many challenges facing entrepreneurs who are trying to launch and grow high potential businesses. Securing financial resources generally tops the list and is often considered the major problem inhibiting high growth (Bhide, 2000; Brush *et al.*, 2004a). While sources of growth capital vary widely across countries, some having specified programmes for debt financing, others offering incubator space or government funded equity, for fast growth ventures the typical source is a form of private equity. These investments can come from multiple sources, including private venture capital partnerships, partnerships affiliated with financial corporations and investment banks, corporate venturing programmes, individuals, and direct investments from banks and financial corporations (Bhide, 2000).[2] Access to these investment pools is difficult under the best of circumstances but, for women entrepreneurs, the doorway is almost completely closed. In spite of increased availability of equity funds during the 1990s, venture capital investment in US women-led businesses is a small percentage of overall investments. In 1998, women-led firms in the US received only about 4.1 per cent of all venture capital investments (Greene *et al.*, 2001; Brush *et al.*, 2004a). This finding is startling because in 2004 there were 6.7 million majority-owned, privately held women-owned business in the US, employing nearly 10.6 million workers and generating nearly $2.46 trillion in sales, up 40 per cent nationwide from 1997 (Center for Women's Business Research, 2004).

The funding gap is problematic for both equity investors and for women-led ventures. For equity investors the gap represents investment opportunities that are overlooked and unrealized, diminishing their ability to achieve top returns on their money. For women-owned businesses the gap signifies limitations for wealth creation, technology development and innovation, to name but a few. Given its deleterious effect, why does the funding gap exist?

Financing strategies of women-owned businesses

The size differential between men- and women-owned businesses may be a function of the resources available at start-up and through the growth phases of the businesses. Research shows that women use less capital in starting or acquiring their businesses than men (Carter *et al.*, 1997; Verheul and Thurik, 2001). Because the majority of businesses are started with the personal savings of the founders (Bhide, 1992), normally accumulated over time, women may be handicapped because of the differential in pay structures between men and women. For example, women are less likely to have high incomes and more likely to have very low incomes than men (Minneti *et al.*, 2005). Women are not only more likely to start their businesses on a shoestring, but also more likely to operate on a shoestring. Some research shows that men and women use different financing strategies, and that this may affect women entrepreneurs' ability to grow their businesses. For example, Chaganti *et al.* (1996) found that women preferred internal rather than external sources of equity for their businesses – a strategy that may place greater limits on the amount of capital available for expansion. However, there are contradictory findings about whether men and women are as likely to use lending institutions for financing their businesses. Carter *et al.* (1997) found that men and women were just as likely to use formal lending institutions for starting their businesses, while Cole and Wolkin (1995) found that women were less likely to use banks as a source of capital and used less trade credit than their male counterparts.

In any case, some form of financial resource is crucial to both start-up and growth. Lack of capital at initial stages can delay or preclude start-up, and may have a long-term impact on the firm. Less capital at start-up influences the ability of the entrepreneur to raise bank financing (Storey, 1994). Carter and Allen (1997) show that undercapitalization at firm founding has a long-term negative effect on the performance of women-owned firms. Carter and Rosa (1998) found that the size of initial capital was positively related to future capital assets, sales, total number of employees and core full-time employees. Although no correlation is shown for the amount of debt a business carries and its financial success (Haynes and Haynes, 1999), it is likely that there is a relationship because of the potential impact on profitability. Without bank financing, women owners may have to resort to other more costly forms of financing. Even the type of funding may have a differential effect, for example, use of bank funding at start-up for men and women had a significant and positive effect on future sales levels in one particular study (Haynes and Helms, 2000).

One explanation for continuation of this funding gap is that women may develop financing strategies for their businesses that inadvertently limit growth. High potential ventures, in particular, often require outside investments in the form of equity capital. In exchange for investment of outside equity, the entrepreneur gives up ownership. At some point, the entrepreneur becomes a minority owner and, eventually, if the business grows as expected, there will be a liquidity event (acquisition, merger, sale or public offering) where returns on investment will be returned to investors. For some entrepreneurs, both male and female, ownership and control are important and, therefore, equity financing is not an option. But, if the choice is to seek growth, access to multiple sources of capital requires that an entrepreneur demonstrates his/her financial savvy and the new firm's capabilities and potential (Brush *et al.*, 2004a). A well-disciplined financing strategy that facilitates proof of the business concept, establishment of channels of supply and distribution, and satisfaction of early customers goes a long way in inspiriting investor confidence. Thus, we ask the question, what are the components of a successful financing strategy and to what extent do women develop such strategies?

Rarely is equity the first, or only, source of capital in a new firm's financing structure. Instead, early capital is likely to come from many sources, including personal savings, banks, government programmes, venture capital funds and business angels (Bhide, 2000). Drawing on each of these sources will have different ramifications for both the business and the business owner. Decisions regarding the sequencing of capital sources, and the resulting capital structure of the business is crucial to a venture's success. Scherr *et al.* (1993) suggested that new ventures should follow Myers' (1984) "Pecking Order" and finance their businesses in a hierarchical fashion. Florin and Schulze (2000) supported this perspective, finding that the most common financing strategy for IPO (initial public offering) firms began with the founding team's reliance on personal savings, bank loans and/or government programmes. As the business grew, the founders then used bootstrapping techniques to build the business while they gained additional experience and achieved the legitimacy desired by external stakeholders.

Bootstrapping involves the use of personal and internally generated funds for business investment, the control of costs and the delay of capital expenditure until sufficient funds to support growth are available (Van Osnabrugge and Robinson, 2000). Often bootstrapping involves a high reliance on internally generated retained earnings, leasing of equipment, customer advances, second mortgages and even the use of credit cards to finance the business' operation (Coleman and Cohn, 1999). Cash flow or retained earnings subsequently fuels the business, as owners position the venture for success in the private equity markets. Bootstrapping can free the venture from excessive debt loads that may constrain the company in its early years and hamper its growth. Bootstrapping can also prepare the venture for outside investments at a later time.

Freear *et al.* (1991) identified bootstrapping as the most likely source of initial equity for 94 per cent of new technology-based firms, and Bhide (1992) found bootstrapping as the preferred source by more than 80 per cent of the 500 fastest-growing privately held firms in the US. Similarly Van Osnabrugge and Robinson (2000) saw bootstrapping as an effective strategy for financing a new enterprise's growth that could position the firm to be attractive to outside investors, and thus, better position the company to receive private equity investments.

Freear *et al.* (1995) and Winborg and Landstrom (1997) identified four types of bootstrapping options: (1) bootstrapping product development, (2) bootstrapping business development, (3) bootstrapping to minimize the need for capital and (4) bootstrapping to meet capital needs. Examples of bootstrapping product development include using existing relationships with customers and suppliers to make ends meet while the company works to roll out the product or service. Bootstrapping business development focuses on options that can be used to grow the firm as a whole, like delaying compensation for the founding team or using personal savings or credit cards rather than taking on business debt. Bootstrapping to minimize the need for capital involves reducing the level of monetary expenses for the young business. Often this includes controlling rather than owning resources. Examples include leasing equipment, rather than purchasing it, using credit from vendors to extend cash flow, or using temporary personnel rather than carrying the expense of full-time employees. Bootstrapping to meet the need for capital includes options that allow the business to raise capital quickly, often to meet short-term material costs, or to minimize the need for capital flow. Business credit cards, loans from family and friends, selling or pledging accounts receivables are often favourite approaches. A recent study found that bootstrap financing is a common source of financing among both technology and non-technology firms, and that technology-based firms perceived a higher importance of bootstrap methods (Van Auken, 2005).

Thus, if bootstrapping is critical for positioning the business for subsequent investment by external investors, a well-disciplined financing strategy should increase the chances of the firm's later success and increase the venture's access to outside investors. Based on this argument, we expect that women-led businesses that use bootstrapping as part of their financing strategy are more likely to be successful in securing equity financing than those that do not use these financing techniques. To test this proposition we studied the financing strategies of women-led businesses that had applied to the Springboard 2000 Venture Forums in search of equity investments. We hypothesize (H1) that those that use bootstrap financing better position the business for equity investment.

> H1: Woman-led businesses that use bootstrapping techniques to finance their high potential, high growth businesses are more likely to secure outside equity funding than women-led business that do not use these financing techniques.

Methodology

The sample for this study was women entrepreneurs who applied to Springboard 2000 Venture Forums in Silicon Valley (San Francisco) and Mid-Atlantic (Washington, DC) during 1999. Each woman entrepreneur had applied to make a presentation requesting an equity investment for her business before an audience made up of venture capitalists, "angels" and corporate fund managers. From the 659 applications, we selected the 466 businesses founded between 1995 and 2000 (224 applications from Silicon Valley; 242 from Mid-Atlantic) to participate in the study. Founders in the companies were sent a letter and e-mail asking them to participate in a study on how more assistance could be provided to business owners seeking venture capital. The letter informed them that they would be contacted within a few days for a phone interview and offered a $25 gratuity for their participation. A second e-mail was sent reminding them of the upcoming phone call and distributing visual aids that would be used during the interview process. The respondents were encouraged to keep the aids handy to their phone so they could refer to them during the call, shortening the amount of time needed to complete the interview.

Phone interviews were conducted by a national, independent market research firm. Of the 466 eligible businesses, 171 of the entrepreneurs could not be reached because the application listed a wrong phone number, a fax or international phone number; the phone had been disconnected; or the female entrepreneur was not available during the study period (e.g. out of the country). Interviews averaging sixty-two minutes (thirty-six minutes shortest; 113 minutes longest) were completed with 100 entrepreneurs.

The bootstrap financing measures of interest in the present study were only contained on the long-form interview schedule; thus, data from only 100 respondents were available for consideration. Additionally, eight of the 100 interviews were discarded because the respondents indicated they had not been a founder on the start-up team, leaving data from ninety-two interviews to consider.

Measures

Dependent variable

After verifying that the respondent was part of the founding team of the business, the interviewer asked whether the business had ever received an equity investment prior to their application to the Springboard 2000 forum and, if so, when each round of equity investment had been received. The interviewer defined equity for the respondent by stating that

> most businesses have two types of investments: 1) ownership or equity, and 2) loans or debt. Those that own equity in the business usually expect to receive a share of the profits. Loans or debt usually must be paid back and often there is interest. Has this business ever received an equity investment other than from yourself or the start-up team, or not?

The business was determined to have an equity investment if the respondent gave a date for when the initial equity round had been received, and they had used at least one of six equity sources listed. The variable was dummy coded one if they met the equity funding criteria, or zero if they had yet to receive an equity investment. Forty of the respondents met the equity funding requirement. Fifty-two were still seeking their first external equity investment when they submitted their Springboard application.

Independent variables

The financing strategy was determined by asking respondents about nineteen different sources of bootstrapping options. Interviewers instructed respondents to refer to a list of potential sources of funding and were told, "I will read you a list of different sources entrepreneurs sometimes use to meet their business capital needs. Please indicate whether or not you used each source to fund your company." Each option was dummy coded: used equalled one; not used equalled zero.

Findings

Table 8.1 reports the sources of the equity investments. Among those who had secured equity funding, over 9 per cent reported securing an investment from private investors, individuals or groups, and over 50 per cent had received equity from venture capital firms.

The findings displayed in Table 8.2 indicate significant differences in the use of bootstrapping options by women-led ventures with equity investments and those yet to receive outside equity. The most common options used by both groups were techniques for business development, or bootstrapping to grow the business as a whole. Fifty per cent or more of both groups used four of the five business development options, but those with equity investments were significantly more likely to delay compensation for the founding team, whereas those without equity were significantly more likely to rely on personal savings. Those with equity funding were also significantly more likely to use bootstrapping to fund product development than those yet to receive external equity. Over 30 per cent of the ventures with equity reported using prepaid licences, royalties, advances from customers or customer funded research and development in comparison to only about 15 per cent of those yet to get outside equity. Similarly, those with external equity were significantly more likely to minimize their need for capital by controlling resources without owning them. More than 50 per cent of those with equity investments leased equipment or used credit from vendors in comparison to only about 10 per cent of those yet to get outside equity funding. Finally, almost 75 per cent of those with equity were paying employees with company stock, more than twice that of those yet to receive outside equity. On the other hand, almost 60 per cent of both groups used temporary personnel to minimize need for capital rather than undertake the cost of full-time employees.

Almost 50 per cent of both groups used credit cards, both personal and business credit cards, to bootstrap the business, and almost 40 per cent of both groups used loans from family and friends to meet the capital needs of the business. Interestingly, the level of credit card usage among these women-led businesses is somewhat higher than that reported by small businesses in general. The US Small Business Administration reported that credit card use to finance busi-

Table 8.1 Sources of equity investments

Sources of equity	Got equity n = 40 (%)
Private investors – individuals or groups	93
Bank where you had debt	8
Venture capital firms	50
From pension/funds/insurance companies	5
Publicly issued stock	5
Investment from a Small Business Investment Corporation	8

Table 8.2 Use of bootstrapping sources to predict equity investment

	No equity n = 51 (%)	Got equity n = 40 (%)	Total n = 91 (%)	Chi-square
Bootstrapping product development				
Prepaid licences, royalties, or advances from customers	16	35	24	$p < 0.03$
Customer funded R&D	14	33	22	$p < 0.03$
Bootstrapping business development				
Delayed compensation for founding team	61	88	73	$p < 0.01$
Personal savings	94	80	88	$p < 0.04$
Deals with service providers (e.g. lawyers) at below competitive rates	52	58	54	
Personal credit cards	57	60	58	
Personal bank loans	16	20	18	
Minimizing need for capital				
Leasing equipment	16	60	35	$p < 0.000$
Interest on overdue payments from customers	4	8	6	
Temp. personnel	57	60	58	
Credit from vendors	12	53	30	$p < 0.000$
Using retained earnings	26	18	23	
Meeting need for capital				
Business credit cards	47	55	51	
Loans from family and friends	39	38	39	
Loans from partner's families and friends	20	18	19	
Loans from previous employers	2	5	3	
Business/commercial bank loan	8	15	11	
Selling or pledging accounts receivable (factoring)	4	5	4	
Paying employees with company stock	33	75	52	$p < 0.000$

Note
Bootstrapping typology adapted from Freear *et al.* (1995) and Winborg and Landstrom (1997).

ness increased from 16 per cent in 1995 to an estimated 47 per cent in 2000 (The State of Small Business, 1999). Findings in this study show that on average 51 per cent use business credit cards, and 58 per cent use personal credit cards.

Discussion

Despite some progress, our understanding of the financing strategies of women-led ventures is based upon only a few studies about the relationship between gender and access to debt financing, and many of the results are inconclusive (Greene *et al.*, 2001). Indeed, the percentage of studies about women entrepreneurs/business owners comprise less than 10 per cent of published work in the field (Baker *et al.*, 1997; Brush and Edelman, 2000).

For women entrepreneurs in the US, bank financing is accessible through government initiatives (such as the US Small Business Administration's Women's Prequalification Loan Program) and private banking programmes (such as, Wells Fargo Bank and Bank Boston programmes for women business owners). Women's business organizations (e.g. Women Inc.) sponsor training programmes, and assistance centres offer workshops about the availability of commercial credit and attempt to demystify the application process. The result is that in 1998, 52 per cent of women business owners in the United States reported that they had used bank credit (as compared to 59 per cent of male business owners). Approximately one third of women-owned businesses had credit lines of $50,000 or more, 16 per cent had $100,000–500,000, and 7 per cent had credit lines in excess of $500,000 (Center for Women's Business Research, 2001). However, we know very little about whether these debt-financing decisions position the businesses for subsequent equity investment that would facilitate the growth of a high potential venture. The lack of knowledge about the financing strategies of women business owners has given rise to a mythology about women entrepreneurs and their access to financing in general, and equity capital in particular (Brush *et al.*, 2004a).

In this study we argued that a financing strategy that includes bootstrapping can be used to position the business for external equity investment. The effective use of bootstrap financing likely depends on both the human capital and social capital of the management team. Whether the bootstrapping involves managing internal cash flow, sharing premises with others, bartering underused services, or forming partnerships/business alliances, financial acumen, managerial skills and social networks would seem foundational. Previous research on the effect of human capital shows that, although female entrepreneurs have higher levels of formal education than male entrepreneurs, they often have not focused their studies on business or finance, nor have they acquired these skills in their work experiences or in training programmes. Although we could find no other study that examined women business owners' experience in using bootstrap financing to effectively grow their companies, intuitively it would seem that women business owners who have higher levels of financial acumen, together with diverse social networks, would be better equipped to use bootstrapping effectively to position their businesses as attractive investment opportunities for outside investors. The question is whether this acumen can only be achieved "on the job", or whether intervention strategies can be developed that would assist women in acquiring the critical human and social capital. Such strategies could provide women entrepreneurs leading high potential, high growth ventures with valuable knowledge about bootstrapping strategies, financing and managerial capabilities, access to leasing opportunities, or the business alliances needed to generate revenue and reduce costs, in other words, all bootstrapping techniques that can minimize business risk and demonstrate the "hustle" that outside equity investors reward.

Recommendations

To ensure that all entrepreneurial ventures, not just those led by men, have the opportunity to contribute to personal, economic and national well-being, we see programmes that provide enhanced *access*, *networks* and *education* as beneficial to individuals, economies and to national competitiveness.

Enhanced access

Among the women-led ventures receiving an equity investment in this study, over 90 per cent reported getting the funding from private investors, individuals or groups. This reliance on "angel" funding corresponds to findings in other studies. The GEM Study (Zacharakis *et al.*, 2001), for example, reported that in some nations more than 90 per cent of investment capital in entrepreneurial companies comes from informal "angel" investors. In addition, 50 per cent of the entrepreneurs in our study reported funding from venture capital firms. Sponsoring forums like Springboard 2000 (now named Springboard Enterprises, see www.springboardenterprises.org/) that link women entrepreneurs with potential investors can greatly increase the odds of funding success. Since the initial Springboard forum in Silicon Valley in 1999, more than 320 women-owned businesses have presented at fourteen venture forums in seven US markets, and have secured, to date, more than $2 billion in investments (www.springboardenterprises.org/about/default.asp).

The success of Springboard Enterprises undoubtedly can be replicated wher-ever the largely anonymous "angel" investing community is linked to the equally anonymous women-led high potential ventures. Zacharakis *et al.* (2001) illustrate the potential impact of angel investment and classic venture capital as a per cent of GDP for the fifteen GEM countries in their study, and how, when it represents as little as 1 or 2 per cent of a nation's GDP, it is still a significant factor in that nation's economy. Between 1970 and 2000, US venture capital-backed companies created 7.6 million jobs in the United States and more than $1.3 trillion in revenue as of the end of 2000 (www.nvca.com/, press release, 22 October). Clearly, opening access for high potential women-led ventures to equity capital sources can lead to impressive revenues, jobs, new products and services, and improvement in productivity and quality of life.

Networking opportunities

The venture industry is male-dominated, small and geographically concentrated. A study conducted by the *Diana Project* mapped the US venture capital industry by gender composition for the years 1995 and 2000 (Brush *et al.*, 2004b). They found that women are extremely under-represented in the industry and are not making great strides in increasing those numbers. Between 1995 and 2000 the number of venture capital firms employing women increased by 37 per cent. However, women's representation in the industry fell from 9.8 per cent to 8.8

per cent during that time frame. Furthermore, women were significantly more likely to exit the industry during the five-year time frame than were men. Sixty-five per cent of the women identified in decision-making positions in venture capital firms could no longer be found in the industry in 2000, while only 30 per cent of the men identified in management positions in 1995 were not found in the industry in 2000.

Why is the gender distribution in the venture capital industry important? It is widely acknowledged that who you know is critical in gaining access to the venture capital community. Furthermore, research shows that women are more likely to have more women in their networks than men. If men are more likely to be venture capitalists than women, then the likelihood that the social networks of women entrepreneurs and women venture capitalists will overlap will be quite small. More bluntly, it is unlikely that women will know the people who will make the equity investment decision. Unless forums are developed that can facilitate the introduction of women entrepreneurs to venture capitalists, the likelihood that high potential women-led ventures will find a conduit into the capital pool is quite small. Additionally, ways to encourage investors to seek out and consider investment in women-led ventures by expanding their networks beyond their traditional contacts must be found.

Education

This study demonstrated that commonalities in the bootstrap financing strategy among high potential, high growth, women-led ventures exist. Nearly 90 per cent of the ventures use personal savings of the start-up team as part of their financing strategy, followed in popularity by delaying compensation for the founding team to help build the business (73 per cent). But there are also distinct strategies that differentiate those ventures that succeeded in getting equity investments from those that are still trying. Among these are bootstrapping options that use "other people's money" (i.e. customers, vendors and employees), and resources the business does not own (e.g. leasing equipment). If women have not had the opportunity to learn how to plan and execute bootstrap financing through first-hand industry and start-up experience, developing pro-grammes to educate and prepare women to lead fast growth businesses may help compensate for the lack of experience. Programmes that foster the development of relevant education and experiential programmes could broaden the participation base for these opportunities.

Furthermore, women need to be encouraged and educated to participate in the investment process (i.e. as angels, corporate venture funds and venture capital firms). Since women are under-represented in the venture capital community, programmes are needed that can systematically increase their numbers and expertise. One such programme dedicated to the advancement of the venture capital practice in the US is the Kauffman Institute for Venture Education. Formerly known as the Kauffman Fellows Program, (www.kauffmanfellows.org/main/index.php?id=1) the Institute is now an independent educational institute.

It is the only institute recognized by the US Internal Revenue Service (taxing agency) to specialize in educating venture capitalists. The mission is to be the leading educational institution for the global advancement of the venture capital process. Its objective is to double the size and reach of the programme within the US, and to establish additional fellowships for venture capital trainees in three other countries or regions within the next five years. But what does this programme mean for women business owners?

In the US approximately 9 per cent of venture capitalists are women. However, of the sixty-one venture capital fellows that the Kauffman programme has trained to date, 25 per cent of the fellows are women. While functioning much like the search for venture capital, looking only for the best, the fellows' network has been successful in recruiting and retaining a diverse programme membership. By increasing the number of women in decision-making positions in the venture capital industry, we increase the odds that women entrepreneurs will connect with these women venture capitalists and enhance the odds that both parties will benefit from the high potential deals that may otherwise go unrealized.

Finally, an important part of education is research that provides knowledge to be used in training and development programmes. Rigorous research, that can answer questions about what works and what does not, can arm entrepreneurs in their efforts to build more successful ventures. For example, concern about why women are getting such a tiny share of equity investments in the US led to the creation of the *Diana Project* and *Diana International,*[3] two research initiatives dedicated to learning more about growth strategies that result in successful, high potential women-owned businesses.

In this chapter, we identified, through an exploratory study, that early financial strategies of bootstrapping are associated with equity capital investments for women-led firms. Equity capital is an important resource for high growth businesses. We also acknowledge that women entrepreneurs may face significant personal and institutional barriers in financing and growing their businesses. We argue that training and development interventions are important to expand women's knowledge of and access to sources of financing, in particular, equity resources. We recommend ways for increasing access, expanding networks and developing education and awareness programmes – all mechanisms that have the potential to reduce the equity-funding gap that beleaguers high potential women-led ventures.

Conclusions

Why is all of this important? First, in terms of wealth creation, it must be acknowledged that the lack of investment in women-led ventures limits the opportunity for women to grow their businesses and create wealth. This, in turn, diminishes opportunities to build wealth and create assets for future generations. Second, in terms of competitiveness, the lack of equity for women-led ventures may limit growth and diffusion of innovations, job creation, and contributions to regional and country economies. Third, in terms of opportunity, the lack of investment in women-led ventures may mean that the venture community is missing out on the chance to fund and receive returns from good investments.

In conclusion, what do we do? We focus on *access*, *networks*, and *education*. As discussed above, in order to improve access, we need to have a good understanding of the current situation. This involves having appropriate systems in place to track investments in and performance of venture funded companies, in order to encourage investors to seek out and invest in women-led ventures. We need to support education on both sides of the deal. For example, we need to encourage programmes like the Kauffman Institute for Venture Education, to improve gender representation in the Venture Capital industry and to help venture capitalists recognize that there are good investment deals to be made by expanding their networks. On the demand side, women entrepreneurs need to understand the equity process as one aspect of a full capitalization strategy. And, finally, we need to encourage the sponsorship and dissemination of research about women's entrepreneurship and comparative research on the financing and growth of women-owned and men-owned ventures. Rigorous research provides a powerful base for influencing systems. Information and knowledge derived from solid data can have irrefutable effects on changing attitudes, opinions and practices.

Notes

1 The term women-owned business includes those businesses that are partly or completely owned by women. There is variation by country in the unit of analysis, and in most European countries, the highest percentage of women-owned businesses are sole proprietorships and self-employed businesses (Brush *et al.*, 2006).
2 For additional information on the venture capital industry, the National Venture Capital Association, www.nvca.org and its partner organizations, the European Venture Capital Association, www.evca.com as well as individual country associations are suggested resources.
3 The *Diana Project* and *Diana International* (www.esbri.se/diana.asp) are research consortiums created to undertake rigorous research that can provide a base for influencing policy and systems. The consortium partners believe that information and knowledge that come from solid data can have irrefutable effects on changing attitudes, opinions and practices. Founders of the Diana Project include Dr Candida G. Brush, Babson College; Dr Nancy M. Carter, Catalyst, Inc. and University of St Thomas; Dr Elizabeth J. Gatewood, Wake Forest University; Dr Patricia G. Greene, Babson College; and Dr Myra M. Hart, Harvard Business School. Their efforts coincided with those of other groups around the world to support and advance the growth and development of women-owned businesses.

References

Acs, Z.J. (1999). *Are Small Firms Important? Their Role and Impact*, Boston, Kluwer Academic Publishers.
Acs, Z., Arenius, P., Hay, M. and Minnetti, M. (2005). "2004 Global Entrepreneurship Monitor Executive Report", Babson Park, MA and London, Babson College and London Business School.

Audretsch, D. and Thurick, R. (2001). "Linking Entrepreneurship to Growth". STI Working Papers 2001/2. OECT: Directorate for Science, Technology and Industry.

Baker, T., Aldrich, H.E. and Liou, N. (1997). "Invisible Entrepreneurs: The Neglect of Women Business Owners by Mass Media and Scholarly Journals in the USA". *Entrepreneurship and Regional Development*, 9, 221–238.

Bhide, A. (1992). "Bootstrap Finance: The Art of Start-Ups". *Harvard Business Review*, Nov–Dec, 109–117.

Bhide, A. (2000). *The Origin and Evolution of New Businesses*, New York, Oxford Press.

Birch, D.L. (1979). "The Job Generation Process". Unpublished Report. Massachusetts Institute of Technology Program on Neighborhood and Regional Change for the Economic Development Administration, US Department of Commerce, Washington, DC.

Brush, C.G. and Edelman, L.F. (2000). "Women Entrepreneurs: Opportunities for Database Research". In Katz, J.A. (ed.), *Advances in Entrepreneurship Firm Emergence and Growth: Databases in SME Research*, Greenwich, CT: JAI Press, 445–484.

Brush, C.G., Carter, N.M., Gatwood, E.J., Greene, P.G. and Hart, M. (2004a). *Clearing the Hurdles: Women Building High Growth Businesses*, Englewood Cliffs, NJ, Prentice Hall.

Brush, C.G., Carter, N.M., Gatwood, E.J., Greene, P.G. and Hart, M. (2004b). *Gatekeepers of Venture Growth: A Diana Project Report on the Role and Participation of Women in the Venture Capital Industry*, Kansas City, MO, The Kauffman Foundation.

Brush, C.G., Carter, N.M., Gatwood, E.J., Greene, P.G. and Hart, M. (eds) (2006). *Diana Project International: Growth Oriented Women Entrepreneurs and their Businesses*, Cheltenham, Edward F. Elgar Publishing.

Carter, N.M. and Allen, K.R. (1997). "Size Determinants of Women-Owned Businesses: Choice or Barriers to Resources?" *Entrepreneurship and Regional Development*, 9, 211–220.

Carter, N.M., Williams, M. and Reynolds, P.D. (1997). "Discontinuance Among New Firms in Retail: The Influence of Initial Resources, Strategy, and Gender". *Journal of Business Venturing*, 12, 125–145.

Carter, S. and Rosa, P. (1998). "The Financing of Male- and Female-Owned Businesses". *Entrepreneurship and Regional Development*, 10, 3, 225–241.

Center for Women's Business Research (2001). *Removing the Boundaries: The Continued Progress and Achievement of Women-Owned Enterprises*, Washington, DC, Center for Women's Business Research.

Center for Women's Business Research (2004). *Women-Owned Business in the United States: A Fact Sheet*, Silver Spring, MD, Center for Women's Business Research.

Chaganti, R. and Parasuraman, S. (1996). "A Study of the Impact of Gender on Business Performance and Management Patterns in Small Businesses". *Entrepreneurship Theory and Practice*, 2, 2, 73–75.

Chaganti, R., DeCarolis, D. and Deeds, D. (1996). "Predictors of Capital Structure in Small Ventures". *Entrepreneurship Theory and Practice*, 20, 2, 7–18.

Cliff, J.E. (1998). "Does One Size Fit All? Exploring the Relationship Between Attitudes Towards Growth, Gender and Business Size". *Journal of Venturing*, 13, 523–542.

Cliff, J.E. and Cash, M.P. (2006). "Women's Entrepreneurship in Canada." In Brush, C.G., Carter, N.M., Gatwood, E.J., Greene, P.G. and Hart, M. (eds), 2005. *Diana Project International: Growth Oriented Women Entrepreneurs and their Businesses*. Cheltenham: Edward F. Elgar Publishing.

Cole, R.A. and Wolken, J.D. (1995). "Financial Services Used by Small Businesses:

Evidence from the 1993 National Survey of Small Business Finance". *Federal Reserve Bulletin*, 81, 7, 629–667.

Coleman, S. and Cohn, R. (1999). "Small Firms' Use of Financial Leverage: Evidence from the 1993 National Survey of Small Business Finances". In Reynolds, P.D., Bygrave, W.D., Manigart, S., Mason, C.M., Meyer, G.D., Sapienza, H.J. and Shaver, K.G. (eds), *Frontiers of Entrepreneurship Research*. Wellesley, MA: Babson College, 354–368.

Ehlers, T.B. and Main, K. (1998). "Women and False Promise of Micro-Enterprise". *Gender and Society*, 12, 4, 424–440.

Florin, J. and Schulze, B. (2000). "Born to Go Public? Founder Performance in New, High Growth, Technology Ventures". Babson College–Kauffman Foundation Entrepreneurship Conference, Wellesley, MA, June.

Freear, J., Sohl, J.L. and Wetzel, W.E. Jr (1990). "Raising Venture Capital: Entrepreneurs' Views of the Process". In Churchill, N.C., Bygrave, W.D., Muzyka, D.F., Vesper, K.H. and Wetzel, W.E. Jr (eds), *Frontiers of Entrepreneurship Research*. Wellesley, MA: Babson College, 223–237.

Freear, J., Sohl, J. and Wetzel, W. (1995). "Angels: Personal Investors in the Venture Capital Market". *Entrepreneurship and Regional Development*, 7, 1, 85–94.

Gatewood, E.J., Carter, N.M., Brush, C.J., Greene, P.G. and Hart, M.M. (2002). *Venture Capital, Women's Entrepreneurship And High Growth Ventures: An Annotated Bibliography*, Stockholm, ESBRI.

Greene, P., Brush, C., Hart, M. and Saparito, P. (2001). "Patterns of Venture Capital Funding: Is Gender a Factor?" *Venture Capital*, 3, 63–83.

Haynes, G.W. and Haynes, D.C. (1999). "The Debt Structure of Small Business Owned by Women in 1987 and 1993". *Journal of Small Business Management*, 37, 2, 1–19.

Haynes, P.J. and Helms, M.M. (2000). "A Profile of the Growing Female Entrepreneur Segment". *Bank Marketing*, May, 29–35.

Loscosso, K.A. and Robinson, J. (1991). "Barriers to Women's Small-Business Success in the United States". *Gender and Society*, 5, 511–532.

Loscocco, K.A., Robinson, J., Hall, R.H. and Allen, J.K. (1991). "Gender and Small Business Success: An Inquiry into Women's Relative Disadvantage". *Social Forces*, 70, 1, 65–85.

Minitti, M., Arenius, P. and Langowitz, N. (2005). *Global Entrepreneurship Monitor: 2004 Report on Women and Entrepreneurship*, Babson Park, MA and London, Babson College and London Business School.

Myers, S.C. (1984). "The Capital Structure Puzzle". *Journal of Finance*, 39, 3, 575–592.

Neergard, H., Nielsen, K. and Kjeldsen, J. (2006). "The State of Women's Entrepreneurship in Denmark". In Brush, C.G., Carter, N.M., Gatwood, E.J., Greene, P.G. and Hart, M. (eds), *Diana Project International: Growth Oriented Women Entrepreneurs and their Businesses*. Cheltenham: Edward F. Elgar Publishing.

Reynolds, P.D., Bygrave, W.P., Autio, E. and others (2003). "Global Entrepreneurship Monitor". Available: www.gemconsortium.org/download/1104613418953/ReplacementFINALExecutiveReport.pdf.

Scherr, F.C., Sugrue, T.F. and Ward, J.B. (1993). "Financing the Small Firm Start-Up: Determinants of Debts". *Journal of Small Business Finance*, 3, 1, 17–36.

Storey, D. (1994). "New Firm Growth and Bank Financing". *Small Business Economics*, 6, 2, 139–150.

The State of Small Business (1999). "A Report to the President", Washington, DC, US Government Printing Office.

Van Auken, H. (2005). "Differences in Usage of Bootstrap Financing Among Technology-Based and Non-Technology Based Firms". *Journal of Small Business Management*, 43, 1, 93–104.

Van Osnabrugge, M. and Robinson, R.J. (2000). *Angel Investing: Matching Start-up Funds with Start Up Companies*, San Francisco, Jossey-Bass.

Verheul, I. and Thurik, R. (2001). "Start-Up Capital: Does Gender Matter?" *Small Business Economics*, 16, 4, 329–345.

Welter, F. (2006). "Women's Entrepreneurship in Germany". In Brush, C.G., Carter, N.M., Gatewood, E.J., Greene, P.G. and Hart, M. (eds), *Diana Project International: Growth Oriented Women Entrepreneurs and their Businesses*. Cheltenham: Edward F. Elgar Publishing.

Winborg, J. and Landstrom, H. (1997). "Financial Bootstrapping in Small Businesses: A Resource Based View of Small Business Finance". Paper presented at the Babson College–Kauffman Foundation Research Conference, Babson College, Babson Park, MA, April.

Zacharakis, A.L., Neck, H.M., Bygrave, W.D. and Cox, L.W. (2001). "Global Entrepreneurship Monitor: National Entrepreneurship Assessment – United States, 2001 Executive Report". Kauffman Center for Kansas City, MO: Entrepreneurial Leadership at the Ewing Marion Kauffman Foundation.

9 Women in engineering and technological entrepreneurship

Exploring initiatives to overcome the obstacles

Ita Richardson and Briga Hynes

Introduction

In both the national and international context, the number of females entering technology professions is very low. For example, a recent report from the European Commission (2003:45) stated that: 'Men graduates are consistently more likely than women graduates to be graduating from Engineering programmes, and, with the only exceptions of Belgium and Spain, from Science, Mathematics and Computing programmes.'

Indeed, contrary to expectations in the late twentieth century, there continues to be an unbalanced ratio of males to females both studying and working in technological positions, and the current situation differs little from what we were experiencing a decade ago (O'Dubhchair and Hunter, 1995; Klawe and Levenson, 1995). For example, computer science is a relatively new discipline and, when it first emerged, it was hoped that it could provide a new technical discipline where women could establish themselves and could 'break new ground in professional access and equity for women' (Pearl, 1995). However, this has not been the case. Due to the variety of courses and titles in the technology and engineering disciplines it can be difficult to present exact figures, but generally, it is accepted that about 20 per cent or fewer places on engineering and technology courses are filled by women (Richardson *et al.*, 2002). Due to the low numbers of women accessing technological careers, many women's organisations, educational institutions, government organisations and individual women themselves feel it necessary to promote such careers among other women.

Furthermore, as a result of low levels of female participation in engineering and technology jobs, we recognise that there are corresponding low levels of female participation in entrepreneurship within technical fields. This can be attributed to specific factors where females do not have the necessary technical and/or business education or background, and also to gender issues common to the more general female population. These more generic factors include personal profile and personality characteristics, and are prominent factors which emerge as barriers to female participation in enterprising activity. To overcome this scarcity of technologically knowledgeable females in self-employment, and to rectify the imbalance in the levels and type of start-ups relative to the male population, it is necessary to determine the source of this problem. To achieve this requires interlinked research to determine more explicitly the factors that inhibit this career choice and their origins. This information will provide important baseline data for the design of interventions to alleviate the shortage of women in technological self-employment overall.

This chapter sets out to address these issues by specifically focusing on the barriers to female entrepreneurship and the establishment of technology-related businesses. These topics are generally researched independently. However, the authors recognise that the merging of these topics could add value to and further inform the debate in this under-researched topic, specifically in the Irish context. The chapter begins by examining the current status of female participation in both engineering and technical disciplines and in self-employment. This is followed by an examination of the design, development, implementation and evaluation of three particular corrective interventions undertaken at the University of Limerick in Ireland. Analysing such interventions not only serves to identify the potential for further development, but also highlights policy issues which need to be considered by others, including educational institutions and government agencies. Following an examination and analysis of these initiatives as examples of good practices for improving women's participation levels in both technical education and technology-based self-employment, a tentative framework is presented for supporting and strengthening high technology entrepreneurship educational modules. Finally, some conclusions are presented.

Current status of female participation in engineering and technical education

When we look at the second-level school system in Ireland, we can see that there has been a marked improvement in the uptake of science subjects among women in recent years. For example, in 2000, 47 per cent of those taking higher-level mathematics, 30 per cent of those taking higher-level physics, 56 per cent of those taking higher-level chemistry and 71 per cent of those taking higher-level biology were women (Forfás, 2003a). However, when we consider subjects which are the basis for further study in engineering and technology, the figures are not so healthy. These constitute mathematics and physics, as applied mathematics (21 per cent women), engineering (4 per cent women), technical drawing (8 per cent women) and construction studies (5 per cent women). Indeed, even with this increase in the numbers taking science subjects, the input to engineering and technology subjects in third-level remains low.

Because of the variety of courses and titles in the engineering and technology disciplines, it can be difficult to present figures from the third-level undergraduate sector. A recent report (McDonagh and Patterson, 2002) stated that, for every seventy-seven males accepting Central Applications Office places this year,[1] 100 females accepted places. However, in engineering or technology courses, only one female accepted a place for every four males. Taking the University of Limerick in Ireland as an example, female graduates have consistently numbered less than 10 per cent across engineering courses over the past six years (University of Limerick, 1999–2004). The BSc in Computer Systems, for example, is a technology course with one of the highest participation levels of women in such courses within the university. Yet, the number of women studying this subject remains lower than 20 per cent. This reflects the national trend and, consequently, the numbers of young women graduating from third-level engineering and technology courses continues to be low.

Similarly, when we examine postgraduate statistics, we can see that this downward trend continues, although it is not as significant as between second-level and third-level undergraduate education. According to a report issued by Forfás (2005), only 18.1 per cent of PhD researchers and 20.5 per cent of non-PhD researchers are female. Within the 'Engineering, Manufacturing and Construction' category, 22.2 per cent of postgraduates are women (European Commission, 2003). On the positive side, while women constitute 39.6 per cent of higher level graduates overall within Europe, their numbers are increasing by an annual average of 4.8 per cent as opposed to 0.9 per cent for men (European Commission, 2003). The growth difference in Ireland is not as great, with 6.9 per cent growth for women and 6.0 per cent growth for men.

Implications for business and society

Why do we consider women's involvement in technology and engineering to be so important? Although, in practice, women's influence on project teams has often caused quite significant changes in product design, their numbers are too small (even at 20 per cent) to have a continuous significant effect on design teams. The construction of infrastructure, both physical and technological, is being carried out mainly by men, yet women make up over 50 per cent of the population (CSO, 2005). While it is now recognised that a women's perspective can be quite different from, and indeed complementary to, that of men, there are many signs of the lack of women's influence all around us. For example, the late Anita Borg from Xerox has been quoted as saying: 'If women were more involved in creating new technologies, cars would have a place for you to put your handbag' (Smith, 2002).

Florida (2002) argues that 'diversity and concentration work together to speed the flow of knowledge'. Or, as Trauth (2002) states: 'women in the IT profession, as a group, are different from men, as a group, in the profession, albeit for sociological rather than biological or psychological reasons'. Ultimately, the diversity offered by female influence during technological design is often missing.

Another effect is that technology-based policies which have an influence on society are being made without women's input to their debate. Current debates include the issue of privacy/security and the misuse of the Internet. Another is the placing of physical telecommunications infrastructure nationally. The number of women who are currently working in the engineering and technology sectors of government are in the minority, thus, they can only exert influence in some cases. However, women's influence must become more far reaching. Indeed, in Ireland, although there is a government target to have State Boards composed of at least 40 per cent women, the actual figure is closer to 27 per cent (WITS, 2004). Without increasing the numbers of women involved in the sector, there will continually be excuses for excluding women from relevant decision-making boards.

For the individual women who are turning their backs on technological careers, the effects are very significant. Mathematics skill is no longer a 'recognised' hindrance – we have already noted that over 47 per cent of higher-level leaving certificate mathematics students are women. They are missing out on what are considered to be very rewarding positions, offering a variety of tasks and an opportunity to work with a range of people. These jobs are often highly paid (CSO, 2005), with new learning always possible. Contrary to common belief, it is unusual for careers in this area to be geeky, anti-social and boring. Furthermore, the Irish and world economy is losing out because of the lack of involvement of women in the development of that economy, facilitating a 'brain-drain' or waste of human talent that should not be acceptable.

A recent report published by Berg (2003) identifies four reasons why more women should be encouraged to consider computer science and engineering: justice, equal opportunity, resource and labour market. *Justice* points to women being deprived of an opportunity to contribute to an important segment of society. *Equal opportunity* considers women's rights to the benefits offered by the growth in information and communications technology. The *resource* argument considers the loss to society when women's input is not utilised. Finally, the *labour market* loses out when there is a large number of potential employees who do not have the skills required.

This loss is further encountered and recognised within the discipline of entrepreneurship, where potential for women to become entrepreneurs in high-technology industries is lost. Many young women are capable of pursuing technological careers in established firms but fail to transfer this knowledge to the establishment of a business owned and managed by themselves. This is generally due to factors such as lack of encouragement towards entrepreneurship, lack of role models and a general lack of the relevant information to consider such a career option.

Current status of female participation in entrepreneurship

Henry and Johnston (2003) suggest that there is conflicting and, overall, a lack of evidence regarding the specific number of female-owned and female-managed enterprises in Ireland. For example, the Organisation for Economic Cooperation and Development Report (2000) found that women make up only 15 per cent of Irish entrepreneurs, while other statistics suggest that the level of entrepreneurial participation by Irish females is 3.7 per cent, which is lower than in the UK or in the US (Fitzsimons *et al.*, 2003). In Ireland, entrepreneurial participation by women halved between 2001 and 2003, while that of men declined by 26 per cent. Furthermore, according to Fitzsimons *et al.* (2003), women in Ireland are 2.6 times less likely to start a business than their male counterparts, as females in Ireland tend to be more averse to risk-taking and more cautious than men. However, more educated women are more likely to engage in entrepreneurial activity. If the current decline, as evidenced by Fitzsimons *et al.* (2003) continues, then this percentage will decline further in the next few years. This is a worrying trend, which necessitates remedial action.

The above compares to an average of 29 per cent of females in Europe who are engaged in enterprising activity (Observatory of European SMEs, 2003). In 2003, Ireland ranked sixth among the twenty-two OECD countries in terms of women who were thinking of starting a business. However, this ranking slips to seventeenth place when comparing the percentage of women who had actually started a new business (GEM, 2004).

So why do so few women consider self-employment as a career option? Findings from empirical research studies, such as the Industrial Society Report (2001), as cited by Goodbody Economic Consultants (2002), provide an insight into the factors contributing to women's low level of participation in entrepreneurship. The general trends emerging from this research are:

- *Age*: women in Ireland appear to be starting businesses at an older age than men.
- *Type of business*: women in Ireland are more likely to start a service business, whereas men are more likely to start a high-technology business.
- *Reasons for leaving previous employment*: women in Ireland are much less likely than men to start their own business as a result of being made redundant.
- *Future plans*: more men than women plan to set up another business, or franchise their existing one.
- *Finance*: women in Ireland have less access to finance than men.
- *Business structure*: women often tend to go into a business or partnership with their husband/partner, rather than starting their own business.
- *Confidence and skills*: women are less confident than men when starting a new business.

In their own specific research with female entrepreneurs, Goodbody Economic Consultants (2002) summarised the primary reasons for lower levels of female participation in entrepreneurship.

- Social conditioning – in Ireland women are still perceived as having a supportive rather than a leadership role, which results in fewer women considering self-employment as a career option.
- Perceptions of the demands of an entrepreneur in Ireland – the current perception is that entrepreneurs work very long hours and may have to travel and sacrifice personal and family life to ensure business objectives are met.

- Glass ceilings – it is more difficult for women to achieve career advancement to management, resulting in them having less management experience and fewer skills.
- There is a lack of female role models.
- There is a low proportion of women pursuing science engineering and technology programmes and courses.
- There is a lack of self-confidence.
- Difficulties exist for women in reconciling work and family life.

Henry and Johnston (2003) found that the main barriers and challenges to self-employment were associated with funding, not being taken seriously and time management. The time management issue centred on the need to balance business activities around family demands and circumstances. These findings are also reflected in research completed by Limerick City Enterprise Board (2003) which found that female entrepreneurs' business choice was related to their interests, hobbies and values. Factors, such as previous work experience, were not rated highly by women as influencing their choice or type of business venture. Rather, it was considered more important to have a flexible type of business which would allow them to accommodate personal family circumstances. The Enterprise Board's research also found that women tended to be less confident and assertive in the initial researching and selling of their business idea, and in the acquisition of resources. Survey respondents did not have previous management positions prior to start up, which they felt was a disadvantage. However, by the same token, it can also be argued that many men entering self-employment do not have management experience or skills, but they do not perceive this as a barrier in the development of their business. This relates to the broader debate on the role of women in the workplace, particularly with regard to their role in management positions, and how, in many instances, current management roles, practices and values are still male dominated. The female entrepreneurs surveyed by the Limerick City Enterprise Board (2003) considered that they could benefit from enhanced management skills and greater confidence, as well as an improved ability to network and sell, not just their business idea, but also themselves in a confident manner.

Other research would also suggest that such issues influence the type and profile of new businesses established. For example, Goodbody Economic Consultants (2002) and the Gender Equality Unit (National Development Plan, 2000) claim that women tend to start businesses in the general services, tourism and financial services sectors, while men tend to start more businesses in manufacturing, construction and technology. It has also been suggested that a range of personal profile and personality characteristics, along with educational and industrial/work experience greatly influence the attitudes, perceptions, knowledge and exposure to self-employment and choice of career options for women. The challenge for policy makers and educationalists, therefore, is to determine how these obstacles can be best addressed and overcome.

In recent years, the University of Limerick has been involved in the instigation and development of a number of initiatives in the promotion of engineering and technology to women, and the provision of entrepreneurship education. Through the evaluation of these initiatives, we examine how more females may be encouraged to choose engineering and technology education, and ultimately pursue self-employment as one of the career options available to them. The following sections provide a more detailed insight into the delivery and implementation of these initiatives.

Educational initiatives for engineering and technology

A number of initiatives exist internationally which attempt to improve the choices available to young women. However, it is not simply a case of requiring all women to take engineering and technology options; one cannot force 'square pegs' into 'round holes'. Rather, what is required is that young women are given choices and can make those choices freely. Organisations, such as Women in Technology and Science (WITS) in Ireland; Women in Science and Engineering (WISE) in the UK; the Women's Chapter within the Institute of Electrical and Electronic Engineers; the International Network of Women Engineers and Scientists, and the British Computer Society's (BCS) women's group, which provide networks and support for women already in science, engineering and technology, and also, as part of their mandate, promote the field to young women. Initiatives in these organisations take place both nationally and internationally, with, for example, 'Role Model Days', mentoring systems (such as MentorLink), the provision of five National Science and Education Research Council/Petro-Canada Chairs to Women in Science and Engineering in Canada, residential schools offered for women, science road shows, such as those offered by WISE, and education and training courses run especially for women, such as the Foundation Course in Science, Engineering and Technology offered by the University of Limerick and funded by the National Development Plan. This chapter details three examples of such initiatives which have been recently held in Ireland: Role Model Days, a Technical Foundation Course specifically designed for women, and an Interdisciplinary Entrepreneurship Education Module.

Example 1: Role Model Days

Acknowledging that second-level female students do not pursue careers in science and technology, WITS instigated Role Model Days. Such days provide transition fifth and sixth year female students with an opportunity to meet working women scientists, technologists and engineers. These women are not expected to be 'over-achievers'; rather, they demonstrate 'normality' to the young women in attendance (Kavanagh and Richardson, 1997).

Major influencers for students making career and subject choices are peers, parents, teachers and role models, not necessarily in that order. Research has shown that many girls considering scientific, technological or engineering careers can be put off by people who are just not familiar with current careers and hold stereotyped views, perhaps of an engineer in oily overalls, with filthy hands who, of course, is male – the 'mad scientist' of Hollywood fame. Thus, a lack of suitable role models has been identified as one of the main reasons why female students do not pursue careers in science and technology (Murphy, 1996). In a study of Irish women in management, 47 per cent of respondents quoted lack of female role models as a reason for the failure of women to break into managerial ranks (McGann, 1996). Similarly, in 1990, a study sponsored by the American Association of University Women concluded that one of the major problems with attracting and keeping women and minorities in computer science is the lack of role models at all levels, particularly senior levels (Pfleeger and Mertz, 1995). During a study compiled with fifty members of WITS in Ireland by Allan (1995), 88 per cent of those interviewed identified the need for inter-action between schoolgirls and people working in science and technology careers. These studies indicate the importance of role models to schoolgirls when making their career choices. This is consistent with findings of research previously referred to by Goodbody Economic Consultants (2002), who found that the lack of role models was a barrier to the encouragement of female entrepreneurs.

At one of the Role Model Days, the 126 attendees were asked to complete a questionnaire before they left. Overall, the comments were very positive, with 87 per cent of respondents saying that they would recommend the day to others. This also resulted in requests for more information on particular careers and courses, as well as requests to visit schools. Students found that the role models were supportive and encouraging, providing them with a recognition that what they would have perceived as 'male' careers are indeed available to them as young women.

At a follow-up feedback session held with fourteen students (9 per cent of attendance at the Role Model Day) specific outcomes were discussed. Since the Role Model Day, these students were required to make subject choices, or even make college choices within the three months that followed. Seven (50 per cent) of the students had since requested information from other sources, either about or similar to those careers discussed on the day. Three students changed the careers that they were originally considering to science or techno-logy options. Examining why students have decided to pursue a particular career, be it in science, technology or otherwise, the role models were found to have directly influenced nine (64 per cent) of the students. Although a small sample, this figure supports the rationale for students to meet with women who have pursued careers in the non-traditional areas, as indeed has been emphas-ised by other researchers (see, for example, Trauth *et al.*, 2004). Unless we pursue activities of this nature, we will not influence younger women to embark on engineering and technology careers. This ultimately will have a negative effect on the numbers of women entering high-technology entrepre-neurial careers.

Example 2: Technical Foundation Course in Science, Engineering and Technology for women

The Certificate in Foundation Studies in Science, Engineering and Technology for women is a joint initiative run by two third-level institutions – the University of Limerick and Limerick Institute of Technology. This course was originally run during the academic year 1999/2000 and, due to its success and the funding received from the Irish Government's National Development plan, is now in its fifth year. This initiative in third-level access was targeted at women aged twenty-two and over who were unable to avail of third-level education through the traditional routes for a variety of reasons. Provision of a third-level foundation course is central to the strategy for improving access to third-level education for the targeted group, and students who successfully complete this course are able to progress through the Certificate, Diploma or Degree route into courses in either of the two third-level institutions involved. The Foundation course was designed and developed by an *ad hoc* working group, consisting of four women and one man, drawn from key departments in both institutions. The aims of the course are to:

- introduce female students to a third-level environment;
- equip them with requisite knowledge for moving into third-level education;
- equip them with skills which help to further their knowledge;
- build up their confidence in their ability;
- expose the female students to the basics of science and technology.

Upon completion, students were expected to be confident about progressing directly into one of the institutions in order to embark on a longer-term course. Since the course began, forty-five women have successfully completed it, with a dropout rate of 10 per cent from the initial enrolment numbers. The number progressing to third-level mainstream education justified the running of the Foundation course. During this time, approximately 60 per cent of students have commenced studies within third-level institutions, and a further 30 per cent have commenced either full-time or part-time employment.

Based on the progress of the students who have completed the course, the following issues have emerged.

- It is important for students to be able to attend the course on campus, particularly in light of the aim of students to continue into third-level education.
- Further research into the effectiveness of this, and other similar programmes, is needed.
- The level of computing skills among the participants can be disparate.
- Science, computing and engineering facilities in the third-level institutes (particularly for science) are inadequate. However, the logistical difficulties in utilising an additional location (i.e. involving a third partner institution) need to be considered.

Notwithstanding the above, the following outcomes were noted:

- the spirit within the class and the feedback from the students was very positive and encouraging;
- as a joint venture between two institutes, it was highly successful;
- on a personal level, staff in the two institutions enjoyed the opportunity for
collaboration.

As stated by one of the external examiners involved in the programme, this was
'a very worthwhile course which seems to have been well received by the students'. Some of the students have gone on to related further studies, thus indicating the overall success of the course.

Example 3: Interdisciplinary Entrepreneurship Education Module

Education (in its broadest sense) should stimulate enterprising behaviour, as it
provides individuals with a sense of autonomy, independence and self-
confidence (Garavan and Ó Cinnéide, 1994). These qualities are particularly
important when starting a business (Deakins and Freel, 2003). Education broad-
ens the horizons of individuals, thereby making the student better equipped to
perceive opportunities in the environment around them. Education should make
people aware of alternative career choices, one such alternative being self-
employment. Findings reported in GEM (2004) suggested that the Irish educational system did not have a developed or focused strategy to expose students
sufficiently to entrepreneurship as a career alternative.

Entrepreneurship education should also adopt an integrated approach and
make enterprise courses available across disciplines (Hynes, 1996; Fleming,
1999). This interdisciplinary approach encourages the use of interdisciplinary
student teams comprising of non-business and business studies students working
together. This interaction provides students with a very 'real life' experience,
and enhances not just knowledge acquisition, but also skills development in the
areas of communication, negotiation and conflict management, as well as in
project and people management. Furthermore, entrepreneurship education is
process driven, and the process needs to consider three central players – the
students, teachers (trainers) and the business community (Hynes, 1996; Daly,
2004).

Entrepreneurship education programmes at the University of Limerick have
been designed with a number of objectives in mind, focusing not just on knowledge accumulation but on skills acquisition, increasing awareness of alternative
career options, enhancing personal and professional skills and competency base
and, more specifically, providing the students with the knowledge and
experience of the entrepreneurial process through the generation of a new business idea and the completion of a business plan. Linkages between students,
teachers and business ensure programmes are balanced between theory and
practice.

Integrating entrepreneurship and technology

The aim of entrepreneurship education at the University of Limerick is to produce graduates who are capable of being innovative, who can recognise and create opportunities, take risks, make decisions, analyse and solve problems and communicate clearly and effectively. It provides students with an insight into the role of the entrepreneur and the entrepreneurial process, and induces enterprising behaviour. It also attempts to focus students' business vision to think strategically and to generate and manage business opportunities.

The university's entrepreneurship programme is inter-collegiate and university-wide, and includes not only courses in business, but also those in engineering, science, information technology and humanities at undergraduate and postgraduate levels. The following is an example of how this integrated and inter-collegiate approach is practised to encourage more entrepreneurial activity, with particular emphasis on encouraging more enterprising behaviour in female students without isolating them from their male counterparts in the science and engineering fields.

Enterprise formation and product design and development

This programme adopts an integrated approach to learning and incorporates objectives for knowledge, skills and attribute learning. Emphasis is placed on not just learning the 'what' but also the 'how'. The primary objectives of the module are:

*   to develop in students the knowledge and skills to create a more rounded graduate who is more equipped for the changing world of work (i.e. through developing core skills such as creativity, critical thinking, analytical skills, problem solving, communication and teamwork skills);
*   to provide students with an insight into enterprise and entrepreneurial activity, as it applies to the workplace or as a means of self-employment;
*   to provide students with experience of working in an interdisciplinary team, reflective of the 'real' world of work;
*   to facilitate students in the identification of a business idea and in the development of a business plan.

Module delivery methods

As the emphasis of the programme is on learning 'how' as well as 'what', it is important that the delivery methods are appropriate and allow for subsequent monitoring and evaluation. Therefore, the role of the trainer/lecturer is that of a facilitator who encourages interaction between the students and the lecturers, and between students themselves, through the development of an informal learning environment. Delivery methods encourage action learning where students are actively involved in group work, role playing exercises, presentations, report writing and analysis of case studies.

A series of lectures provide the students with the necessary fundamental theory and knowledge underpinning and directing the various stages of the process of developing and researching their potential business idea. The lectures are supported by web-based notes, and by other relevant information sources, such as websites, etc. which provide the student with extra information on the various topics, if required.

A core element of the module is the development of a business plan, which students work on in teams. Workshops are key in the delivery process to identify and accommodate the more specific needs of the various students. The workshops provide each team with feedback on progress, identify milestones for the development of the business plan and provide contacts to relevant external organisations.

An important and novel element of the delivery is the team teaching concept, where the engineering faculty is involved in assisting the business faculty in the workshop sessions. This team teaching ensures that the students have access to both the business and technical experience and expertise necessary to realistically develop their business plan. This sort of interdisciplinary team teaching is somewhat unique within the sector, and something entirely new, both for faculty and students.

Assessment/examination of module

Due to the multiple objectives driving the module, the various delivery methods employed and the diversity of the participating students, the assessment methods used must be relevant and equitable. In this context, multiple assessment criteria, which are both individual and team-focused, are incorporated. The module is 100 per cent project-based (as opposed to the more traditional exam-based approach), designed around the 'Enterprise Ireland – Student Enterprise Awards' competition (www.enterprise-ireland.com/newsworld). The assessment mechanisms include written and verbal progress reports, a final report, presentation and participation in an exhibition.

To date, feedback from students and faculty has been very positive. For example, student feedback has indicated that they were exposed to new and different teaching and learning methods. Positive indicators as to the level of satisfaction with the programme are evidenced in the following comments:

'It helped me think in a broader way.'
'Improved my team working skills and people skills in general.'
'Provided a greater awareness of what starting a business is about.'
'Improved my knowledge and understanding of the importance of elements such as market research, how to access finance, the role of development agencies.'
'Obtained new knowledge on patents, trademarks and their importance in protecting a new idea.'
'Improved decision-making abilities.'

'Ability to get used to rejection, people saying "no".'
'Encouraged and allowed us to be creative and innovative in how we presented the idea.'
'Taught us valuable lessons on not just selling the product but how we needed to sell ourselves.'

Feedback would suggest that the module provided the relevant theory and knowledge necessary to develop a new business idea, and equally important, facilitated skills enhancement, which in turn facilitates the development of lifelong competencies in the individual.

The module also exposes students to the realities of establishing a new business in a team scenario. In this regard, it takes the 'mystery' out of self-employment by getting students to realise that this can be a realistic employment alternative at some stage of their career cycle.

A framework for supporting high-technology entrepreneurship

Feedback to date suggests that initiatives, such as those described in this chapter provide very important, albeit sometimes intangible learning outcomes. These include personal development, confidence building, self-esteem and skills enhancement. It is considered that these skills are very important in encouraging greater participation among women in both the technology and engineering disciplines, as well as in self-employment in these disciplines.

Through studying the process model of Entrepreneurship Education (Hynes, 1996), it can be seen that engineering and technology initiatives, such as those discussed above, can support entrepreneurship within the high-technology arena. Such initiatives should consider three significant components – inputs, process and output. Adopting such a structure helps to provide a useful template within which such initiatives can be integrated, as illustrated in Table 9.1.

It is important to define the personal profile and personality characteristics of the 'inputs' or students before finally deciding upon the content or teaching focus. It is at this stage that many of the aforementioned obstacles discussed can be accounted for and accommodated in the content, teaching and delivery process. One way of ensuring that such details are collected in advance is to get the students to complete an 'entry questionnaire' at the beginning of the module. This also helps students to determine their own levels of self-awareness and interest in both disciplines.

Students should also have a prior knowledge base, without which they will not focus on the science/engineering/technology industry base. Courses, such as the Foundation Certificate, can help to build up the engineering and technology knowledge base within the female community. Other inputs, such as needs/ interest, can be provided through these courses. The promotion of initiatives such as Role Model Days can influence motivation, attitudes and parental influence. As female participation in engineering and technology is not occurring

Table 9.1 Framework for developing entrepreneurship modules

Inputs	Process		Outputs
Students	*Content focus*	*Teaching focus*	*Outputs*
Prior knowledge base	Entrepreneurship	Didactic	Personal (confidence
Motivation	defined	(reading/lectures)	communication)
Personality	Intrapreneurship	Skill building	Knowledge
Needs/interests	Innovation	(case studies,	(enterprise, initiative,
Independence	New product	group	self-employment,
Attitudes	development	discussions,	business,
Parent influence	Idea generation	presentations,	management and
Self-esteem	Market research	problem solving,	market skills,
Values	Feasibility of idea	simulations,	analytical, problem
Work experience	Finance	teamwork,	solving, decision
	Production	projects)	making,
	Regulations	Discovery	communication,
	People management	(brainstorming,	presentation, risk-
	Teamwork	personal	taking)
	Business	goalsetting,	Career (improved
	Marketing	career planning,	knowledge, broader
	Management	consultancy)	career options,
			broader less
			structured career
			perspectives)

Source: (Hynes, 1996).

'naturally', a focus must be maintained on the promotion of these disciplines to women through such initiatives; otherwise, there will never be significant female participation in high-technology entrepreneurship.

The content focus provides students with an understanding of the stages of the entrepreneurial process. Other 'content focus' topics, such as people management, teamwork, business, marketing and management, are often not associated with the study of engineering and technology. The provision of these elements within entrepreneurship modules serve to add value to the skills base to encourage more enterprising behaviour.

The teaching process aspect is also critical, particularly in ensuring that identified skills and knowledge objectives are achieved. In this regard, the teaching focus should also take into consideration the obstacles that militate against female participation in engineering, technology and entrepreneurship. Therefore, the focus should combine both formal and informal teaching methods, encouraging topics such as problem solving and career planning. The teaching focus should also provide students with the knowledge of not just 'what' to do but 'how' to do it.

The combination of content and teaching elements provides students with an understanding of the stages of the entrepreneurial process. Furthermore, the completion of a business plan in an interdisciplinary team also provides the student with a practical and realistic insight into how self-employment in the engineering and technology fields can, at some stage, be a career option for them.

Given that the initiatives discussed in the chapter all focus on inputs, content and teaching, we expect that a combination of such initiatives would give the desired outputs. Therefore, we consider that the integration and linking of these types of programmes will result in key initiatives, where the inputs can be provided through the effects of engineering and technology initiatives, and the content and teaching focus through entrepreneurship education. This, in turn, should provide female graduates with the relevant personal knowledge, and indeed, career aspirations, thus facilitating them to become high-technology entrepreneurs.

Policy issues

Whether initiatives promoting engineering and technology are effective is difficult to ascertain. For example, we can quantify success at one level by looking at the individuals who have entered technological careers having been influenced by particular initiatives. We can even point to these individual successes. However, a second level of determining success is to consider the statistics. Indeed, when examining figures over the past six years, we do not seem to be showing significant improvement in Ireland. Therefore, the question must be asked, would these figures be much lower in the absence of the types of initiatives previously discussed? In promoting these disciplines, we must continue to include a research element. The involvement of social science researchers to carry out analysis of the effects of these initiatives is imperative. Other questions need to be asked, including: why do people participate? Is there a wider effect, such as peer-support, that we do not recognise? How can such programmes be improved? In the past, funding has been mainly used to implement programmes and initiatives rather than to measure their effectiveness. However, recently funded initiatives include a requirement for such measurement.

Notwithstanding the above, a difficulty that often arises is that many of these initiatives are run on a voluntary or semi-voluntary basis. Indeed, the authors are not aware of any scheme, other than the Chairs for Women in Science and Engineering in Canada, where this is not the case. Many women currently employed in the engineering and technology educational or industry sectors get involved in such initiatives, often in addition to their career and family duties, because they recognise the importance of presenting choices to female students that they may not otherwise consider. It is interesting to note that there have been some recent changes, particularly in the computing discipline, which ensure that more women are becoming involved at a technical level. Computing is becoming more interdisciplinary, and backgrounds that are being sought include languages, as well as music and art. These have traditionally been areas associated with women, and they are now experiencing increasing numbers of women becoming involved in computing through their involvement in these disciplines. Perhaps there are other sub-disciplines within engineering and technology which will help to increase this effect.

The promotion of engineering and technology initiatives should continue if there is to be a growth in the number of women participating in these sectors and, indeed, the continued government funding for these and other initiatives supports this argument. While the same type of programme can be applicable and relevant to both genders on a generic basis, the promotion of female entrepreneurship in engineering and technology sectors requires some level of customisation to cater for the more specific attitudinal and confidence issues which tend to be more prevalent with females students. We suggest, therefore, that programmes to foster female engineering and technology entrepreneurship can be adopted to suit most school curricula and can have positive benefits for each of the sectors.

The above should also help to reverse the fact that much of Ireland's female population are turning their backs on engineering and technology, on entrepreneurship and, consequently, on high-technology entrepreneurship. Ireland's economic change over the past decade has meant that we are faced with an increased demand and a shortage of skills in the technology and engineering sectors. Indeed, Ireland's overall level of entrepreneurial activity in the establishment of new enterprises has decreased during the early 2000s, and this prompts questions such as: are women losing out? Is society losing out? Is our economy losing out?

In addition, to ensure a competitive business environment the shortages in both of these areas need to be rectified in the short term. The economy needs a supply of skilled graduates and successful growth-potential business. Since both areas display a low level of female participation, it suggests an area for potential development. As has been discussed, a number of fundamental practical barriers exist that militate against females entering these disciplines. Many of the barriers centre around personal and social conditioning. Any corrective interventions need to focus on the source of the perceived barriers. The authors consider education as a primary mechanism that can influence, either positively or negatively, the choice made by females to enter the technology and engineering sectors and/or self-employment.

Conclusions

This chapter has sought to further the ongoing debate surrounding the issues and barriers associated with female entrepreneurship in the high-technology sector. It has also discussed how the promotion of engineering and technology educational initiatives can support the development of high-technology female entrepreneurship. The chapter presented a number of suitable interventions that cater for both entrepreneurship and technical disciplines, and these can and should be further developed. Through our examination of these initiatives, we considered some of the key priority issues which need to be addressed in any future entrepreneurship programme so that the barriers that militate against females participating in engineering and technology entrepreneurial activity can be reduced. The development of such initiatives should have broad application; should assist in reversing negative trends, as identified, for example, by Fitzsimons *et al.* (2003) and, finally, should ultimately contribute to the pool of Irish female entrepreneurs willing to and capable of starting high-technology companies.

Note

1 The Central Applications Office (CAO) is the office to which higher education institutions in the Republic of Ireland have delegated the task of centrally processing applications to their first year undergraduate courses (see, www.cao.ie).

References

Allan, J. (1995). Presented at *Forfas STI Awareness Campaign*, Dublin City University, Dublin, Ireland.

Berg, V.L. (2003). 'Getting More Women into Computer Science and Engineering, SIGIS, Strategies of Inclusion: Gender and the Information Society'. Supported by the European Commission Information Society Technology (IST) Programme.

CSO (2005). Central Statistics Office, Dublin, Ireland, available: www.cso.ie.

Daly, S. (2004). 'Entrepreneurship Education at Postgraduate Level in Ireland'. MBS thesis (unpublished) University of Limerick.

Deakins, D. and Freel, M. (2003). *Entrepreneurship and Small Firms*, London, McGraw Hill Education, Chapter 1.

European Commission (2003). 'Women and Science, Statistics and Indicators: She Figures 2003'. Community Research, Science and Society, Luxembourg: Office for Official Publications of the European Communities.

Fitzsimons, P., O'Gorman, C. and Roche, F. (2003). 'The Global Entrepreneurship Monitor, The Irish Report – How Entrepreneurial is Ireland?' UCD Business School, Dublin, Ireland.

Fleming, P. (1999). 'Developing Graduate Entrepreneurs. An Analysis of Entrepreneurship Education Programme in Ireland'. University of Limerick, PhD Thesis, unpublished.

Florida, R. (2002). *The Rise of the Creative Class*, New York, Basic Books.

Forfás (2003). 'Strategy to Maximise the Potential Contribution of Women in the Science, Engineering and Technology Sectors', Paper submitted to the Department of Enterprise, Trade and Employment, October, 2003, Ireland.

Forfás (2005). 'Business Expenditure on Research and Development (BERD) Ireland, 2003/2004'. Science and Technology Indicators Unit, April 2005, Ireland.

Garavan, T. and Ó Cinnéide, B. (1994). 'Entrepreneurship Education and Training Programmes – A Review and Evaluation, Part 1'. *Journal of European Industrial Training*, 18, 8.

GEM (2004). 'How Entrepreneurial was Ireland in 2004?' The Irish Annual Report, Enterprise Ireland, Dublin, Ireland. Available: www.gemconsortium.org.

Goodbody Economic Consultants (2002).'Entrepreneurship in Ireland', Dublin, Ireland.

Henry, C. and Johnston, K. (2003). 'State of the Art of Women's Entrepreneurship in Ireland: Access to Financing and Financing Strategies'. Centre for Entrepreneurship Research, Dundalk Institute of Technology, Ireland.

Hynes, B. (1996). 'Entrepreneurship Education and Training – Introducing Entrepreneurship into Non-Business Disciplines'. *Journal of European Industrial Training*, 20, 8.

Kavanagh, I. and Richardson, I. (1997). 'Positive Action: Promoting Technology and Science through Female Role Models'. Proceedings of Women into Computing Conference, Progression: From Where to What, De Montfort University, 10–12 July, Milton-Keynes, 173–180.

Klawe, M. and Levenson, N. (1995). 'Women in Computing: Where are We Now?' *Communications of the ACM*, 38, 1, 29–35.

Limerick City Enterprise Board (2003). 'Captains of Enterprise – An Entrepreneurship Education Programme for Female Students'. Unpublished Report, Limerick, Ireland.

McDonagh, S. and Patterson, V. (2002). 'The Expert Group on Future Skills Needs'. SkillsNet, Deptartment of Education and Science, Dublin.

McGann, K. (1996). 'Irish Women Who have Broken Through the Glass Ceiling in Business'. MBS Thesis, Michael Smurfit Graduate School of Business, University College, Dublin.

Murphy, C. (1996). 'Limiting Choice – The Least Productive Course'. *Irish Times*, 9 January.

National Development Plan (2000). 'Women and Men in Ireland as Entrepreneurs and Business Managers'. Gender Equality Unit, Department of Justice, Equality and Law Reform, Dublin, Ireland.

O'Dubhchair, K. and Hunter, N. (1995). 'Gender Issues in Computing'. In Proceedings of Third Annual Conference on the Teaching of Computing, Dublin, 244–249.

Observatory of European SMEs (2003) 'SMEs in Focus – Results from the 2002 Survey'. European Commission Enterprise Publications.

OECD (2000). 'Small and Medium-sized Enterprises: Local Strengths, Global Reach Policy Brief'. Available: www.oecd.org/.

Pearl, A. (1995). 'Introduction to Women in Computing'. *Communications of the ACM*, 38, 1, 26–28.

Pfleeger, S.L. and Mertz, N. (1995). 'Executive Mentoring What Makes it Work?' *Communications of the ACM*, 38, 1, 63–73.

Richardson, I., O'Brien, M. and Moore, P.A. (2002). 'Foundation Course in Science, Engineering and Technology for Women'. ICWES12, 12th International Conference on Women in Engineering and Science, Women in a Knowledge-Based Society, Ottawa, Canada, 27–30 July, Reference No. 71 (published on CD-rom).

Smith, E. (2002). 'Women Look to Shape the Future'. *Technology*, 25 July.

Trauth, E.M. (2002). 'Odd Girl Out: An Individual Differences Perspective on Women in the IT Profession'. *Information Technology and People*, 15, 2, 98–118.

Trauth, E.M., Quesenberry, J.L. and Morgan, A.J. (2004). 'Understanding the Underrepresentation of Women in IT: Toward a Theory of Individual Differences'. Proceedings of the ACM SIGMIS Computer Personnel Research Conference, Tucson, Arizona, U.S.A.

University of Limerick (1999–2004). *Graduation Booklets*, Limerick, Ireland.

WITS (2004). 'Women in Technology and Science'. Available: www.witsireland.com/talentbankbackground.html (accessed May 2006).

For an international perspective see Proceedings of ICWES12, 12th International Conference on Women in Engineering and Science, Women in a Knowledge-Based Society, Ottawa, Canada, 27–30 July (published on CD-rom).

For an insight into National Development Plan funding 2000–2006, see Annual Reports, Equality for Women Measure, Government of Ireland.

10 Identifying good practice in the promotion of female entrepreneurship

Petra Puechner and Christine Diegelmann

Introduction

The number of women who are self-employed across the European Union is significantly lower than that of men, and the number of women entrepreneurs with employees is lower still. In 2000, only 8 per cent of the total number of women in work were self-employed. The comparable figure for men was around 16 per cent. However, there is increasing evidence that more and more women are becoming interested in starting a business (Franco and Winqvist, 2002). The Global Entrepreneurship Monitor (GEM; Minitti *et al.*, 2004) states, that 'There are almost twice as many men who are active entrepreneurs than women' (Minitti, 2005). Due to a strong correlation between the emancipation and working conditions of women and the well-being of a country, GEM released a special report dedicated to women and entrepreneurship in March 2005 (Minitti *et al.*, 2005).

In innovative sectors, women entrepreneurs face the same barriers as women working in other areas. The advantages of education and experience do not totally compensate for the disadvantages they have to face because of their gender. Women lack the support and role model effect of other women, and typically need to develop business credibility on their own. The single entrepreneur style favoured by women is the antithesis of the teams required by university and commercial science. There are fewer women in innovative sectors, but this is less related to personal characteristics and abilities, and more related to structural and experiential factors (Carter, 2003).

In 2001, a European network called ProWomEn – Promotion of Female Entrepreneurship – was established with the support of the European Commission (DG Enterprise) in the framework of its Innovation Programme. The network involves sixteen European regions and is coordinated by the Ministry of Economic Affairs, Baden-Württemberg and Steinbeis-Europa-Zentrum. Its remit was to identify good practice in the promotion of female start-ups, to establish innovative support schemes and to generate ideas for new support models. The member regions include those that have already implemented structures to promote female entrepreneurship, as well as regions without such experience, but where encouraging female entrepreneurship is recognised as a need. Besides the German States of Baden-Württemberg, North Rhine Westphalia and Thuringia, regions from the Czech Republic, Belgium, England, France, Hungary, Italy, Ireland, Poland, Spain and Sweden have contributed to the ProWomEn initiative. Among the members are organisations for economic development and technology transfer, as well as four universities (Linköping University, Polytechnical University of Barcelona, Czech Technical University Prague and Dundalk Institute of Technology).

By way of recognising the need to identify good practices in the promotion of female entrepreneurship internationally, this chapter reports on a study conducted by the ProWomEn network between 2001 and 2004. The chapter begins by explaining the key objectives of the project and outlines the various thematic areas upon which the project focused. This is followed by an explanation of the methodology adopted by the ProWomEn team for the study. The findings of this international study are then presented, highlighting a range of examples of good practice in the promotion of female entrepreneurship across a number of different regions and countries. Following a discussion of the findings, some conclusions are drawn and areas in need of further research are identified.

Objectives and focus of the ProWomEn initiative

The key objective of the ProWomEn initiative is essentially the promotion of women entrepreneurs. This in itself is quite a broad area and can include a number of different themes, ranging from educational systems which serve to develop self-confidence in young girls, through to child care responsibilities for working women. Among the range of possible themes to be investigated, ProWomEn focused on the following for their research:

- *Problem awareness.* This thematic area seeks to determine the differences that exist between men and women entrepreneurs. Questions in this regard include how to sensitise support organisations to women-specific approaches, and how to encourage women to consider self-employment in their private and professional decisions. The general opinion among some policy makers has been that women entrepreneurs face the same challenges as men; therefore, there is no need for specific support structures. The objective of the ProWomEn network was to challenge this general opinion and deliver arguments which would create awareness of the specific problems women face when starting a business.
- *Instruments of support.* This thematic area considered the particular support women entrepreneurs need to consider self-employment. In this regard, the research sought to address questions such as how to respect gender-related differences in entrepreneurship support, and how to engender mainstream support schemes. There are many different support systems for starting a business already in place; however, women do not seem to use these systems to the same degree as their male counterparts. A key question to be

addressed here was how to design enterprise support systems that are effective in reaching women.

- *Regional networks.* This thematic area concentrated on the benefits of networking. For example, how can female-led start-ups and established women entrepreneurs network effectively? How can they best network with intermediary organisations? Typically, women entrepreneurs do not have the same support networks as men. Whether this is due to the non-existence of networks or is due to the nature of the network organisation and services offered, is also a question for investigation.
- *Education and training.* Within this thematic area, the issue of how to accommodate gender-related aspects within entrepreneurship education was considered. The issues examined included determining how education might help to reduce the gender-related difficulties encountered in entrepreneurship. The education market offers several courses on entrepreneurship which are not typically availed of by women. ProWomEn decided to investigate the appropriateness of different education structures and tools so that women might be better trained for a career in entrepreneurship.

Methodology

Employing a methodology specially designed for the ProWomEn project, the network members identified critical success factors and selected good practice examples. As indicated in Figure 10.1, the starting point of the project was a detailed survey on the general state of female entrepreneurship in the participating regions by means of a series of questionnaires. Each of the four thematic areas discussed above were investigated in a separate questionnaire, as follows.

- Questionnaire 1 dealt with the theme of 'problem awareness' and sought mainly statistical data, for example, the percentage of women starting a business in each of the participating countries, the number of women receiving bank loans, women's participation levels on entrepreneurship courses, etc. In addition, information on existing studies and details of any promotional campaigns in each of the countries to raise awareness about women's entrepreneurship was also sought.
- Questionnaire 2 dealt with 'instruments of support' and sought information pertaining to the general role of female entrepreneurship in regional policy, details of existing support measures for entrepreneurship in general and

Figure 10.1 ProWomEn learning process.

female entrepreneurs (target groups, success rates, etc), and financial support structures for female entrepreneurs.

- Questionnaire 3 addressed the theme of 'regional networking', and sought details of existing networks for female entrepreneurs in each of the regions (including the nature of the networks, i.e. whether there were 'real' or virtual network meetings), target groups, geographical coverage, coordination and cooperation structures/services and the success levels of the networks.
- Questionnaire 4 focused on 'education and training initiatives', and sought details on the role of entrepreneurship in education and training structures in the region (at university, in schools, in training programmes and existing strategies and models for entrepreneurship education (including the specific target groups, tools used, etc.)).

Each of the questionnaires were sent to all member regions and completed by the network partners. The results of the fifteen member regions were summarised in a database. Additional desk research using the Internet supplemented the information collected via the questionnaires.

The next step, as illustrated in Figure 10.1, identified the critical success factors for the four key themes. Critical success factors in this context are seen as a small number of topics that are influential in determining the positive outcome of an activity. The critical success factors should, on the one hand, meet the requirements of tried and tested scientific methods and, on the other hand, be flexible enough to respect individual regional or personal aspects. Therefore, a two-step approach to identify critical success factors was chosen. Assisted by creativity methods, the network members looked for factors which appeared important to them, both personally and with regard to their regional framework conditions. The success factors identified were then evaluated against standard project evaluation criteria used by the European Commission (1997). These criteria are intended for use on a post and intermediate evaluation basis, and focus on relevance, effectiveness, efficiency, utility or sustainability. By means of this two-step procedure, regional peculiarities and supra-regional aspects could equally be considered.

For each of the four thematic areas, up to fourteen critical success factors were identified. These were prioritised and the three to four most critical factors were selected (see Table 10.1). To identify good practice the data collection was

Table 10.1 Important critical success factors

Problem awareness	Instruments of support	Regional networks	Education and training
Communication/ visibility	Flexibility	Publicity	Meets the needs
Shows realistic role models	Supports different phases of the enterprise	Defined target group	For different phases of the enterprise
Involves partners	Practical approach	Defined organisational	Involves women
	Involves experts	structure	entrepreneurs

screened according to the critical success factors determined above. All examples that met at least half of the critical success factors were considered as 'good practice'. This exercise resulted in a database of eighty examples of good practice, covering all four thematic areas.

Examples of international good practice

Out of the eighty examples of good practice identified by the research, the network members were asked to select those practices which would best meet their regional needs. It was clear that this decision depended on the particular organisation's operational framework, as well as the local conditions and economic/political objectives in the region. For instance, support organisations having to achieve certain objectives within a given budget, might have a different opinion on this question than decision makers who seek an activity that creates strong publicity. In this regard, through open discussions and group analysis, the ProWomEn members jointly selected three to four examples for each of the thematic areas (see Table 10.2).

Problem awareness

The types of barriers and problems women face when starting their own business do not appear to differ too much from country to country; however, their intensity varies from region to region. In general, two types of problem can be identified: those that prevent women from starting a business and those that arise during the actual start-up process. For example, the lack of role models, difficulties in balancing family and work commitments, or economic problems in the particular business sectors are all valid reasons why women do not start their own business. Those who take the chance often have to face new problems, such as the absence of business networks, male dominated support systems or even real discrimination. While long-term solutions need to be embedded within the educational system, there are several short-term solutions which could be

Table 10.2 Selected examples of good practice

Problem awareness	Instruments of support	Regional networks	Education and training
Campaign of information days (D)	Support of information and qualification (S, D)	Network for intermediaries (D)	Modular qualification schemes (D, B, E)
Information service for women entrepreneurs (D)	Micro-financing and alternative financing (UK, S, PL, E, D)	Virtual networks (D, E)	Mentoring (D)
Exhibition on women entrepreneurs (S) Awards (PL, IRL, B)	'Women Resource Centres' (S)	Networks for women entrepreneurs (UK)	School projects (country specific)

adopted. For example, role models who portray a realistic picture of female entrepreneurship can effectively encourage women to take the option of being self-employed. A campaign of information days, similar to those in Baden-Württemberg, awards and competitions such as those in Ireland and Poland, or a Swedish exhibition on women entrepreneurs, are practical examples of how female entrepreneurship can be made more visible. Each of these examples is discussed in more detail below.

Good practice example: information days for women entrepreneurs, Germany

The campaign of information days for women entrepreneurs was part of a start-up initiative of the State Government of Baden-Württemberg, in Germany. At that time (1995), a distinct spirit of entrepreneurship and extensive entrepreneurship support was lacking in Baden-Württemberg. Awareness of the specific situation of women entrepreneurs was almost non-existent, and only a few general support programmes and information services were available. Women were not equally represented among business start-ups, and indeed many Chambers of Commerce and Business Associations initially refused to approach this target group differently, if at all.

Thus, part of the initiative was to conduct a campaign of information days for women entrepreneurs, with the aim of raising awareness among potential support organisations and, at the same time, informing potential female business founders about the start-up process, funding and other available support services. Landesgewerbeamt Baden-Württemberg (Office for the Promotion of Trade and Industry) – a public body supporting small and medium sized enterprises and directly subordinated to the regional Ministry of Economic Affairs – with its department *ifex* (initiative for start-ups and business transfer) was in charge of implementing the actions of the initiative and reaching the targets set.

The objectives of this information day campaign for women entrepreneurs included:

- *To provide information.* An information day designed to give aspiring and established women entrepreneurs a general idea about the start-up process and the thematic issues linked to it. Support organisations present their support mechanisms through talks and information stands.
- *To offer role models.* Women entrepreneurs from several sectors and with different biographical backgrounds talk about their experiences during keynote speeches and panel discussions.
- *To raise awareness among decision makers and experts.* By critically discussing the specifics of female entrepreneurship in a team setting and jointly organising the information day, regional decision makers and entrepreneurship experts become aware of the particular gender aspects in entrepreneurship, and the fact that women entrepreneurs require specific support.

- *To raise awareness among women* to think about entrepreneurship as a job opportunity.
- *To support regional economic development* by setting up activities for women entrepreneurs.
- *To obtain media coverage.* A series of forty information days for women entrepreneurs held between 1995 and 2000 ensured a permanent communication with the media. By involving high rank politicians and women entrepreneurs, the media were encouraged to report about the events.

The information days' programme was designed to reach all women, especially women entrepreneurs, as well as key decision makers in regional development agencies, politicians, experts in entrepreneurship support, intermediary organisations and, of course, the media. The idea was to enable regional institutions to organise information days to promote female entrepreneurship, while at the same time educating regional players on the specific situation of women entrepreneurs.

Example of the agenda for the information days:

- *Formal opening and welcome.* Speeches by high rank politicians in order to outline the importance of the event (e.g. regional Ministers and local politicians).
- *Key note speech* on the specifics of female entrepreneurship (e.g. a researcher who has gained interesting insights in this field).
- *Workshops* on the most important thematic issues of business start-up for women (e.g. 'how to start a business', financing, marketing, 'how to handle the dual role').
- *Lunch and networking.* Time to view the exhibitions of support institutions and network with other women.
- *Panel session and discussion* with regional women entrepreneurs in order to showcase different role models.

On average, *ifex* initiated fifteen information days per year all over Baden-Württemberg, a region of 35.8 square kilometres with ten million inhabitants. This required a full-time project manager to plan, carry out and control the entire campaign. *Ifex* started its series of information days with two initial events in Stuttgart and Karlsruhe, the two major cities in the region.

The most important resources in Baden-Württemberg proved to be the personnel costs for the campaign's project manager at *ifex* and the in-kind resources delivered by regional partners. Due to the extensive use of in-kind resources, such as rooms, personnel or mailing actions from stakeholder organisations, the amount that subsequently had to be paid in cash could be kept down to about 20 per cent of all costs (see www.ifex.de for further information).

Instruments of support

In the long term, successful support programmes must pursue the objective of equal opportunities for both women and men, as well as promoting a culture of female entrepreneurship. Women's resource centres at local level, national competence centres, agencies for female entrepreneurship, purposeful public relations and projects in schools can all contribute to achieving these goals. However, in the short to medium term, women still need individual help when translating their plans into action, i.e. when financing their projects or accessing networks. Examples like the Swedish Women's Resource Centre, or microfinancing programmes for women entrepreneurs in England and Spain can act as good practice just as the 'Women Entrepreneurs' meetings existing in various regions of Baden-Württemberg.

Good practice example: Women's Resource Centres, Sweden

Sweden has a strong political movement in supporting women, especially in rural and less developed areas, where the work of organisations such as the Rural Women's Association served to highlight the fact that women were not treated equally and, thus, were not offered the sort of chances and opportunities often offered to men. As a result of their work, several governmental initiatives on female entrepreneurship support were introduced in the early 1990s. In 1992, NUTEK – the Swedish Business Development Agency – received an assignment from the government to map out obstacles and opportunities faced by female entrepreneurs in sparsely inhabited areas. This was an area never explored before, and at that time, society's understanding of women as entrepreneurs was limited. Ninety women entrepreneurs were interviewed, and the findings from these interviews resulted in twenty proposals being put forward to the Government. The most vital information gained from the interviews was that women who think about starting a business prefer female advisors. Thus, the Government asked NUTEK to make sure that business consultants for women were hired in sixty-two municipalities all over Sweden. The municipalities set up their own programmes to achieve this. One example of a very successful programme was the Business Advisors for Women initiative, which was set up in Dalarna between 1994 and 1996. The female advisors were part of their municipality and formed a critical network, keeping in touch through electronic means and county-wide meetings. The advisors worked for between one and three days a week for the project. After three years, not only had 176 new companies been started by women but, more importantly, women and their skills had been made more visible, and women's participation on all levels of trade and commerce had increased.

In 1995, the Women's Resource Centres were established by the government through the support of NUTEK. Their objectives were:

• to draw attention to and make female competence more visible in society,
• to increase the number of businesses run by women,

- to influence the situation for women in the regional/municipal labour market,
- to promote integration of gender equality in regional development by creating positive examples and activities in the region,
- to increase women's participation in regional and local development at all levels,
- to specifically increase women's participation in the labour force in less traditional areas such as technology,
- to desegregate the labour market.

The resource centres are targeted at women of all ages and backgrounds (e.g. regardless of ethnic and social status), especially existing women entrepreneurs or women who would simply like to start a business or change their job situation. In 1995, the Swedish national rural development agency (Women in Rural and Agricultural Areas), together with NUTEK, created the Women's Resource Centre Programme. By 1999, 150 Resource Centres were established and financed by governmental and county administrations, with NUTEK being the overall coordinator of the programme. In 1999, the programme became one of NUTEK's core projects with a €1.6 million budget. The project came to an end in 1999, with the political decision to mainstream the work performed within the Resource Centres into the core work of business and regional development. In this unstable and insecure situation, the number of Resource Centres was reduced from 150 to about fifty. Some of the Resource Centres then decided to act independently, starting a National Resource Centre Association (NRC) as a non-profit, non-governmental organisation with elected board members and an elected chairperson. The NRC began actively lobbying for the Resource Centres, and eventually, the government asked them to put forward a proposal for a financing budget. This was implemented at the end of 2001 and the Government decided to deliver an annual financing budget of €1 million, with an additional €2.6 million for Resource Centre projects over a period of three years. Today, Sweden has about 120 Resource Centres in two thirds of its municipalities.

The typical activities of a Resource Centre include:

- provision of information (education and business opportunities),
- support and advice on how to start or develop a business,
- education of women and women entrepreneurs,
- networking and information dissemination at the political and operational levels in the region (e.g. seminars to increase knowledge on gender equality in regional and local sectors),
- networking with technology-based companies to break down the barriers for women,
- business advice (on an individual or group basis),
- offering support with technical resources, such as computers and Internet (mainly in rural areas),
- creating places for women to meet,

- initiating and implementing projects to promote and support female entre-preneurship,
- participating in and cooperating with national and international networks (e.g. WITEC – Women in Science, Engineering and Technology).

Some of the Resource Centres are organised as NGOs, some operate within a municipality and others act as a network connected to a municipality. Twenty of the Resource Centres act regionally and cover more than one municipality. Women Resource Centres usually have at least two people working on a full-time or part-time basis time as business advisors, trainers or 'first contacts' for aspiring women entrepreneurs. The service offered is very much tailored to the local needs, but business advisory services are the easiest to sell and create additional funding for the centre's activities.

On 16 December 2002, the Swedish government officially declared the Resource Centres as being an important partner within regional development and gender equality. Thus, it is expected that Resource Centres will be more actively involved in the strategy and implementation of regional development planning.

The impact of these resource centres is clearly visible. For instance, the Resource Centre in Eskilstuna County, a municipality with 90,000 inhabitants, has been in operation since 1996. In five years, sixty-four training seminars were held with nearly 2,000 women participating. A total of 520 individual business advice meetings were held, resulting in sixty-five jobs being created and fifty new start-ups supported (see www.nrckvinnor.org).

Regional networks

While men have always used their 'old boys network' to initiate business, to generate business contacts and to collect information, women often have reservations about using networks for the benefit of their enterprises. They tend to think that being a network member means permanent active collaboration, and they often underestimate the strategic aspect of networking. However, support organisations have a need for regional and trans-regional networking in order to build up competence and to back up and strengthen their activities. Successful networks need clearly defined objectives, target groups and organisational structures. Visions, strategies and openness for changes are crucial elements of thriving networks. Good examples in this context can be found in some of the UK networks, such as 'WIN' (Women into the Network – see: www.networkingwomen.co.uk), and 'Prowess' (described below), as well as virtual 'Women Entrepreneurs' Portals' in the German states Baden-Württemberg and North Rhine Westphalia (see, for example, www.gruenderinnenagentur.de and www.u-netz.de).

Good practice example: Prowess, the UK

Although a number of organisations have been working for many years to support women's enterprise development in the UK, it is only within recent years that the policy environment has been conducive to a coordinated national approach. In 1999/2000, women's enterprise practitioners and researchers across the UK were brought together for the first time in events organised by the Women's Unit (now the Women and Equality Unit) and the DTI (Department of Trade and Industry). These included consultation meetings around the development of the DTI's Small Business Service (SBS). By sharing knowledge and experience, it became clear that provision of support for the start-up and development of women's businesses was evolving in a patchy and non-strategic manner. The need for a structured network to help share and develop good practice and to promote a coherent web of support structures for women's enterprise within the UK was identified.

The need for an organisation like Prowess, therefore, became increasingly evident, particularly as the UK government had already made a commitment to increasing the numbers of women starting businesses and had acknowledged that a more cohesive strategy was needed at both regional and national level. Wales, Northern Ireland and Scotland were included in this strategy, but the devolved nature of their administrations means that each region is responsible for its own strategic delivery. Prowess has been able to support policy development based on the experience and expertise of its members, and is playing a key role in ensuring that good practice is identified and disseminated nationally.

Prowess can be described as a UK-wide trade association for organisations providing business support to women. It started its activities early in 2002, and is structured as a non-profit making company limited by guarantee. Prowess has seed funding from the UK DTI Phoenix Development Fund and the European Social Fund. It generates income from membership fees and events, and it has also attracted corporate sponsorship. The administration headquarters of the organisation are situated in Norwich in the east of England, but Prowess operates as a virtual company with key personnel located around the country. The Prowess vision is to create an environment where equal numbers of women and men are starting and growing businesses. As an umbrella organisation, Prowess aims to achieve this by promoting and raising awareness of women's enterprise and the organisations that support this key area of economic growth, lobbying on their behalf to create a policy environment and opportunities which support the development of women's enterprise.

The key objectives of Prowess include:

- *Promotion and awareness raising* to raise the profile of women's enterprise and the organisations that support women entrepreneurs, bringing women's enterprise into the public arena and providing strong role models for future entrepreneurs.
- *Policy development and research.* As an independent organisation, Prowess plays a leading role in educating and influencing policy makers about the economic impact of women's business ownership, coordinating research and disseminating results on the subject of women's enterprise.
- *Information.* Newsletters, websites and events, providing and sharing

information about women's enterprise support in the UK and internationally (relevant government initiatives, funding opportunities, details of new research, information about training and conferences, etc.).

- *Quality.* To improve the quality of women's enterprise support throughout the UK, and to provide appropriate advice and information to women on the best possible business support.
- *Consultancy and development* to assist business support agencies and development organisations to review and develop women-friendly services.
- *Networking and sharing best practice* among members through networking and good communication links wherever possible.

Prowess is directed at organisations who work directly with businesses and want to develop and improve their services for women entrepreneurs. Members include:

- business support and enterprise agencies,
- women's enterprise initiatives,
- associations and networks of women entrepreneurs,
- banks and other financing organisations,
- business centres and business parks including incubators,
- Chambers of Commerce,
- economic and regional development agencies,
- science and education institutions.

Before Prowess was established, a national consultation exercise was carried out in May 2001, and the feedback of more than 30 organisations who responded to the questionnaires showed there was strong support for a UK-wide 'umbrella' organisation. The original name proposed for the network was NAPWE – the National Association for the Promotion of Women's Enterprise. But 'Prowess' emerged as a more appropriate and user-friendly name, and after a successful bid to the DTI's Phoenix Development Fund in the autumn of 2001, a steering committee representing the five founder members (organisations supporting women entrepreneurs) was formed. The company was formally constituted, as a Company Limited by Guarantee and the steering members became interim directors. Prowess appointed its first Executive Director, Erika Watson, in January 2002 and an operations office was established in Norwich. In addition to its small, professional team, Prowess contracts with specialists in other parts of the UK to provide a truly 'virtual' national network. Prowess was formally launched in October 2002.

Prowess works at both a strategic and an operational level. The strategic level involves consulting and influencing key government bodies concerning the promotion and support of women's enterprise development. For example, Prowess assisted the DTI's Small Business Service (SBS) in the development of the 'Strategic Framework for Women's Enterprise'. This framework provides a collaborative and long-term approach to the development of women's enterprise in the UK. Prowess continues to cooperate closely with the SBS, and the collaboration includes a part-time secondment of one of Prowess's advisors to the SBS, working as an intern. This arrangement helps to ensure effective sharing of information and communication and provides additional experience and expertise which is of mutual benefit to both organisations. On an operational level, Prowess as an umbrella organisation, promotes and supports targeted and mainstream initiatives. It has also developed best practice criteria for business support organisations and networks and is delivering practical events and workshops aimed at improving the quality of services provided to women entrepreneurs. Its best practice mark or 'Flagship' status is typically awarded to those organisations which provide established women-friendly services at the very highest level. Flagship status entitles organisations to become voting members of Prowess. The assessment for the best practice mark takes place following the receipt of application according to the criteria indicated in Table 10.3. If members fail to meet the criteria, they are informed of the areas in which they have weaknesses and are encouraged to apply again. They continue to receive membership benefits and to play a full part in member consultations and activities. Prowess members are entitled to the following benefits and services:

- free introductory half-day seminar on women's enterprise (held regionally),
- free monthly women's enterprise e-mail newsletter,
- regular policy briefings,
- access to dedicated membership section on the Prowess website,
- reduced rates for events and annual conference organised by Prowess,
- access to Prowess's specialist consultancy services (first half-day free of charge),
- discounts on associated economic development seminars and events throughout the UK.

Table 10.3 Prowess criteria for assessment of best practice

Area	Criteria
Inclusion	A commitment to serve diverse communities and recognition of the importance of social and economic inclusion for under-represented groups.
Quality	A commitment to excellence in the provision of enterprise support for women, supported by an appropriate level and quantity of activity and service.
Equality	Commitment to improving equal opportunities.
Client-focused	Demonstrable responsiveness to clients in the form of regular consultation, client feedback, etc.

Prowess has established a team of consultants which includes former CEOs of women's enterprise organisations, accomplished researchers, programme development and women's business training and counselling specialists as well as consultants with track records in organisational capacity building, business planning and fund-raising.

Within a year, Prowess has attracted more than 100 full members from across the UK. These include enterprise agencies, Business Link Operators, academic institutions, banks and networks. Client evaluations of events and services are consistently positive and Prowess is recognised as the UK's 'lead' organisation in terms of awareness raising, policy development and dissemination in the area of women's enterprise. Prowess has had fewer problems than anticipated in terms of influencing the women's enterprise agenda in the UK. Given the current government's commitment to this area, the timing of Prowess's establishment has been fortuitous, and, in the main, it has been 'pushing at an open door'. The organisation's biggest challenge is how to satisfy the many demands on its resources. It has to be careful to retain a strategic, national approach, along with a facilitating role in terms of regional development (www.prowess.org.uk).

Education and training

It is generally agreed that entrepreneurship education should be a long-term objective and must start as early as possible in the education process. 'School firms'[1] and business games support entrepreneurial thinking and acting, promote personality development and help to reduce gender-related problems in an early stage. When preparing for the actual start-up, women require specific training. Training activities are based on an interdisciplinary approach that builds on both hard facts and soft skills, and also involves successful women entrepreneurs. In this context, imparting theoretical knowledge and sharing hands-on experience is equally important. The 'PriManager' competition in Baden-Württemberg (www.primanager.de) and the Belgian 'DREAM' (www.dream-it.be) project are good examples of school initiatives. Modular training schemes in Belgium, Spain and Baden-Württemberg, as well as the 'TWIN' mentoring project in North Rhine Westphalia, can offer practical ideas for the design of qualification activities.

Good practice example: the TWIN mentoring project, Germany

TWIN is essentially a mentoring project which aims to support young women entrepreneurs with the help of experienced entrepreneurs. The idea behind the project is to bring the inexperienced into contact with experienced entrepreneurs through a mentoring process. The young entrepreneur can apply for the programme as soon as her company is set up (for entrepreneurs with companies between one and three years old).

The most important aspect in the mentoring approach is the direct and open relationship between the mentor and the mentee. This one-to-one relationship is the element which makes this initiative different from all the other existing networking frameworks. For this purpose, the project managers organise meetings for the exchange of experience between the experienced entrepreneur and the 'beginner', as well as different possibilities for further professional training. Gesellschaft für Innovative Beschäftigungsförderung (GIB – Organisation for Innovative Employment Promotion), a state-owned counselling organisation in North Rhine Westphalia Germany, and Käte Ahlmann Foundation realised through contacts with young female entrepreneurs that there was a lack of experienced women who had the necessary time available to be contacted for specific business advice and help. This gap was specially noticed among female entrepreneurs who had started their own business within the last few months. The help they were looking for could not be found within networks of other business start-ups or from consultants.

TWIN started in September 2001 and is promoted as a model project by the Ministry of Economy and Labour of the state of North Rhine Westphalia and the European Union under the European Social Fund with the goals of:

- bringing together a young woman entrepreneur (mentee) with an experienced woman entrepreneur (mentor),
- giving young women entrepreneurs and start-ups the possibility to meet experienced entrepreneurs who could share their positive and negative experiences,
- supporting young women entrepreneurs in the growing process and help with their business development and growth potential,
- attracting the attention of the public to the competency of women entrepreneurs,
- complementing the existing advice services by the provision of experience and know-how of the mentors.

The mentees should be young entrepreneurs who have been active in their own company for at least one year but no longer than three years. If possible, before participating in the project, the young entrepreneurs should have participated in start-up consultation. The business can be from any sector. The mentors should be experienced women entrepreneurs who have been self-employed for at least five years. They should agree to work on a voluntary basis, support the mentees with advice and services, open doors for them and help in establishing contacts. Mentees should be aware of the difference between mentoring and consulting, they must possess the earnestness to enter into a relationship of one-year duration, they should aim at full-time employment and their company should be growth-oriented.

The concept behind this project is the intensive exchange of professional experience between mentors who know how to avoid the problems which are faced by nearly all women who start a business. Both parties benefit from this short, uncomplicated process and direct experience exchange. For example, on the one hand, the young entrepreneur learns the professional and life 'lessons' from the mentor and, on the other hand, the mentor uses her contacts with the entrepreneurs of the younger generation which can be useful in deliberating about the future of her own professional and personal situation.

The process of matching mentors and mentees starts with the presentation of TWIN during regional information sessions which are held in offices for business development as well as Chambers of Commerce. The information sessions are directed at both business start-ups looking for a mentor, and women entrepreneurs wishing to act as mentors. Interested young entrepreneurs can apply by providing the following details on herself and her business:

- general background information about the mentee and her company,
- profile, objectives and goals of the company,
- reasons for starting the company and the rationale for the chosen industry sector,
- past experience of managing a company,
- whether any type of consultation services have been approached or availed of,
- the economic situation of the company,
- personal expectations from TWIN,
- the kind of mentor they would like to have.

The entrepreneurs who wish to act as mentors can apply by presenting themselves through a company portrait. Before a female mentor can be found for a business start-up, a detailed discussion will be carried out with the mentee. The women introduce themselves and discuss the background to their enterprises, while expressing their expectations concerning the type of mentor. The project managers then select matching mentors and invite them to a joint discussion in the office of the mentee. At the end of this meeting, both parties can decide if they would like to start working together. It is advisable that the mentor and mentee do not work in the same business sector, as they may become competitors. It is also beneficial if the personal situation of the mentee is considered when choosing a mentor.

As soon as both parties decide to work together they sign an agreement. The mentor agrees to accompany the mentee on a voluntary basis for a period of one year. At least four meetings are planned, for which time and content are discussed by the entrepreneurs themselves, as well as aspects of confidentiality. At the end of the relationship, the Project Manager of TWIN will interview the mentor and mentee to learn about the experiences of the mentorship. Of course, both entrepreneurs can decide to continue their cooperation for longer periods. Where the relationship ends, the mentor has the opportunity to start assisting another mentee.

One of the most important conditions of the successful mentoring process is the trusting relationship between the two parties. The mentor can support the mentee only if she knows the situation and the problems of the mentee. The task of the mentee is to ask the mentor for advice and support. Respect, understanding and fair criticism should be integral parts of the relationship. The expectations of both parties should be realistic – mentoring is not consulting. The mentors should help in personal development and building up a company by supplying their personal knowledge and their experience. They should give advice on how to use relevant networks, offer contacts and know-how, as well as specific strategies e.g. in management, customer service and building-up contacts.

By the end of April 2003, the project had delivered sixty 'twins'. The feedback received from mentees has been very positive. Almost all mentees who received support managed to achieve a better basis for their business.

One factor that makes this initiative so successful is the pre-selection of mentors. Selection is done by someone who, in most cases, knows the mentors personally and also has knowledge of their company. The mentors have also been recruited with the support of VDU Verband Deutscher Unternehmerinnen (German Association of Women Entrepreneurs), an organisation with 1,700 associated women entrepreneurs (450 of whom are located in the North Rhine Westphalia region) (www.u-netz.de/twin).

Conclusions

The study conducted by the ProWomEn network helped to identify a range of gender-specific support activities, as well as a number of general support schemes with a strong gender mainstreaming dimension, which seek to promote female entrepreneurship. From the data gathered through their international study, the ProWomen team reviewed a number of good practice projects in women's entrepreneurship across the network member countries. Using standard project evaluation criteria and discussion groups, a number of projects were selected as examples of good practice within each of the four thematic areas of: problem awareness, instruments of support, regional networks and education and training. Notwithstanding the inherent subjective assessment element of the study, as well as the potential discrepancies in the nature and extent of the information gathered (due as much to the newness of the research topic, as to the data limitations in some regions), it was possible to identify several examples of how to promote female entrepreneurship. This information will be of value to policy makers and enterprise agencies and can easily be transferred across different regions. The good practice examples discussed in this chapter included: Women's Resource Centres in Sweden, the WIN networking initiative in the UK, and the Information Days for Women and the TWIN mentoring project, both in Germany.

The ProWomEn project has also influenced the creation and implementation of national and other European projects. For example, on a national level in Germany, the three ministries in charge of Economics/Labour, Education/ Research and Social Affairs joined forces to create a national agency for female start-ups. Since 2004 this agency has offered women a national helpline for all questions relating to business start-up, collects data on statistics and research results, and disseminates information through an Internet-portal (www.gruen-derinnenagentur.de).

In 1998, a European Commission Report on 'Employment – NOW – Business Creation by Women' suggested that SME agencies should take account of women-specific needs when designing training or support programmes. More recently, the BEST Report (2004:20) stated that: 'Gender awareness in designing and delivering support measures targeted at female entrepreneurs is ... essential ... agencies must always be aware of the differing characteristics of their female and male clients when designing respective support measures'. The knowledge gained in the ProWomEn project is available on the public website. Twenty-two case studies with hands on advice are described in detail. They can be used by development agencies to incorporate women-specific needs in their own support measures.

Further research is needed, however, to evaluate the effectiveness of the transfer of good practice examples to other regions, and to determine the quantifiable economic impact of such initiatives in terms of the improvement in awareness about entrepreneurship among women; the overall increase in the number of women entrepreneurs; the range of industry sectors in which they are setting up; survival and growth rates, as well as continuing support needs. Such research needs to be conducted on an international level so that support organisations in different countries can exchange experiences and learn from each other.

Acknowledgements

The authors are especially grateful to all of the ProWomEn network members. Special thanks goes to Marianne Karlberg from NUTEK and her team for the data and information given on the Women Resource Centres in Sweden, and to Erika Watson and her team for the information on Prowess.

The authors thank the European Commission, DG Enterprise, for financing the thematic Network ProWomEn under their Innovation Programme (FP5). All results presented in this chapter have been achieved during this project.

Note

1 A school firm is an expression for pupils' entrepreneurial activities, i.e. they start a business within a school project.

References

BEST (2002). 'Good Practices in the Promotion of Female Entrepreneurship'. Austrian Institute for Small Business Research, published on the Internet, online, available at www.europa.eu.int/comm/enterprise/entrepreneurship/craft/craft-women/bestproject-women.htm.

BEST (2004). Report No. 2. 'Promoting Entrepreneurship Amongst Women'. European

Commission, DG Enterprise, published on the Internet, online, available at www.europa.eu.int/comm/enterprise/entrepreneurship/craft/craft-women/bestproject-women.htm.

Carter, N. (2003). 'Female Entrepreneurship and Innovation'. Paper presented at the International WIR Conference, Berlin.

European Commission (1997). 'Evaluating EU Expenditure Programmes – *Ex Post* and Intermediate Evaluation'. DGXIX/02, January, Luxembourg: EC.

European Commission (1998). Employment-NOW (Community Initiative) Business Creation by Women: Measure to Support the Creation, Consolidation and Growth of Women-Owned businesses. DG Employment.

Franco, A. and Winqvist, K. (2002). 'The Entrepreneurial Gap Between Women and Men'. In Statistics in Focus Theme 3-9/2002, Women and Men Reconciling Work and Family Life, Eurostat, European Communities.

Minitti, M. (2005). 'Characteristics of the Entrepreneur'. GEM 2004 Global Report Launch in London, 20 January, 2005.

Minitti, M., Arenius, P. and Langowith, N. (2005). GEM 2004 'Report on Women and Entrepreneurship', Center for Women's Leadership, Babson College, MA, and London Business School. Available: www.gemconsortium.org.

Websites

www.prowomen-eu.net – European Network for the Promotion of Women Entrepreneurship

www.innovating-regions.org – website of the European Commission on all Innovating Regions Initiatives

www.gruenderinnenagentur.de – German agency for female start-ups

www.u-netz.de – platform for women entrepreneurs in North Rhine Westphalia, Germany with information on the TWIN initiative

www.newcome.de – entrepreneurship portal in Baden-Württemberg, Germany

www.nrckvinnorg.org – National Resource Centres for Women in Sweden

www.prowess.org.uk – women's enterprise support portal in UK

www.networkingwomen.co.uk – women into the network: a network of female entrepreneurship support networks

www.dream-it.be – entrepreneurship promotion programme in Belgium schools

www.exist.de – German national programme for university-based start-ups

www.primanager.de – virtual business game competition for secondary schools

11 Conclusions
Implications for education, training and policy

Nancy M. Carter and Barra Ó Cinnéide

Introduction

It is believed that the book's span of topics and geographical spread of authors provide new opportunities for readers to understand issues involved in the important field of female entrepreneurship. In particular, the contributors' analyses of the subject are seen to make an important contribution to understanding the current status of female entrepreneurship, as well as providing recommendations on how the growth of women business organisations (WBOs) may be enhanced globally.

Modern management/organisation theory is often criticised for being based on masculine values and concepts. "Men seem to be the norm and women are 'the other' " (Lamsa *et al.*, 2000:203), as quoted by John Watson and Rick Newby in Chapter 3 which considers the extent to which male and female SME owner–operators differ in terms of the importance they attach to various financial and non-financial goals. Chapter 3 also suggests that biological sex might not be an appropriate proxy to use when testing for the influence of gender on an entrepreneur's goals and expectations. Research has typically, but not always, found that male-owned businesses outperform female-owned businesses in economic terms, even after controlling for variables such as industry, business age, business size, owner–operator experience, desire for business growth, and ownership structure.

Research work by John Watson, one of the Chapter 3 authors, has argued that (i) this apparent underperformance was a function of male-owned enterprises having greater economic inputs and, therefore, greater economic outputs and (ii) might also be a function of female-owned enterprises (on average) having less risk and, therefore, lower returns. In Chapter 3 a third option is proposed, that male and female business owners attach different levels of importance to "hard" (objective/financial) and "soft" (subjective/intrinsic) goals. This might be said to parallel Buttner and Moore's (1997:34) finding that female entrepreneurs measured success in terms of "self-fulfilment and goal achievement. Profits and business growth, while important, were less substantial measures of their success."

Status of female entrepreneurship

In the last two decades in the US, women-owned businesses outpaced the overall growth of businesses by nearly two to one. In Europe, while there has been an increase in female entrepreneurial activity, the rate of growth has not been so rapid as in the US (Carter *et al.*, 2003). For example, in the Netherlands, females comprise 34 per cent of all those who are self-employed while in Finland, Denmark, Spain, Belgium and the UK the percentage is somewhat lower, with average figures of around 25 per cent (Duchenaut, 1997; Nilsson, 1997). Based on the data generated as a result of the GEM (Global Entrepreneurship Monitor) studies in 2003, the UK was found to rank sixteenth out of a possible thirty-four countries in terms of this ratio (Minniti *et al.*, 2005).

In Chapter 2, Sara Carter and Susan Marlow cited empirical evidence on the state of female entrepreneurship and considered widely-held theoretical perspectives on the subject, particularly in terms of its comparison with counterparts. Research investigating gender and enterprise in the UK has expanded and matured considerably over the past fifteen years. There has been a major refocusing of attention from early studies of women's business ownership which considered female experiences entirely in relation to male norms. Now there is an increasing awareness of gender differences within entrepreneurship which are socially constructed and negotiated. In addition, research investigating gender and enterprise has opened up the field to include insights into race, class and family issues, and is starting to produce a more complete and nuanced picture of women's participation in the small firms sector, while the research effort has improved as a result of growing specialised studies.

Shirley-Ann Hazlett *et al.* in Chapter 4, report on an empirical study of entrepreneurship attitudes of undergraduates in Northern Ireland, and comment on data gleaned from GEM findings. The TEA (Total Entrepreneurial Activity) index of females in Northern Ireland is estimated at only 2.3 per cent in comparison with a figure of 7.8 per cent for male entrepreneurial activity (O'Reilly and Hart, 2004). The authors show women in Northern Ireland as more likely than women in any other region of the UK to report fear of failure as preventing them from starting a new business venture (O'Reilly and Hart, 2003). It should be noted, however, that generally a higher fear of failure exists in Northern Ireland among potential entrepreneurs of both sexes: 43 per cent in Northern Ireland compared with 32.9 per cent in Britain (O'Reilly and Hart, 2004). Moreover, fewer women in Northern Ireland compared to the majority of regions elsewhere in the UK believe they have the skills to start a business. These beliefs are in contrast to those held by males, with just over half of men, compared to less than one-third of women, perceiving that they had the necessary skills to start a business or were less likely to fear failure.

Social networks

It is generally held that networks can be an important means of enhancing self-conviction. For example, Fielden *et al.* (2003) found that moral support is more pivotal than financial help to WBOs.

The important role of networks in the survival and success of individual firms has been a recurrent theme in small firm literature. Gender differences in the way networks are created and used have been cited as having an influence on certain aspects of the management process. Networking remains a seriously under-researched area. Studies undertaken in a diverse variety of contexts and countries, including the USA, Italy and Northern Ireland, have all concluded that there is a great deal of similarity in the networking behaviour of men and women. However, women are more likely to have networks composed entirely of other women, and men are more likely to have networks composed entirely of other men.

In Chapter 6, Pauric McGowan and Alison Hampton indicated that the greater majority of women entrepreneurs in their research sample value contact networks as a key resource and seek to utilise networks to their full potential. The following quotes provide a useful insight to the mindset of the women new venturers involved in this research: "If I need anything, I know I can lift the phone and call Joanne in the enterprise centre, she's always there to help." "There are a lot of people out there who can help but the real trick is knowing who to ask in the first place."

One key difference between men and women in business is in the key areas for network development and approaches to mentoring (Aldrich, 1989). "The first erroneous assumption held by men ... is that women operate their businesses the same way that men do and have the same thought processes" (Davis and Long, 1999:26). There is a need to gain greater insights to the potential of networks and networking to female entrepreneurs in both establishing their ventures and in sustaining and maintaining the growth of existing enterprises. Research by Hill and McGowan (1996) suggests that personal contact networking is viewed increasingly as an essential entrepreneurial competence, the mastery of which is a core determinant of an enterprise's potential for initial as well as future growth. The benefits of networking are: providing information on a dynamic environment (Birley, 1985); identifying new product ideas (Carson *et al.*, 1995); and developing new contacts, particularly with new customers (Dodd, 1997): "It's knowing that there are other women doing the same thing who found a way to overcome difficulties" (Chapter 6).

Media and female/male entrepreneurship

Factors such as role models, cultural variables and attitudes towards entrepreneurship have been shown to affect the number of business start-ups in general. Media, also, have an important impact regarding creation of attitudes as well as making potential role models visible. Elisabet Ljunggren and Gry Agnete Alsos in Chapter 5 investigate the images a Norwegian newspaper creates and expresses of entrepreneurs; in particular, the differences in describing female and male entrepreneurs.

In media portrayals of entrepreneurs, the differences in regard to gender are particularly evident when it comes to the "additional information" published, e.g. personal characteristics of the entrepreneur. Topics which do not directly relate to business issues, but are included to make the article more "spicy", are more often found when female entrepreneurs are presented. Regularly, female entrepreneurs are described and characterised distinctively from male entrepreneurs. For instance, in referring to female entrepreneurs the journalist in several cases publicises to whom she is married, as well as the number of children, etc. This kind of information is less frequently added to articles when male entrepreneurs are featured.

In addition, features on a female entrepreneur more often include information on how she personally views her own business and her personal goals, (e.g. self-realisation). In contrast, media coverage of male entrepreneurs along these dimensions is generally infrequent. They are more often featured in terms of issues such as financial figures, size of the business, financial goals, etc.

Entrepreneurs, particularly small and new entrepreneurs, seldom are exposed in the newspaper and are consequently "invisible", particularly in female ventures. A small group of male entrepreneurs (four to five men) get most of the media exposure, representing "big business". Female entrepreneurs are seldom featured.

Chapter 5 proposed that the media contribute to women's alienation to entrepreneurship, since the media's exposure of entrepreneurs mainly refers to male entrepreneurs with distinct risk-taking behaviour, heavy involvement in the stock market, and is usually confined to those representing strongly growing firms. Additionally, it is suggested that the media disregard female entrepreneurs, hence failing to expose female entrepreneurial role models. As the chapter's authors, Elisabet Ljunggren and Gry Agnete Alsos, succinctly comment: "They are so seldom exposed that they are made invisible in the media." They conclude that the media articles may reflect not only journalist's perceptions of male and female entrepreneurs but also society's understanding and image of them.

Financing

It would seem that over the last three decades the differences between men and women have narrowed such that, in today's society, male and female SME owners score similarly in terms of their "masculine" traits. While the results presented in the Watson and Newby study, see Chapter 3, support the view that male and female SME owner–operators differ in terms of the importance they attach to various non-financial goals, it was found that the proposition that females attach less importance (than males) to financial goals could not be supported. An interesting conclusion in Chapter 3 is that the display of masculine traits is considered necessary for career advancement, consistent with the evidence of Kolb (1999) and Kirchmeyer (2002).

However, in recent studies, Grant (2003, 2004) identified that the approach to business start-ups and growth by WBOs dramatically differed from that of their male counterparts, with female start-ups tending to be largely low risk, low investment ventures. Perceptions of financial risk, growth intentions and access to capital are pivotal in the relationship between self-employed women and those from whom they seek financial advice. Female entrepreneurs appear to be at a disadvantage from the outset, particularly given the dearth of female network brokers or mentors, such as female bankers or female venture capitalists. This has led to a major research theme concerning the effect of gender differences in business financing. Four areas of the financing process have been consistently noted as posing particular problems for women:

1   women may be disadvantaged in their ability to raise start up finance,
2   guarantees required for external financing may be beyond the scope of most women's personal assets and credit track record,
3   finance for the ongoing business may be less available for female-owned firms than it is for male enterprises (largely due to women's inability to penetrate informal financial networks), and
4   female entrepreneurs' relationships with bankers may suffer because of sexual stereotyping and discrimination.

In relation to the fourth point above, 37 per cent of women reported that they have actually experienced sexual discrimination over the last five years (Barclays Bank Plc, 2000), as cited in Chapter 7. Between 1995 and 2000 the number of venture capital firms employing women increased by 37 per cent. However, women's representation in the industry fell from 9.8 per cent to 8.8 per cent during that time frame, (see Candida Brush *et al.*, Chapter 8).

Why is financing strategy particularly important in terms of female entrepreneurship? The following have been highlighted in Chapter 8 as determining factors:

- *Wealth Creation.* The lack of investment in women-led ventures limits the opportunity for women to grow their businesses and create wealth.
- *Competitiveness.* Scarcity of equity for women-led ventures may limit growth and diffusion of innovations, job creation, and can stunt regional/ national development.
- *Opportunity.* The lack of investment in women-led ventures may mean the venture community is missing out on potentially attractive investments.

In Ireland, research has provided insights into the factors contributing to the low level of participation by females in self-employment. Ita Richardson and Briga Hynes in Chapter 9 set out to address these issues by specifically focusing on the barriers to female entrepreneurship, particularly in relation to the establishment of technology-related businesses. General trends that emerge from research in Ireland include the following (Goodbody Economic Consultants, 2002):

Age. Women in Ireland appear to be starting businesses at an older age than men.

Type of business. Women in Ireland are more likely to start a service business whereas, men are more likely to start a high-technology business.

Reasons for leaving previous employment. Women are much less likely than men in Ireland to have chosen to start their own business as a result of being made redundant.

Future plans. More men plan to set up another business or franchise their current one.

Finance. Women have less access to finance.

Business structure. Women often tend to go into a business or partnership with their husband/partner rather than starting their own business.

Confidence and skills. Women are less confident than men when starting a new business.

What has to be done?

We need to have a good understanding of the current situation, entailing having systems in place to track, for instance, the performance of venture funded companies so as to encourage investors to seek out/invest in women-led ventures.

The reports of the Northern Ireland GEM studies conducted in the years 2002–2004 highlight the need to tailor educational curricula to raise the TEA index for Northern Ireland students at tertiary level (Kourilsky and Walstad, 1998). This is particularly necessary in relation to female students, as women are currently only one-third as likely as men to start a business. Among the best known educational programmes dedicated to the advancement of the venture capital practice in the US is the Kauffman Institute for Venture Education, described by Candida Brush *et al.* in Chapter 8. An important part of the educational process is the research element that provides knowledge to be used in training and development programmes. Rigorous research that can answer questions about what works and what does not work, can arm entrepreneurs to have more successful ventures.

In identifying best practice in promoting female enterprise in Chapter 10, Petra Puechner and Christine Diegelmann emphasise the importance within the education and training domains of respecting gender-related aspects. They also allude to the influential role that programmes can play in reducing gender-related problems through appropriate pedagogic approaches. Chapter 10 provides many interesting examples of good ("Best") practice in promoting Female Entrepreneurship, including the ProWomEn initiative. The ProWomEn network involves sixteen European regions. Among the members are organisations for economic development and technology transfer. A core feature of ProWomEn is that its members identify critical success factors and select good practice examples to implement their approach, not just to education and training but to the network's other three key components: problem awareness, instruments of support and regional networks. TWIN, another German initiative, is a mentoring project which aims to support young women entrepreneurs with the help of experienced entrepreneurs.

Women's involvement in technology and engineering has been considered an important future direction for education and training initiatives. In this context, Ita Richardson and Briga Hynes in Chapter 9 quote Smith to argue:

> The construction of infrastructure, both physical and technological, is being carried out mainly by men – yet women make up over 50% of the population. There are many signs of the lack of women's influence all around us. A woman's perspective can be different from that of men. Anita Borg from Xerox has been quoted as saying "If women were more involved in creating new technologies, cars would have a place for you to put your handbag".
>
> (Smith, 2002)

Conclusions

Despite a growing enthusiasm among researchers and policy makers for focusing on issues relating to gender and enterprise and a marked increase in the number of studies investigating the area, there has been a failure to build adequate explanatory theories, particularly around the concept of gender and how the experiences of women entrepreneurs reflect those within the wider socio-economic context. By comparison with the volume of academic research that has been undertaken on the small firms' sector, the female business owner has been "neglected" by both the mass media and the academic community (Baker *et al.*, 1997). There can be little doubt that self-employed women, as a relatively new group operating significantly younger businesses, may not yet have attained the same level of achievement as those owned by men, but over time they will catch up. This would be progress!

In light of a recommendation in Brush *et al.* (1995), the authors of Chapter 4, Shirley-Ann Hazlett *et al.*, recommend an educational policy which would incorporate a variety of pedagogies to meet the needs of both female and male students. This would entail designing a suite of activities to develop appropriate entrepreneurial skills at each level of the management study programme, in order to address the major deficiency issues that have been identified.

The McGowan–Hampton conceptual model (see Chapter 6), suggests that the optimum approach for female entrepreneurial networking is a move, in the new venture stage, from all-female networking towards a model of mixed gender networks. It links:

1 reliance on all-female contacts/networks,
2 the length of time in business, and
3 the confidence levels of female entrepreneurs.

It would appear that the value of all-female networking is useful in the early stages of the firm's venture set-up, in providing advice, increasing self-confidence and legitimising aspirations for entrepreneurial success. However, as the female entrepreneurial firm develops, the value of all-female organised networks, as sole source of networking, reduces substantially with the enterprise's growth and development.

Whether initiatives promoting engineering and technology are working or not may be difficult to ascertain but, by identifying individuals who have entered technological careers as a result of being influenced by particular initiatives, it is possible to quantify success at one level at least. Questions need to be asked, such as: is there a wider effect, such as peer-support/peer-pressure that is not recognised? and how can such programmes be improved? In the past, funding has been mainly used to implement the programmes, rather than to study their effects. It is clear that there is a major research lacuna in the field of female entrepreneurship in the technology sector.

Concern about why women are getting such a tiny share of equity investments in the US led to the creation of the *Diana Project* and *Diana International*, research initiatives dedicated to learning more about growth strategies that result in successful high potential women-owned businesses. The *Diana Project* (Brush *et al.*, 2004) found that women are extremely under-represented in the industry and are not making great strides in increasing those numbers, since the venture industry is male-dominated, small and geographically concentrated, as indicated by Candida Brush *et al.* in Chapter 8. Why is the gender distribution in the venture capital industry important? It is widely acknowledged that who you know is critical in gaining access to the venture capital community.

Barriers and problems which women face when starting their own business do not seem to differ too much in Europe, although their formidableness varies from region to region. In general, two types of problems can be identified: obstacles that prevent women from starting an enterprise and problems which arise during the starting process. Lack of role models, difficulties in balancing family and work, or economic problems in the sectors they would prefer, are all prospective reasons why women do not start their own business. Those who take the chance often have to face new problems like non-existent networks, male-dominated support systems or even real discrimination. Long-term solutions have to start in the educational system, while initiatives such as information days carried out in Baden-Württemberg, awards as in Ireland and Poland, and the specialised Swedish exhibitions dedicated to female start-up ventures exemplify how a wide range of women's entrepreneurship promotion options can be devised for the short term.

Discussing the findings of their empirical research described in Chapter 5,

Elizabet Ljunggren and Gry Agnete Alsos look forward to the raising of journalists' consciousness about their role as creators and mediators of images/understandings of entrepreneurs, especially regarding the gender dimension.

Finally, there is a critical need to sponsor and disseminate the results of research about women's entrepreneurship, including comparative research on women-owned and men-owned ventures. Rigorous research provides a powerful base for influencing systems, since information and knowledge derived from solid data can have untold effects on changing attitudes, opinions and practices.

Hopefully, this book's publication will add even further to this!

References

Aldrich, H.E. (1989). "Networking Among Women Entrepreneurs". In Hagan, O., Rivchum, C. and Sexton, D. (eds), *Women Owned Businesses*. New York: Praeger, 105–107.

Barclays Bank Plc (2000). "Women in Business – the Barriers Start to Fall". Available: www.smallbusiness.barclays.co.uk.

Baker, T., Aldrich, H.E. and Liou, N. (1997). "Invisible Entrepreneurs: The Neglect of Women Business Owners by Mass Media and Scholarly Journals in the United States". *Entrepreneurship and Regional Development*, 9, 3, 221–238.

Birley, S. (1985). "The Role of Networks in the Female Entrepreneurial Process". *Journal of Business Venturing*, 1, 2, 107–117.

Buttner, E.H. and Moore, D.P. (1997). "Women's Organisational Exodus to Entrepreneurship: Self-Reported Motivations and Correlates with Success". *Journal of Small Business Management*, 35, 1, 34–46.

Brush, C.G., Carter, N.M., Gatwood, E.J., Greene, P.G. and Hart, M. (2004). *Gatekeepers of Venture Growth: A Diana Project Report on the Role and Participation of Women in the Venture Capital Industry*, Kansas City, MO, The Kauffman Foundation.

Brush, C., Griffin, J. and Smith, C. (1995). "Perceived Value of Entrepreneurship Course Content and Pedagogy". Available: www.sbaer.uca.edu/research/sbida/1995/pdf/10.pdf (accessed 25 April 2005).

Carter, S., Anderson, S. and Shaw, E. (2003). "Women's Business Ownership: A Review of the Academic, Popular and Internet Literature with a UK Policy Focus". In Watkins, D. (ed.), *ARPENT: Annual Review of Progress in Entrepreneurship*. Brussels: The European Foundation for Management Development, 66–157.

Davis, S.E.M. and Long, D.D. (1999). "Women Entrepreneurs: What do They Need?" *Business and Economic Review*, 45, 4, 25–26.

Dodd, S.D. (1997). "Social Network Membership and Activity Rates: Some Comparative Data". *International Small Business Journal*, 11, 2, 13–25.

Duchenaut, B. (1997). "Women Entrepreneurs in SMEs". Report prepared for the OECD Conference on Women Entrepreneurs in Small and Medium Sized Enterprises: A Major Force for Innovation and Job Creation, Paris: OECD.

Fielden, S.L., Davidson, M.J., Dawe, A.J. and Makin, P.J. (2003). "Factors Inhibiting the Economic Growth of Female-Owned Small Businesses in North West England". *Journal of Small Business and Enterprise Development*, 10, 2, 152–166.

GEM (2004). "How Entrepreneurial was Ireland in 2004?" The Irish Annual Report, Enterprise Ireland, www.gemconsortium.org, Dublin, Ireland.

Grant, J. (2003). "Growing Rural Female Entrepreneurs: Are They Starved of ICT Skills?" ICSB 48th World Conference Proceedings, June.

Grant, J. (2004). "Farmers' Markets: Are They Growing Female Entrepreneurs?" Third International Conference in Business and Economics, Amsterdam, July.

Goodbody Economic Consultants (2002). "Entrepreneurship in Ireland". Dublin, Ireland.

Hill, J. and McGowan, P. (1996). "Developing a Networking Competency for Effective Enterprise Development". *Journal of Small Business and Enterprise Development*, 3, 3, 148–157.

Kirchmeyer, C. (2002). "Gender Differences in Managerial Careers: Yesterday, Today, and Tomorrow". *Journal of Business Ethics*, 37, 1, 5–24.

Kolb, J.A. (1999). "The Effect of Gender Role, Attitude Toward Leadership, and Self-Confidence on Leader Emergence: Implications for Leadership Development". *Human Resource Development Quarterly*, 10, 4, 305–320.

Kourilsky, M. and Walstad, W.B. (1998). "Executive Forum: Entrepreneurship and Female Youth: Knowledge, Attitudes, Gender Differences, and Educational Practices". *Journal of Business Venturing*, 13, 77–88.

Lamsa, A.M., Sakkinen, A. and Turjanmaa, P. (2000). "Values and Their Change During the Business Education – a Gender Perspective". *International Journal of Value-Based Management*, 13, 3, 203–213.

Minitti, M., Arenius, P. and Langowitz, N. (2005). "Global Entrepreneurship Monitor: 2004 Report on Women and Entrepreneurship". Babson Park, MA and London: Babson College and London Business School.

Nilsson, P. (1997). "Business Counseling Directed Towards Female Entrepreneurs – Some Legitimacy Dilemmas". *Entrepreneurship and Regional Development*, 9, 3, 239–257.

O'Reilly, M. and Hart, M. (2003). *Global Entrepreneurship Monitor, Northern Ireland*, Dublin and London, InvestNI and London Business School.

O'Reilly, M. and Hart, M. (2004). *Global Entrepreneurship Monitor, Northern Ireland*, Dublin and London, InvestNI and London Business School.

Smith, E. (2002). "Women Look to Shape the Future". *Technology*, 25 July.

Index

References to tables and figures are given in *italic*.

220   *Index*

Helms, M.M. 154
Helson, R. 39
Henderson, J. 3
Henkens, K. 40
Henrekson, M. 38
Henry, C. 1, 2, 69, 110, 171, 173
Hill, F. 3
Hill, J. 113, 116, 117
Hirschman, E. 116, 118
Hisrich, R.D. 12, 16, 17, 18, 20, 22, 93
Hoang, H. 112
Hofer, C.H. 97
Hofstede, G. 37
Hogarth-Scott, S. 38
Holliday, R. 19
Holmquist, C. 11, 12, 15, 18, 89, 105
home/work balance 4
Hong Kong 16
Household Entrepreneurship Survey 75
Huberman, A.M. 116, 118
Hunt, S.D. 111
Hunter, N. 168
Hurtz, G.M. 41
Hynes, B. 5, 177, 180, 181, 210, 212

Ibarra, H. 112
Ilies, R. 41
India 16
Industrial Society Report (2001) 172
Information Days for Women 192–3, 202
innovation 44–5
Institute of Electrical and Electronic
  Engineers 174
International Network of Women
  Engineers and Scientists 174
investment, informal 143, 161
InvestNI 72–3
investor role 98
Ireland, Republic of: awards 213; barriers
  to female entrepreneurship 169;
  comparisons with Northern Ireland 74;
  current status of female participation in
  entrepreneurship 171–4; gender trends
  210–11; percentage of women-owned
  businesses 151
Israel 151
Italy 21
Izyumov, A. 16

Jackson, D.N. 44, 45
Jackson Personality Inventory 44, 45
Jaumotte, F. 40
Jelinek, M. 37
Jensen, R.S. 94
Johannisson, B. 111, 113
Johnson, J.E.V. 140, 142, 144
Johnson, S. 20, 22, 94

Johnston, K. 171, 173
Jones, K. 16
Jørgensen, M.W. 96
Jover, M.A. 139
Judge, T.A. 41, 59
Julien, P.-A. 97
justice 171

Kaiser, H.F. 46
Kalleberg, A.L. 43, 92, 94
Kanter, R.M. 39
Kao, J.J. 117
Käte Ahlmann Foundation 201
Katz, J.A. 19
Kauffman Institute for Venture Education
  162–3, 164, 211
Kaufmann, P.J. 43
Kavanagh, I. 174
Keats, B.W. 37
Kennedy, S. 2, 110
Kickul, J. 59
King, K.M. 140
Kirchmeyer, C. 40, 48, 58, 209
Kitching, J. 141, 146
Klawe, M. 168
Knight, F.H. 139
Knouse, S.B. 112
Kolb, J.A. 40, 48, 209
Kolvereid, L.: (1995) 58; (1996) 105;
  Alsos and (2004) 99; and Alsos (2005)
  88; Alsos and (1998) 92; Carter and
  (1997) 17; Ljunggren and (1996) 17, 92,
  93, 94, 105; *et al.* (1993) 17
Konrad, A.M. 40
Koper, G. 20
Kourilsky, M.L. 15, 70, 85, 211
Kuratko, D.F. 37, 38, 45

Labour Force Survey 16
labour market 16, 90–1, 92, 171
Lamsa, A.M. 37, 206
Landström, H. 97, 155, 159
Langan-Fox, J. 15
Langowitz, N. 1
leadership 18–19
Leahy, K.T. 18
Lee, J. 16
Lee-Gosselin, H. 15, 16
Lefkowitz, J. 43
Leicht, K.T. 43, 92, 94
Leighton, L.S. 97
Leitch, C. 3
LePine, J.A. 41
Lerner, M. 22
Levenson, H. 44
Levenson, N. 168
Levent, T.B. 142